The Origins and Legacies of World War I

The Origins and Legacies
of World War I

D. F. Fleming
Emeritus Professor
of International Relations,
Vanderbilt University

Doubleday & Company, Inc. Garden City, New York

To my wife Doris
never-failing helper on all my books
at every stage

Library of Congress Catalog Card Number 68-27116
Copyright © 1968 by D. F. Fleming
All Rights Reserved
Printed in the United States of America
First Edition

More and more historians look back upon World War I as the great turning point of modern history, the catastrophic collapse which opened the way for others, perhaps the final one.

Why did a great and flourishing civilization suddenly break down in its very heart and center? How could such an event occur? This question has increasing relevance as governments now equipped with the power to destroy all that matters continue to exert their potent wills against each other in a steadily shrinking world.

Yet no period of modern history, indeed of any history, has been the subject of so much controversy as the origins of World War I. The fall of the Hapsburg, Hohenzollern, and Romanov governments and the prompt opening of their archives forced the victorious powers to do the same, if somewhat more grudgingly, and supplied scholars with a vast mass of documentation such as no previous historians had even had in their own day. At the same time Article 231 of the Treaty of Versailles, which laid the responsibility for the war upon Germany and her allies, became the focus of an international controversy over the degrees of responsibility for the war which should fall upon the various governments.

These factors led to the publication of many weighty volumes about the origins of the war in all the chief countries concerned, a mass of evidence too great to be wrestled with as the period recedes, even if it were not progressively less available. Accordingly, this book is offered as an attempt to digest this enormous receding literature and to reduce it to a narrative small enough for the college student or the general reader to cover in a few hours. The author does not suppose that he has settled all details of the many controversial elements dealt with, but he has tried to give an evaluation of the events and decisions involved based upon many years of study, and of discussion of the issues involved with his students at Vanderbilt University over a long period.

I hope to be able to save generations of oncoming students some of the great labor of perusing numerous volumes that I and my students have undergone, and to provide an introduction to a very large field for those who wish to study it more deeply.

In the same way, I have tried to deal with the vigorous controversy which produced many works about the entry of the United States into the Great War, making it the First World War.

The first chapter describes the world-wide ferment of relatively orderly change, mainly by legislative process, which characterized the decade before 1914. This parallel movement, which accompanied the series of power politics plunges that preceded the deluge, has received much less attention. Of course it should have established the trend of the century. Did its very existence contribute to the resort to blood and iron?

Finally, the concluding chapter endeavors to describe the chain of disasters which flowed from World War I and the failure to make peace after it, and to come to grips with the issues which in 1968 depend for their solution upon the avoidance of a final World War III. A prudent reading of the evidence recorded here concerning World War I, and to a lesser degree about World War II and the Cold War, will tell us that the definitive disaster will occur. Yet it must not happen, and it need not if enough of us are determined that the final folly must be averted.

This is not a book for the ivory tower. It is an urgent message addressed to each citizen who wishes to see succeeding generations of our youth fulfill their destinies.

D. F. FLEMING

Palo Alto
June 1968

Contents

I. The Twilight of Aristocratic Rule in the Old World 1900–1914

As the twentieth century opened, it could not be said that the world had been made safe for democracy. In the newly developed continents the forms of political democracy were well established in the United States and the British Dominions, but the abundance of free natural resources had postponed any real test of the ability of these peoples to organize a permanent economy which would perpetuate freedom. In Latin America the same issue was complicated by the presence of large numbers of subservient Indians and the determination of aristocratic social elements to rule, by military force whenever necessary.

In the old world a small fringe of democratic peoples clung to the western edge of the vast Eurasian continent. The British, French, and Swiss, together with the small nations of the Low Countries and Scandinavia, had developed democratic institutions to the point where they seemed established. Elsewhere, from Hamburg to Canton, the bulk of the human race lived under varying degrees of autocratic control. If Italy offered an apparent exception it was hardly of a nature to establish the permanence of democracy as a way of life. Yet among every people, from Switzerland to Japan, there was a powerful ferment operating, a striving for free institutions and the end of arbitrary government. Even the presence of efficient administration and economic prosperity, as in Germany and to a large extent in Austria-Hungary, did not stop the advance of democratic desire. Eastward, the huge masses of Russians and Chinese stirred toward the overthrow of autocratic governments which they had ample reason to hate.

A Republic Displaces the Manchus

In China the more vigorous spirits had long felt the urgency of breaking the tyrannies of ancient custom and of freeing China from the sterile rule of the Manchus, who had levied tribute upon the Chinese people since 1644. But it took the bitter experience of the Sino-Japanese War of 1894 to begin the awakening of the whole people to the need of regeneration.

CHINA DESPOILED   The easy defeat of China by Japan was the signal for a descent upon China from all quarters. Korea on her border and Formosa, taken by Japan, were soon followed by the loss of ports to Germany and Great Britain, territory in South China to France and the lease of the Kwangtung Peninsula in Manchuria—denied to Japan by Russia, by Germany and France —to Russia. The anti-foreign rebellion led by the secret society of Boxers which resulted from these spoliations only made matters worse, since the Western Powers combined to rush troops to Peking for the rescue of their legations and nationals. The troops of some nations, notably the Russians, pillaged the Chinese capital, even to the royal palaces. One Russian lieutenant general carried away ten trunks filled with imperial valuables and "unfortunately the general's example was followed by other army men.[1] In the same spirit, the spread of the Boxer movement to Manchuria was made the pretext for rushing large Russian forces into the Chinese towns of the region "with no other end in view than to furnish excuse for promotions and looting."[2] As their

---

[1] *The Memoirs of Count Witte*, Garden City, 1921, p. 108.

[2] *Ibid.*, p. 111. One general, Tzerpitzky, killed the monks of a Mongolian monastery and carried away, as his share, 200 ancient statues of gilt bronze.

The refusal of Russia to withdraw these strange guardians of public or-

contribution to the despoiling and discipline of China, because of the Boxer outbreak, the foreign governments levied upon the Chinese people an exorbitant indemnity of $320,000,000.

A CONSTITUTION PROMISED It was now clear enough that reform must come to China. Even the Manchu court was moved to abolish the ancient system of classical education and send commissions abroad to study the ways of the West. The published reports of these observers were eagerly read. Educated people cried out for a national parliament and, on September 1, 1906, the government announced itself in favor of a constitutional government. Two years later a decree outlined reforms which were to culminate in a constitution in 1917. The first provincial elections were held in 1909. A preliminary national Assembly summoned in 1910 made itself into a constituent Assembly, demanding a responsible cabinet and the abolition of the queue, the badge of servitude to the Manchus, in the army and among the officials. The government thought this gesture unnecessary.

REVOLUTION On May 8, 1911, a cabinet was conceded, but on the German model, with responsibility to the Emperor. The next day the nationalization of railways was proclaimed, a step which followed a period of wildcat railroad building that greatly augmented the national debt by huge sums, improperly used. This issue precipitated revolt and China quickly became a republic.[3] It was to be long before the vicious governmental habits

---

der from Manchuria, was one of the leading causes of the Russo-Japanese War.

The German contribution to this "discipline" of China was equally discreditable. The Kaiser cried to his departing marines: "Give no quarter! Take no prisoners! Kill him when he falls into your hands!" Like the Huns under Attila, he wanted the terror of the German name to "resound through Chinese history a thousand years from now." This German expedition remained in China until 1901, "exacting indemnities and concessions." —Nicholas Mansergh, *The Coming of the First World War*, London, 1949, p. 55.

[3] The declaration of independence published when Dr. Sun was selected as President charged the Manchus with responsibility for the disastrous pol-

of the Manchu era were thrown off. It would take time for a nationalist regeneration to permeate and educate the enormous masses of peasants, with the great difficulties of the Chinese written characters to overcome, but the immense effort of the Chinese to make themselves a free and progressive nation gave to democracy one of its chief hopes of future survival.

War and Revolution in Russia

NAKED IMPERIALISM IN MANCHURIA   Early in 1904, a second war launched by Japan almost brought down another ancient autocracy, the Russian House of Romanov. The Russo-Japanese War was the result of the evident intention of the Tsarist regime in Russia to retain Manchuria and even to push on into Korea. For this imperialistic exploit there was no basis of justification other than the opportunities it would offer the declining ruling class of Russia to recoup its fortunes by seizing the wealth and resources of China. Even the romance of Russia's perennial search for warm-water ports could not justify, from the standpoint of Russia's interests, the Tsar's freebooting adventure in the Far East. Almost unlimited resources awaited development in the vast reaches of Russia, in both Europe and Asia. The attention of the Russian people might be diverted a little from their illimitable woes, but their welfare could not be advanced by exploits in China.

Yet, with complete disregard of the rotten foundations beneath them, the Tsar and his lieutenants in Manchuria persisted in their aggressive tactics until Japan suddenly struck. In attempting to negotiate with Russia the Japanese had encountered little but

icy of seclusion and with a vicious craving for aggrandizement and wealth. It alleged that they had created privilege and monopoly, levied unwholesome taxes, denied justice, inflicted cruel and immoral punishments, connived at official corruption and sold offices to the highest bidders.—Edward J. Dingle, *China's Revolution*, London, 1912, pp. 17–18.

insolence and avoidance. Russian officials openly despised them
as impudent "Yellow monkeys." "Although in no other place in
the civilized world outside Russia was man so oppressed, where
his most pathetic attempts to look up and aspire were crushed
with such vengeance as only despotism could command, these
vice-regents looked down upon the Japanese as from a pure
and lofty eminence."[4] Even the Tsar, with all his weakness,
was confident of his ability to dominate the Far East. The government of his cousin, the Emperor of Germany, had been giving
him every assurance that his western frontier would be protected
during a war with Japan. The Germans felt that it would be a
splendid thing for Russian energies to be expended in the Far
East.[5] Not so the English, who were so alarmed at Russian
encroachments in China that they left their splendid isolation in
1902 and made the alliance with Japan which protected her rear
while she fought Russia.

The war which was made certain by these friendly urgings
and assurances of support opened the eyes of discerning observers to what modern warfare would be like. In Manchuria
there were actually fighting fronts forty miles long! Battles lasted
ten days. Field guns shooting four miles were used and more
ammunition was expended in one day than in the whole of the
Spanish-American War.

WHOLESALE INCOMPETENCE IN WAR Throughout the struggle,

[4] Frederick McCormick, *The Tragedy of Russia in the Pacific*, New York,
1907, Vol. II, p. 231.

[5] Theodore Wolff, *The Eve of 1914*, London, 1935, p. 26; *The Memoirs
of Count Witte*, pp. 107–8; Baron Sergius Korff, *Autocracy and Revolution in Russia*, New York, 1923, p. 57; George Vernadsky, *History of Russia*,
New Haven, 1929, p. 173; Hans von Eckardt, *Russia*, New York, 1932, pp.
70, 245. "I will certainly do everything in my power," wrote the Kaiser to
"Nicky," "to keep Europe quiet and to protect Russia in the rear, so that
nobody shall interfere with your action in the far East. For this is obviously Russia's task in the future, to turn its attention to the Asiatic continent and to protect Europe against the encroachment of the great yellow
race. In this you will always find me at your side and prepared to help
you to the best of my power." (Korff, p. 245.)

too, the Russian troops fought far better than could have been expected of them against the enthusiastic, well-equipped Japanese. For the Russians it was a matter of being carted thousands of miles to extend a dominion which was hateful and shockingly ungrateful. The Russian bureaucrats and merchant patrioteers routed one great consignment of food and vodka to the troops by way of Danzig and the supplies found their way into Germany at bargain prices. A little later an extensive shipment of medical supplies going through Memel met the same fate, and a heavy consignment of winter clothing for the troops was dispersed along the trans-Siberian railway during the summer. Boots were delivered with paper soles and tons of sugar were found to be composed of quite equal parts of sand, flour and sugar. Payments sufficient to maintain an army of 1,000,000 men hardly sufficed to support, in this fashion, 250,000 men.[6]

Nor was there greater competence in the field. The officers scorned to learn how to use telescopic sights on the artillery.[7] In Manchuria public moneys were regarded as free plunder. Graft and blackmail were almost universal. Officers continually sent home large sums of money, while the troops were without pay. Yet officers even had to bribe their way to ride on the trains.[8] Jealousy and intrigue were rife in all official circles. The whole of one general's staff had female traveling companions and during the retreat from Mukden the kitchens and harems of the Grand Dukes took up two entire trains.[9] Drunkenness, debauchery, and gambling were the pastimes of all ranks.

It followed naturally enough that the Russian forces were compelled to give way in nearly every case and in every respect before the Japanese.[10] It followed, too, that indignation and

---

[6] Carl Joubert, *The Truth About Russia*, London, 1905, p. 55.

[7] Henry W. Nevinson, *The Dawn in Russia*, London, 1906, p. 231.

[8] McCormick, *The Tragedy of Russia in the Pacific*, Vol. II, pp. 281–82.

[9] Georges Michon, *The Franco-Russian Alliance, 1891–1917*, New York, 1929, p. 122.

[10] This was the terrible Russian bear in action, the fear of which had dominated British policy for the preceding fifty years.

disgust mounted among the people of Russia. To win through, the regime took the most reckless gamble of all, sending its obsolete Baltic fleet on a six months' journey around the world to suicidal annihilation by Japan's navy. At this juncture it became clear even to the muddle-minded men in St. Petersburg that the "victorious little war" which the notorious Minister of the Interior, Wenzel von Plehve, had anticipated as a desirable outlet for popular discontent, had miscarried. Government in Russia had almost ceased to function. Everything had broken down. In the words of Count Witte, to whom it fell to make peace and save the autocracy from the people: "Instead of enhancing the prestige and increasing the physical resources of the regime, the war, with its endless misery and disgrace, completely sapped the system's vitality and laid bare its utter rottenness before the eyes of Russia and of the world generally, so that the population, whose needs had been neglected for many years by a corrupt and inefficient government, finally lost patience and fell into a state of indescribable confusion."[11]

BLOODY SUNDAY The final demonstration of the Tsarist tyranny's ineptitude came on January 22, 1905, Bloody Sunday. On that day Father Gapon led an immense procession of many thousands of St. Petersburg workmen and their families to the Tsar's Winter Palace. The vast host moved in orderly fashion, through unusually bitter cold, led by the Cross, carrying pictures of the Tsar and singing, not the Red Internationale but religious and patriotic songs. Father Gapon had come to be the head of the government-sponsored "Union of Russian Workingmen," organized by one Zubatov, an agent of the police. The purpose of the demonstration was to present a petition to the Tsar, which read in part: "We the workingmen and inhabitants of St. Petersburg of various classes, our wives and children, our helpless old parents, come to Thee, Sire, to seek defense. We have become beggars; we have been oppressed; we are burdened by toil beyond our powers; we are scoffed at; we are not recognized as

[11] *The Memoirs of Count Witte*, p. 250.

human beings; we are treated as slaves who must suffer their bitter fate and keep silence. We are pushed further into the den of beggary, lawlessness and ignorance. We are choked by despotism and irresponsibility—the limit of our patience has been reached. There has arrived for us the tremendous moment when death is better than the continuation of our intolerable tortures."

This last desperate sentence revealed, perhaps, the end toward which all autocracies plunge. The remainder of the petition detailed the specific grievances of the workmen no less clearly. Requests to their masters to discuss grievances had been refused. It was illegal to ask for a shorter day, to agree on wages, even to plead for one ruble a day as a minimum for women, to desire to receive medical attention without insult or to seek to have the workshops arranged "so that death might be avoided from awful draughts, rain and snow." Each of these requests was a crime. "In reality," cried out the petition, "in us, as in all Russian people, there is not recognized any human right, not even the right of speaking, thinking, meeting, discussing our needs, taking measures for the improvement of our condition. We are deprived of the possibility of organizing ourselves into unions for the defense of our interests."[12]

The petition was a cutting indictment of life under the Tsar. His court, formally warned by the organizers of the petition march, chose not to receive the appeal. Instead, troops were assembled and ordered to shoot the demonstrators. They did so until, according to most accounts, upwards of 1500 of the marchers were massacred and about 3000 wounded. Instead of seizing the opportunity at least to pose as the "Little Father" of his people, the Tsar chose to have them shot down. The *Century Magazine* feared that such "blind, brutal and stupid measures of repression" might lead to fearful reprisals by the people and to chimerical solvents of reform.[13]

---

[12] A. J. Sack, *The Birth of Russian Democracy*, New York, 1918, p. 94ff.
[13] Continuing, the editor quoted a paragraph from a Russian lady of high position which revealed vividly the depth of corruption which despotism

THE REVOLUTION OF 1905 The massacre on Bloody Sunday, says Kerensky, created "the Proletariat, as a new anti-dynastic political force."[14] A week later it was found necessary to shoot the workmen of Warsaw, with eight hundred casualties, and Poland fell into a state of revolutionary anarchy. The peasants of the Baltic states turned against their German landlords, who hounded the military on to vengeance. Over all Russia the peasants looted and burned the manor houses, 2000 of them, and months later, when the regime regained enough especially favored troops from Manchuria, many thousands of the peasants were flogged, hanged and shot, their huts burned and their children turned out into the winter to starve.[15]

In the meantime, the navy was affected. On June 14 the sailors of the battleship *Potemkin* mutinied at Odessa against eating spoiled meat and threw their officers into the sea. Three days later the tyrant of Finland was assassinated, and, on July 28, von Plehve, Minister of the Interior, was shot. Grand Duke Sergius, Governor of Moscow, had already been killed in February. The regime was losing its heads, and throughout the summer no help was at hand, so bitter was the hatred of all classes of the population. "The workmen regarded it as the defender of capitalism, harsh, brutal and greedy for profit; the citizens as standing for the suppression of freedom and right, the bourgeoisie as the embodiment of a parasitic bureaucracy," and the peasants as a system based on force which deprived them of the land. Strikes followed in endless succession culmi-

---

breeds. "It is true," said the letter, "that despotism has a demoralizing influence. Men under the yoke end by having no sentiment left of honor or morality; there is a complete lack of ethics—nothing but a fierce desire to grow rich by any possible means. That is what happened to us. For those of us who are serious and thoughtful the outlook is frightful. . . . Despotism cannot be a victor; it is a corrupter of peoples."—*Century Magazine*, April 1905, Vol. 69, pp. 954-56.

[14] Alexander Kerensky, *The Crucifixion of Liberty*, New York, 1934, p. 103.

[15] Henry W. Nevinson, *The Dawn in Russia*, pp. 264-65; 279.

nating on October 20 in a railway stoppage which spread quickly into the most complete general strike ever known in any country. Every means of communication ceased entirely. Street cars stopped. All shops were shut. Every trade came to a halt; every industry closed, even lawyers and housemaids struck. Food became scarce. The government was helpless.

It acknowledged the fact by appointing Count Witte as Premier and he forced from the Tsar the manifesto of October 30, promising a bill of rights and a responsible parliament. This concession split the liberals from the socialists and permitted the government to rally its forces. A soviet, or council of workers, led in part by one Leon Trotsky, which had been meeting openly in St. Petersburg and directing the strikes, was broken up on December 16 and two hundred of its members arrested. Strike funds were confiscated, and strikes provoked spasmodically. A workers' rising in Moscow was ruthlessly stamped out by the use of heavy artillery. Even schoolboys were executed for believing in a better form of government and schoolgirls were handed over to soldiers to be flogged.

To speed the crushing of the rebellion the old reliable device of organizing pogroms was used on a national scale. Gangs of thugs called "Black Hundreds" were assembled and wherever there were Jews they were plundered and massacred. Intellectuals and workers suspected of revolutionary sympathies were attacked until many thousands of innocent people suffered death and outrage. The peasants, forewarned, came with their carts to share in the looting of the Jews, until finally they decided to visit the same treatment upon the landlords and were busy at home.[16]

The pogroms added to the losses which the revolutionary strikes and riots had caused, and when the middle class tradesmen and industrialists saw that revolt stopped all trade and led

[16] William Henry Chamberlin, *The Russian Revolution, 1917–1921*, New York, 1935, Vol. II, p. 47ff.; F. L. Benns, *European History Since 1870*, New York, 1938, p. 276.

to great destruction of property they turned against the revolution. Then it transpired that the returning troops responded to better food and clothing by shooting down their fellows, at the command of those who had so shamelessly left them in the lurch in Manchuria. This fact once proved, the relief of the regime was immense. The troops were at once turned loose from Finland to the Caucasus and from Poland to Siberia. Stern vengeance was taken throughout the empire. "The prisons were crammed, and typhus finished what the rifle and hang-rope had left undone."

FINANCIAL AID FROM THE DEMOCRACIES Then Count Witte performed his last great service to Tsarism, after which he was promptly dropped from power. He persuaded the Western Powers to advance a huge loan to cover the great deficit which war and revolution had bequeathed the Russian treasury. In the autumn of 1905 it had seemed impossible for the bankrupt, discredited Russian Government to obtain a loan anywhere. In the Spring of 1906, after a winter of bloody repression had restored "order" to Russia, the bankers of the democracies advanced $450,000,000 to the Tsar's government—enough to wipe out the deficit and make the government independent of the new Duma before it could meet.[17]

THE DUMA SHORN OF POWER At once the Tsar issued a series of decrees nullifying his October manifesto. It was ordained that the government could itself re-enact the budget on May 1 of each year, and that an upper house, filled with Tsarist appointees, should be created to block the Duma. The elections to the latter were held under severely repressive measures, in spite of which the liberal Constitutional Democratic Party won a large majority. When the Duma petitioned the Tsar to hold to his promise of democratic government, and to expropriate the great landlords, it was dissolved and sporadic revolts were

[17] The French contributed $230,000,000 to relieve their ally, and British bankers, now that the Russian bear had shown his impotence, were willing to supply $65,000,000 to help set him up in business again. Austria's share was $33,000,000 and Holland's $10,000,000.

quickly suppressed. The second Duma being equally unsubmissive, it also was dissolved, in 1907. Then the Tsar further modified his October constitutional pledges by introducing a class system of voting which would give the landlords and other Rightist elements overwhelming control. The Duma thereafter ceased to be a force, except in one respect. Though the Tsar sought constantly and everywhere to get back to autocracy, pure and undefiled, he did not quite dare to abolish the right of opposition members of the Duma to speak against his acts in that body. It thus became one place in Russia where oppression could be denounced. More important still, the denunciations in the Duma were widely heard throughout the nation.[18]

The bureaucracy was in the saddle again and, aided by a secret police which became a state in itself, democratic reforms appeared to be effectively throttled. But in the heart of the bureaucracy itself there were worms of doubt which were eventually fatal to it. Knowing that the system was wrong, many of the bureaucrats continually suggested small compromises which gradually weakened the firm grip of the autocratic machine, for compromise is fatal to autocracy. When autocracy begins to yield rights, however small or grudgingly given, it invalidates its divine right to rule alone and in its own interest. The insistence of the fascist regimes that the alternative to democracy was total autocracy, without any mitigation or compromise, was well grounded.

THE CHURCH AN ENGINE OF TYRANNY Throughout the Revolution of 1905 the corrupt alliance between the Tsarist autocracy and the Russian Church was evident to all foreign observers in Russia. At the height of the disorders, the Tsar issued a manifesto which was read in all the churches. It described the heads of the liberal movement as evil minded leaders, blinded by pride, "who make insolent attacks upon the Holy Orthodox

[18] Paul Miliukov, *Russia, Today and Tomorrow*, New York, 1922, pp. 14–22. Professor Miliukov was the leader of the Constitutional Democrat party (Cadets).

Church and the lawfully established pillars of the Russian state." In commenting upon the message the priests told their flocks that the intellectuals had been bribed by Japan and England to turn the country over to the English, and in some cases the congregations went straight from these exhortations to attack the schools.[19]

The hatred of both the Church and the State for education was deep. Both knew that the perpetuation of their power depended upon keeping the peasants ignorant and the city proletariat as illiterate as possible. The government opposed the efforts of enlightened landlords in many local Zemstvos to promote education, often taking away from the Zemstvos the schools which they had built. The Ministry of Public Education was hostile to all public schools "and frequently where it could not destroy the schools established by the Zemstvos, it sought to undermine and nullify them by creating rival church schools which reduced education to the narrowest limits."[20]

The continuance of both Church and State thus came to depend upon the preservation of ignorance. Educated people forsook religion and despised the Church, regarding the priests as "greedy, grasping merchants, always striving to extort the highest possible price for their wares." Conscientious priests, of which there were a sprinkling, dared not teach the people true religion, lest Church spies bring down vengeance upon them. The Holy Synod was as much a department of the state as the Minister of War. The hierarchy saw to it that monastic prisons swallowed up those clerics who raised doubts, or made

[19] *The North American Review*, May, 1905, Vol. 180, pp. 780–88.

[20] Charles E. Smith, "The Internal Situation in Russia," *The Annals of the American Academy of Political and Social Science*, July, 1905, Vol. 26, p. 98.

Writing from his long sojourn in Russia, Dr. E. J. Dillon records that education was often suppressed by force. He found that in one large area there was an annual expenditure of $150.00 a year on education. In the same district there were 700 liquor houses with an annual turnover of 2,000,000 rubles.—Dillon, *Russia Today and Yesterday*, New York, 1930, p. 94.

the slightest protest against official tyranny. One of the Synod's circulars threatened to excommunicate any priest who voted for a liberal member of parliament, and five who were elected to the Duma with liberal support were unfrocked.

The dogma dinned into benighted minds for generations taught that the Tsar was God's representative on earth, that his word was God's word and his laws God's laws, that to disobey the Tsar was to disobey God. But when misfortunes fell through an act of the Tsar's agents it was to be regarded as merited punishment. God had made some to be masters and some to be servants, some rich and some poor. Naturally this doctrine did not inspire respect from educated people, when taught by priests who were charged on every hand with rapacity, drunkenness, and the grossest immorality.

A BARBAROUS REGIME   It was the peasant's lot to support his betters in the Church and the State. The State levied taxes upon him which were so heavy that he had to sell at harvest the grain needed for his food. The Church then sanctified his hunger by providing long and frequent religious fasts. Even seed grain and horses frequently had to be sold for taxes until whole districts were denuded of both.[21] The peasant, 90,000,000 strong, was thus bound to a life that was merely bestial. He was a grovelling, stupid, inarticulate creature, afraid of the dark, too ignorant even to know anything about the soil he tilled. It was his lot to balance eternally between hunger in good years and famine in bad crop seasons, to live huddled together in dark, foul hovels, which often disabled for life and then left him alone to face his last years in hunger and disease. His children were sold to human hucksters for a trifle, to be hauled off in tumbrils to the factory towns, exactly like the cattle.

Inevitably, says Dr. Dillon, the moral effect upon the younger generations was truly terrible. All ideas of law and justice were torn from their hearts. They became "eternally drunk, with dis-

[21] Joseph Ward Swain, *Beginning the Twentieth Century,* New York, 1933, pp. 115–20.

figured features and averted eyes. Covered with rags, they looked like half-tamed beasts. . . . This was not a proletariat; it was a return to savagery. No trace of anything human remained."

For a few months, during the revolutionary struggle of 1905, the barbarized Russian people did lift themselves and look to the future. In that year "not half as much vodka was drunk in Russia, not half so many suicides took place; there was not half the adultery and immorality." Everybody was waiting to see. Then, after the failure of the revolution, the people plunged so deeply into debauchery that "Our world became hell."[22]

In 1906 the revolution appeared to have been without constructive result. Yet it did win some important gains for the peasants. Count Witte had secured the cancellation of land payments which the former serfs had been making to the government since 1863. In 1906, Premier Piétr Stolypin decreed that the peasants might withdraw from the collectivist villages which controlled their 1863 holdings and buy land also from the nobles, the Church and the Crown. A Peasant Bank was organized to supply funds and a considerable fraction of the abler peasants

[22] Stephen Graham, *Changing Russia*, London, 1913, p. 230. E. J. Dillon, *Russia Today and Yesterday*, p. 94; Leroy Scott, "The Travesty of Christ in Russia," *Everybodys*, July, 1907, Vol. 17, pp. 800–8; Percival Gibbon, "The Church's Blight Upon Russia," *World's Work*, June 1905, Vol. 10, pp. 6243–54. Unforgettable descriptions of the utterly heartless exactions of the priest-official classes, for their own aggrandizement, and of the depths in which the people lived, are contained in: Ernest Poole, "The Night that Made Me a Revolutionist," *Everybodys*, November 1905, Vol. 13, pp. 635–40; Leo Tolstoy, "Must It Be So?," *Independent*, September 3, 1908, Vol. 65, pp. 524–26.
It was perhaps not strange that the developing Russian middle class, living as it did between the utter degradation of the people and the predatory magnificence of the church and lay aristocracy, should be slow in evincing a constructive social conscience. The bourgeoisie cried out against the state of the peasants, but was quite willing to bring them into factory life under the worst industrial conditions. They blamed the government for ruling by brute force, but would calmly see their own strikers shot down.—Graham, *Changing Russia*, p. 61.

acquired larger holdings. Within a few years this process had split the peasants and provided a basis for support of the government.

In the cities there was no corresponding gain for any section of the rapidly growing industrial proletariat. By the summer of 1914 St. Petersburg was again convulsed with revolutionary strikes and rioting. In the opinion of Alexander Kerensky the order for mobilization on July 31 stayed the revolution.[23] At the close of the war a hurricane of revolutionary change was to sweep through Russia, with such violence that it still dominates the international politics of most of the world.

The Sultan's Despotism Overthrown in Turkey

The Russian Revolution of 1905 had stimulated the growth of revolutionary movements in China, in Persia and in Turkey.[24] In the latter country the despotism of Abdul Hamid II was, if possible, worse the tyranny of the Tsar. The Turkish autocrat kept himself in power by pampering a few regiments of guards in Constantinople, by espionage and assassination, and by allowing a large portion of the public revenues to stick to the fingers of his officials. He had learned that he could play the Great Powers of Europe off against each other and that the Concert of Europe would talk much but never take action against him.

ARMENIAN MASSACRES UNPUNISHED   Particularly after William II of Germany and his Empress had singled him out for the honor of their first state visit, in 1889, he felt himself able to treat his subjects as he pleased. Of these he began to fear that the Christian Armenians of Eastern Asia Minor might rebel

[23] Alexander Kerensky, *The Crucifixion of Liberty*, p. 159.
[24] George Vernadsky, *Political and Diplomatic History of Russia*, Boston, 1936, p. 370.

and win the aid of Russia. Hence in 1894 he suddenly began the systematic massacre of the Armenians, burning villages and subjecting the people to the foulest cruelty and outrage. For two years his butchers moved from district to district until finally in 1896 some six thousand Armenians were clubbed to death in the streets of Constantinople under the noses of the protesting ambassadors.

These horrors aroused great indignation in England, which had been primarily responsible for the preservation of Turkish rule. Nor did Britain lack the power to halt the Sultan's savagery. A powerful British fleet lay off the Dardanelles, before the time of heavy howitzers and floating mines. But Britain was governed by the Conservatives, under Lord Salisbury. Urged by great mass meetings of indignant Englishmen, he issued solemn warnings to the Sultan and did nothing. He was filled with "the prudence which could taper off into cowardice."[25] Did he not lack allies? Was not Turkey the affair of the Concert of Europe? And, above all, was there not Russia to dread? Salisbury thus made his excuses and gave a powerful impetus to the feeling in Europe that Britain would not fight, unless for the most selfish and sordid of reasons. "Abdul the Damned" had correctly measured his contemporaries.

During the Armenian massacres he enjoyed the frequent companionship of the German Ambassador. Shortly afterward, in 1898, William II traveled again to Constantinople to kiss "the Red Sultan" and call him brother—also to make himself the protector of all Islam and to advance to a climax the negotiations for the Baghdad railway.

THE YOUNG TURK REVOLT, 1908   The dissolute Sultan did not need to concern himself with the admonitions of the Christian ambassadors about the chronic anarchy in Macedonia. He filled his vizierates with "slippery scoundrels of the most depraved type" and ruled by terror until suddenly, in July 1908, two

[25] William Stearns Davis, *Europe Since Waterloo*, London, 1927, p. 516.

army corps started from Salonika to depose him. Abdul was caught completely unaware. His spies had long followed the "Young Turks," many of whom had fled from his oppression and established a "Committee of Union and Progress" in Paris, but no one had told him that the movement had gained general support throughout Turkey. Repeating the tactics of 1876, the Sultan at once proclaimed again the extremely liberal constitution of 1876 with the intent, of course, again to confine it strictly to paper as in the earlier year. It all seemed so miraculous that celebrations swept the empire, while Abdul Hamid rallied all the noxious elements which had battened on his regime for a counter revolt. On April 13, 1909, the Sultan's troops seized the capital and held it until the Young Turks brought the entire European army to Constantinople and deposed Abdul Hamid, taking him to Salonika for safe keeping.

The Young Turk Revolution did not at once convert Turkey into an advanced democracy. The Turkish rebels were to discover that inexperience and the centuries-old heritage of arbitrary misgovernment could not be overcome at once. During the great wars soon to come they were also to lapse into barbarities greater than those of "Abdul the Damned." Yet none could deny that the beginning of regeneration had occurred in Turkey.

The Disintegration of the Austro-Hungarian Empire

Nowhere in the vast realms of autocracy was the demand for freedom and self-government as insistent or as confident of success as in the Austro-Hungarian Empire. This state was a contradiction of national aspirations which everyone knew could not continue to exist. It might be a desirable economic unit, especially from the standpoint of the German industrialists of Vienna and Bohemia, but in an age when nationalism was the strongest force in the world the Hapsburg monarchy was a survival of the *ancien régime* which only awaited the convenient moment for disintegration—an event, however, which the two ruling races, the Germans and Magyars, were determined to prevent.

In the Austrian half of the Dual Monarchy lived some 28,500,-000 people. According to the census of 1910, taken by German officials, the Germans numbered just over 12,000,000 of which about 2,000,000 were Jews and of which another 2,000,000 lived in Hungary; the Czechs 6,643,000; Poles just under 5,000,-000; and Ukrainians 4,000,000. In Austria and Bosnia-Herzegovina (separately administered) there were 2,600,000 Serbs and 800,-000 Italians. In the Hungarian half of the monarchy dwelt another 6,226,000 Slavs, South and North, and 3,224,000 Rumanians. Of 20,500,000 people in Hungary the Magyars listed 10,000,000 as belonging to their own race, a figure which included 1,000,000 Jews. Accordingly, in both halves of the Empire the ruling race was in a minority.

THE BALANCE OF MINORITIES IN AUSTRIA To preserve their position the two dominant peoples used different tactics. The Austrian Germans, being more heavily outnumbered and obliged to deal with the Czechs, the most unified and advanced minority in the Empire, were compelled to grant various and increasing degrees of governmental and cultural autonomy to the subject peoples. It was necessary to play off Poles against Ruthenians, or *vice versa*, and even, from the Hapsburg standpoint, occasionally to allow the Czechs to balance the Germans. It was essential, too, to maintain a parliament in which the warring nationalities could blow off steam and vent their animosities, even against the government, which could ignore these outbursts so long as it held the power of the purse. Beginning in 1897 with a German riot in the Reichsrat over the proposed equal status of the German and Czech languages in Bohemia, the Austrian Parliament became the scene of perennial riots, every faction being equipped with an arsenal of noise makers, a state

of affairs which enabled the bureaucracy to retain the reins
with ease.

FOUR CLASS VOTING   Election to the Reichsrat was conducted
under a four class system of voting, which was weighted overwhelmingly in favor of the upper bourgeoisie and landowners.
Of the latter, sixty-three voters could elect a deputy, while
it required 11,000 rural voters to choose one. The cities and
the chambers of commerce constituted the other voting classes
until 1897, when a fifth class of voters was created, including
all men over twenty-four years of age. Since the four favored
classes voted also in the fifth, the popular leaven which was
added to the legislature was not large. Dissatisfaction continued
and was brought to a high pitch by the Russian Revolution
of 1905. Great popular demonstrations were repressed only by
bloodshed. Impressed by the widespread demand for reform,
the ministers decided in 1907 to try universal suffrage, with
the result that eighty-seven socialists were elected. But universal
suffrage did not usher in constitutional democracy. "Austria
remained essentially absolutist."[26]

FOUR RULING GROUPS   To govern his turbulent realm the old
Emperor Francis Joseph (1848–1918) relied upon a powerful
army officered by the German nobility, a loyal bureaucracy
and "a Roman Catholic clergy who used their influence to
strengthen the Hapsburg hold on the lesser nationalities."[27] He
could depend also upon the German industrialists. The Emperor
stoutly guarded German as the army language of command,
even against the Hungarians. As the only head of a great
power which was not anti-clerical or non-Catholic, he enjoyed
a strong position with the Church and used it to the full to
preserve his rule.

On its administrative side, the Hapsburg regime was "a

[26] Carlton J. Hayes, *A Political and Cultural History of Modern Europe*,
New York, 1936, Vol. II, p. 639. The universal suffrage reform did not extend to Hungary.
[27] F. L. Benns, *European History Since 1870*, p. 300.

police infested, corrupt government,"[28] though of a far milder type than the Russian despotism. The easygoing Austrians multiplied officials and regulations until any kind of action was difficult. Everything tended to become petty, including the innumerable winkings at bribery and law-breaking. Even the dissolute Hapsburg court, "one of the most immoral and degenerate courts in the world,"[29] was not an effective center for resolute action or repression. The old Emperor so sternly regimented his horde of more than sixty archdukes and archduchesses in busy idleness that the dynasty had little energy for such brutal suppressions of all unwelcome movements as emanated from St. Petersburg.

HUGE ESTATES   Austria-Hungary was, for the most part, a land of "stupid peasants and of great land owners." Prince Schwartzenberg owned 437,000 acres in Bohemia, where the Emperor had an estate of 86,000 acres. The Church held vast estates. Great prelates enjoyed incomes as large as those of the French bishops before 1789. One Austrian archbishop received an income of $300,000 a year and a Hungarian bishop held 266,000 acres of land. Forty percent of the land in Hungary was gathered into huge *latifundia*. One estate contained 570,000 acres, or 890 square miles, while 324 averaged 41,000 acres (64 square miles each).

LANDLORD RULE IN HUNGARY   In the great elliptical area controlled by Hungary the dominance of the Magyar landlords was complete, both economically and politically. Four-fifths of the agricultural population had less than twenty acres per farm. The Magyar aristocracy "made no pretense of sharing the management of Hungary with the masses of their own people, to say nothing of sharing it with any of the subject nationalities."[30] The franchise was so narrow that a bare 6 percent of the people voted, nearly all upper class Magyars. The non-

---

[28] William Stearns Davis, *Europe Since Waterloo*, p. 424.
[29] *Ibid.*, p. 420.
[30] Hayes, Vol. II, p. 639.

Magyar majority in the kingdom could elect only 10 percent of the deputies to parliament. Throughout the thousand-year-old kingdom that the Magyars have lamented so unceasingly since 1919 the policy of the ruling strata was forcibly to Magyarize the subject races and keep them poor and ignorant, along with the bulk of the Magyars. In 1869, when the Slovaks came under Hungarian rule, they had 1921 schools; in 1911 they had only 440, despite a large increase in population. The non-Magyars could obtain but 19 percent of the elementary schools and only 7 percent of the higher schools. Even the German schools in Hungary decreased from 1272 in 1869 to 500 in 1915. The pressure to use the Magyar language was never-ending, in the schools and everywhere else. No means of coercing the "Little Peoples" was omitted. The determination of the Magyar lords to rule supremely and alone was daily illustrated on the faces of the Austro-Hungarian bank notes. On one side, the Austrian, the denominations were printed in eight different languages; on the other side in Magyar alone, notwithstanding the presence of many tongues in Hungary.

The fixed purpose of the Magyar landlords to monopolize the country inevitably led to agitation for electoral reform so intense that in the first decade of the twentieth century it brought the kingdom "to the verge of civil war."[31] Between 1876 and 1910, some 3,500,000 people emigrated from Hungary to escape from the repressive arrogance of the Magyar nobles. More important still for the fate of the proud kingdom, its South Slav subjects were goaded into such a state of complete disaffection that they wanted only to end Hungarian rule over them forever.

THE EMERGING SOUTH SLAVS Since the Slavs in Bosnia and in Austria also felt the benefits of military roads and rule to be a poor substitute for freedom, the existence in Serbia of an independent South Slav kingdom became a standing of-

[31] *Ibid.*

fense both to the German dynasts of Austria and the Magyar rulers of Hungary. The danger of a drawing together of the 13,000,000 South Slavs was not greatly feared until the Austrian-controlled King Milan of Serbia was murdered in 1903, along with his too-ambitious queen and her brothers, who controlled the state, and a pro-Russian dynasty installed. After the "brutal but not unprovoked" crime of 1903 the people of Serbia cele-brated and lifted their heads as free men. If their government was far from an ideal democracy it was so free by comparison that Hapsburg South Slavs felt the contrast with their own condition to be most painful. In Bosnia 85 percent of the people were illiterate; they had but 253 primary state schools, whereas in smaller Serbia there were 1272. In Bosnia the Ortho-dox Church, the chief vehicle of Serb nationalism, was reduced to slavery, while Roman Catholic officials and ecclesiastics ruled and prospered, exporting large fortunes.[32]

Matters became still worse when Serbia endeavored to throw off the economic dominance of Austria. The tariff war which began in 1906 taught them how intensely they needed a seaport and nothing could have made their bitterness deeper in the succeeding years than Austria's repeated blocking of their ef-forts to get one. Even in the Monarchy the railway and economic interests of Bosnia, Herzegovina and Dalmatia were deliberately separated to hinder the unification of the Slavs. Nevertheless, Serbia continued to grow in size and power, as a result of the two Balkan wars, and to magnetize the Slavs under the Hapsburg yoke ever more strongly as she grew. Responding to the divisive tactics of Vienna, representatives of Croatia, Dalmatia, and Istria met at Fiume as early as 1905 and de-manded to be united in one state. During the same year Serbs and Croats met at Zara to proclaim themselves one nation. They gained control of the Diet of Croatia. After repeated dissolutions and many treason trials, the Governor of Croatia

[32] Virginio Gayda, *Modern Austria*, New York, 1915, pp. 114–120. Aus-tria "crushes the other religions until she converts them."—p. 117.

dispensed with the Diet and ruled as a dictator. Attempts to kill him were made in 1912, 1913, and 1914.

The obvious solution of attempting to incorporate all of the Yugoslavs inside the Monarchy into a third kingdom was never tried. The Magyar nobles who were responsible for the bitterest disaffection of the Slavs would not hear of it. The Magyar lords would release no subjects nor share their independent position in the Monarchy with any other people. Besides, if the Yugoslavs received a kingdom of their own would not the powerful Czechs be equally entitled to one? This was a prospect that appealed to no German subjects of the Emperor. And what of the Poles and Rumanians? Because the Hungarians would not begin to democratize the Monarchy, and because the Austrians could not see where the process would end, the two ruling classes united in a policy of scotching independent Serbia, first by diplomacy, and when occasion should offer, by force.

COLLAPSE RESISTED "Thus at the very heart of Europe," in the words of a German statesman, "lay a great state inwardly ripe for collapse, and bearing the outward signs of the approaching calamity."[33] Lacking either the will or the foresight to attempt a genuine liberalization and federalization of their polyglot peoples, the dignitaries of Vienna and Budapest moved toward war, another Balkan war which would end their worst troubles and "save the Monarchy" that most of the Emperor's subjects wished only to destroy. The Archduke Francis Ferdinand might as Emperor have succeeded in forcing a trial of "trialism"; his death furnished the ideal occasion for the war.

For two years the great arc of the Austrian domain, from Ruthenia around to Herzegovina, had been increasingly shaken by riots, dissolutions of diets, arrests and public trials in which the Slavs won the moral verdict. Within the rich oval where the Hungarians ruled, the pressure had likewise mounted danger-

[33] Richard von Kühlmann, *Thoughts on Germany,* London, 1932, p. 78.

ously. "The last attempt of the Hapsburgs to reform and strengthen their empire had ended in failure. . . . The invocation of force alone remained."[34]

The Emperor Francis Joseph was old. His eightieth birthday had been celebrated in 1910. He must soon pass, and his German and Magyar industrialists and nobles were determined that the empire should not pass with him. The rulers of the mighty German Empire also willed that the Dual Monarchy should not dissolve. Germany was tied tightly by diplomatic alliance to that body of death which the flickering spirit of Francis Joseph held together and her masters feared that unless the decay of the Monarchy could be arrested it would be fatal to Germany. When Bismarck broke the connection of Austria with the great mass of Germans, after Sadowa, he doomed the Austrians to submergence in a sea of Slavs and Magyars; now his successors were to risk the empire which he created in order to preserve "our only reliable ally."

The Clash of Militarism and Socialism in Germany

The Germany of the pre-war years was a nation of which any emperor might have been proud. Born in 1871 of Bismarck's union of blood and iron, nourished on the promptly paid gold of the French indemnity, Germany had become a great industrial nation with a rapidity which only the United States could equal. Exhilarated by military victory, she had grasped the advantages of free trade within the empire and, stimulated by protective tariffs against the outside world, German organizing genius, scientific ability, thoroughness and discipline combined to build an empire of coal and iron which had given Germany a splendid and expanding place in the sun of world trade and prosperity. In the words of Chancellor Bernhard von Bülow: "The poor German country has become a rich country.

[34] Joseph Ward Swain, *Beginning the Twentieth Century*, p. 159.

. . . German industry has its customers even in the remotest corners of the earth."[35]

DIVINE RIGHT RULE How did democracy fare in the magnificent empire of William II? In his first address, and in succeeding ones, William had made clear his own attitude: "The soldier and the army, not parliamentary majorities, have welded the German Empire together. My confidence is placed in the army! . . . One shall be master, even I. . . . Everyone who is against me I shall crush."[36]

To make his imperial will effective William discharged the masterful Bismarck from the Chancellorship and made it clear that only viziers could serve him. The number of ministers directly responsible to him was increased to thirteen, among which the military heavily predominated. Apart from these, too, the brilliant, vain Emperor naturally accumulated about him a large court of intriguing flatterers. Eventually, in 1907, exposures of disgusting immorality among his courtiers led to the elimination of some from his circle, after public trials had given the facts to the world, but plenty of other irresponsible advisers remained around the erratic ruler.

THE DAILY TELEGRAPH UPROAR The 1907 scandals had scarcely subsided when the Kaiser himself unwittingly touched off a political bombshell which revealed the lack of responsibility in the German government. In 1908 the London *Daily Telegraph* published an interview with the Kaiser which caused an explosion of indignation in both England and Germany. William had sought to improve the tense relations between the two peoples, but the effect was just the opposite. A storm of fury swept all sections of opinion in Germany from the chauvinists to the socialists, against the "man who autocratically laid down the foreign policy of Germany, unwarrantably provoked Japan, deprived all the Powers of any feeling they may have possessed that they could make a confidential communication to Germany

---

[35] Bernhard von Bülow, *Imperial Germany*, New York, 1914, p. 249.
[36] Davis, *Europe Since Waterloo*, p. 391.

and, finally, boasted that he had betrayed a small and friendly nation (the Boers) by going behind its back to its enemy with his famous Plan of Campaign."[37]

In the Reichstag debates on the *Daily Telegraph* episode it came out that Chancellor von Bülow had seen the proposed interview but had sent it to the Foreign Office without reading it, and the latter, thinking it had been approved, made no objection. However, von Bülow joined in the universal denunciation of the Kaiser's indiscretion and exacted a public declaration from him that he would impose more reserve upon himself in the future. Following this promise another debate was held in the Reichstag, in which the Chancellor led the attack and everybody, including many conservatives, joined in a vote of censure.

For a time the Kaiser was chastened, but his resentment at Bülow only laid him open to the pressure of Admiral Tirpitz and his big-navy men. By August 1910 William was recalling in a speech at Königsberg the time when his grandfather had crowned himself, without reference to "parliaments, national assemblies and popular resolutions" and declaring that "Regarding myself as an instrument of the Lord, I go my way . . . indifferent to the views and opinions of the moment."[38]

THE REICHSTAG CONTROLLED The Imperial Chancellor, who bore alone all the responsibilities carried by the cabinet under parliamentary government, was responsible solely to the Kaiser, not to the Reichstag. Yet he did have to secure from that

[37] Arthur Rosenberg, *The Birth of the German Republic,* London, 1931, p. 52. In his *The Eve of 1914* (London, 1935, p. 42), Theodore Wolff supports a statement by Ernest Jäckh "that behind the apparent solidity of the façade of the German Empire those responsible for the administration were all at sixes and sevens. A perpetual war was going on between all sorts of authorities. The various departments of government and the subservient member of the Court were fighting in utter disorganization for power and influence."

[38] William H. Dawson, *The German Empire,* 1867–1914, New York, 1919, pp. 348–49.

body the approval of appropriations, a task which no Chancellor found especially difficult until after the election of 1912. With five fairly large parties in the Reichstag it was always feasible to construct a coalition of some kind around the Conservatives, with the understanding that the Socialists must never be in it, not only because they were socialists but republicans as well, given to denouncing the whole imperial idea in the Reichstag.[39] The Socialists were also excluded from any share in the government of Prussia, which included three-fifths of the Empire and was controlled by ministers reporting to William as King of Prussia.

THREE CLASS VOTING IN PRUSSIA   Within the Prussia which completely overshadowed the Empire the Socialists and all other popular elements were excluded from power by the three-class system of voting, whereby in every district the large taxpayers who paid one-third of the taxes were given one-third of the votes, and so on down. Though the system undoubtedly promoted the efficient management and development of German cities, it also practically disenfranchised the great bulk of the citizens. In the Prussian election of 1908, the first class voters numbered 293,402, the second class 1,065,242 and the third class 6,324,079. The upper class voters had respectively 22 and 6 times the weight of the third class. This weighting gave the Conservative and Centre parties 316 seats in the Prussian Landtag, the Liberals and Radicals 101 seats and the Socialists a microscopic 7.[40]

[39] "There is no possibility of reconciling them to the State, and of dissolving them in so doing, by tying them to the Government cart for a time," wrote Prince von Bülow in 1914. Our Social Democratic Party "will have nothing to do with German patriotic memories which have a monarchical and military character."—*Imperial Germany*, pp. 221, 223.

[40] J. Ellis Barber, *Modern Germany*, New York, 1915, p. 448. In 2,214 voting precincts the first class votes were cast by one man; in 1,703 precincts by two individuals. In 1907 the third class included 87.5 percent of the voters. Up to 1906 the great city of Berlin was allowed but 9 seats in the Landtag, and afterward only 12.

In 1903 the Socialists tried the system out just to see what would happen.

IMPERIAL ROTTEN BOROUGHS For elections to the Imperial Reichstag universal male suffrage prevailed, even in Prussia.[41] But here the liberal and socialist masses of the cities were disenfranchised almost as successfully as in Prussia, simply by refusing to redistrict the electoral areas. When the Empire was formed in 1871, Germany was an agrarian, provincial country. The remarkable industrial development which followed transformed her into an urbanized nation. Yet decade by decade the government refused to agree to new election districts— down to the verge of the revolution of 1918. Consequently, in the Tetlow district, near Berlin, 197,000 votes were required to elect a member of the Reichstag, but in Schaumburg-Lippe only 10,000 votes were needed; in Berlin VI 195,000 votes, in Launburg 13,000; in Hamburg III 137,000 to 13,000 in a town nearby. The injustice became more glaring and intolerable yearly, until it was fully as scandalous as "the corresponding abuses that once supported in power the landed interest in the British parliament, at the height of parliamentary corruption in that country."[42]

UNPAID MEMBERS As a further device for keeping Socialists out of the Reichstag Bismarck had refused to permit the members to be paid. Later, when the Socialists themselves supported their members, the Imperial Court of Appeal ruled that practice illegal. Then for many years the Reichstag passed laws for the payment of its members, only to have them killed in the Bundesrat. It was not until 1906 that this measure of elementary fairness could be secured.

Their 314,149 votes elected not a single member of the Landtag. But 324,-157 Conservative voters elected 143 members.—F. A. Ogg, *The Governments of Europe*, New York, 1922, pp. 259–60.

[41] Prince von Bülow agreed that no conciliation of the Socialists was possible while the Reichstag elections were carried on "from an absolutely different standpoint from that of the Prussian Diet elections."—*Imperial Germany*, p. 232.

[42] Thorstein Veblen, *Imperial Germany and the Industrial Revolution*, New York, 1915, pp. 207–8.

SOCIALIST GAINS INTERMINABLE   The steady increase in Socialist votes in all German elections was the despair alike of Bismarck and all his successors. Bismarck had sought to forestall the Socialists by establishing a comprehensive system of social insurance. German workmen were the first to have extensive protection against accident, sickness, old age, and unemployment. They accepted these benefits, but did not abate their socialist convictions. After 1881 each succeeding election showed an average gain of about 750,000 Socialist votes. Only in 1907 did Bülow succeed in reducing Socialist strength in the Reichstag sharply, by inducing Conservatives and National Liberals to cooperate against the Socialists, and by promoting the Radicals in other constituencies. He then obtained an increase of Conservatives, who, in spite of their ire over the *Daily Telegraph* affair, would not permit an advance toward ministerial responsibility to the Reichstag or any other step toward democracy. On the contrary, they helped to defeat the budget and Bülow resigned July 14, 1909. His successor, Theobald von Bethmann Hollweg, was careful to state that he would not resign, regardless of Reichstag support, so long as he retained the confidence of the Kaiser.

THE ELECTORAL REVOLT OF 1912   In the 1912 election 4,250,329 Germans voted as Socialists. Polling 35 percent of the total vote, the Socialists won even in the rotten boroughs, advancing their Reichstag strength from 43 to 110, and becoming the largest party in the chamber. While the progressive-minded Radicals held their own, the Junker Conservatives and industrialist National Liberals lost heavily, after a victory over the Social Democrats had been declared to be "a matter of life and death for the Fatherland." The Socialist leader, August Bebel, polled 175 votes to 196 in the balloting for President of the Reichstag— the chamber's intermediary with His Majesty! The Socialist Philipp Scheidemann was actually elected Second Vice-President, and it took a month of jockeying to form a coalition containing nearly all the other parties and get him out.

The great Socialist sweep in the election of 1912 was not a true measure of Socialist strength. In 1911 the party had only 729,000 male members. Perhaps there were many semi-Socialists who were not zealous enough to pay dues. But beyond these a very large part of the huge 4,250,000 vote represented the protest of non-Socialist Germans who were disgusted by the incessant military struttings of the Hohenzollern regime, with its accompaniment of ever higher taxes and mounting ill will abroad. The economic grievances of the prosperous, state-socialized German people were not sufficient to account for the great Socialist vote of 1912, a boom year in Germany, and the imperialists knew it.

The "Security League" was at once founded to propagandize the country heavily for militarism by stressing the danger of attack by Germany's neighbors. The Italo-Turkish and Balkan wars supplied a disquieting background for the campaign. It was featured, at frequent intervals, by great patriotic centennial celebrations of the Napoleonic wars that were prophetic of the patriotic circuses which would rock Germany in the Nazi era.

THE GOVERNMENT REBUKED ON POLISH LANDS In January 1913 a significant clash occurred in the Reichstag. Bethmann Hollweg was pushed by the East Prussian Junkers to begin enforcing the expropriation law of 1908, aimed at the lands owned by Poles. The reaction in the Reichstag was immediate and emphatic. A motion that the policy of the Chancellor was contrary to the views of the Reichstag carried by a vote of more than two to one. The Reichstag has passed its first pointed vote of "no confidence" in an Imperial Chancellor.

In April the new Army bill, with its heavier burdens, was approved only after a bitter debate. Very soon the Socialist leader, Karl Liebknecht, made scandalous revelations of the way in which the Krupp armament works corrupted the government and fomented war scares abroad to frighten it. Liebknecht was excluded from the investigating committee and the affair hushed up, but several convictions resulted.

MILITARISM AT ZABERN   Then, in November 1913, the Zabern incident swiftly followed, emphasizing to the whole German people the full extent to which they were at the mercy of an arrogant military caste. Lieutenant Baron von Forstner was only twenty, but he was an officer in the Alsatian town of Zabern, the only district in Alsace which was Protestant and represented by a Conservative in the Reichstag. Nevertheless, Forstner felt it necessary to address his Alsatian recruits as rowdies and speak of France offensively. He urged his soldiers to use their weapons energetically should they clash with the people and offered a prize of ten marks to those who should succeed in running a man through.

Not unnaturally the remarks of that bloodthirsty young man became the talk of the town, and after the story of a ludicrous mishap which had befallen him while drunk had been circulated, he was teased by people, especially children. The dignity of His Majesty's Imperial Army being thus offended, Forstner's superior officers ordered soldiers with fixed bayonets to guard the officers about town. This, of course, increased the merriment and small crowds began to follow the embattled military parades and to stand before the barracks gates, to see them come and go.

Then, instead of sending Forstner away, Colonel von Reutner mobilized his troops and threatened to shoot the crowd, which by his own testimony numbered forty to a hundred people. Orders were then issued to arrest all who lingered at the barracks or laughed at officers. Thereupon the troops arrested a group of citizens, including three local judges and the prosecuting attorney, who were soon released. The others were locked in the barracks coal cellar all night, until released by the civil magistrates. But even this remarkable sortie failed to make the populace respect Lieutenant Forstner. He was jeered again by a group of youngsters and his troops succeeded in catching only a crippled cobbler who could not get away. It was alleged by the Army that this cripple had presumed on his infirmity to offend

Forstner. If so he miscalculated, for that redoubtable officer avenged his Prussian honor by cutting the lame shoemaker down (though not fatally), while he was held by two soldiers.

"NO CONFIDENCE" AGAIN VOTED The political effect of these events was tremendous. "The majority of the German population felt itself to be physically and legally defenceless against the military aristocracy." In the Reichstag the Minister of War, Erich von Falkenhayn, sharply and brutally defended the Zabern officers and, after Bethmann Hollweg had weakly followed him, "there arose a storm of indignation against the corps of officers the like of which had never been known in the whole history of the German Empire." The Reichstag refused to accept Bethmann's exculpations and promises by a vote of 293 to 54.[43]

IMPERIALIST RULE DISTURBED Of course Bethmann did not resign, even after this second vote of no confidence within the year, but his position was becoming dangerous. Powerful fears and aversions had been aroused. As Swain has pointed out, should the Centre Party decide to oppose the government, Bethmann would either have to resign, thus initiating parliamentary responsibility, or govern in defiance of the Reichstag and bring about a truly grave crisis. The autocratic control of the imperialist classes over the German people was beginning to be uncomfortably shaken. The vast majority of the Germans were too well regimented to think of actual revolution, but they had begun to join peace societies everywhere and to read pacifist literature more than the outpourings of the chauvinists and Pan-Germans.[44]

Early in 1914 the Social Democrats won 150,000 new dues-paying members in a national drive and then defeated the

[43] Rosenberg, *The Birth of the German Republic*, p. 56; Barber, *Modern Germany*, p. 799; Davis, *Europe Since Waterloo*, p. 396; Swain, *Beginning the Twentieth Century*, p. 76. The militarist class thought it essential to keep the civilian population strictly "in its place." Colonel Reutner received 15,000 telegrams of congratulation for his repression of the disrespectful Alsatians.

[44] Swain, *Beginning the Twentieth Century*, p. 76.

president of the National Union Against Social Democracy in
a by-election. Simultaneously, there was a sharp economic slump,
tight money, the withdrawal of French capital and a general
retraction to meet the new taxes for armament. The absence
of return on the huge uneconomic outlays on armaments was
beginning to be strongly felt. Thorstein Veblen thought that the
date when German industry and commerce ceased to gain came
in 1909.[45] By the summer of 1914 both economic and political
tension in Germany menaced the further aggrandizement of the
industrialist classes and the continued dominance of the Junker-
aristocrats who fattened upon the autocratic system. The nation
created by blood and iron was becoming weary of the weight
of iron on its back and of the load of parasitic militarism on
its soul. It was time for the soldiers of Germany to make her
great again.

Democracy Consolidated in France

France also, in the years before 1914, had her militarists and
chauvinists. They, too, attempted to dominate the State, but the
outcome was different. In France the democratic forces were
strong enough to control the military men and to assert the
supremacy of the civil authorities.

THE DREYFUS CONFLICT   The decisive contest in France began
in 1894 with the conviction of Captain Alfred Dreyfus for the
sale of military information to the German military attaché in
Paris. Dreyfus was a wealthy Jew. A violent book by Edouard
Drumont and a campaign by eight leading Paris newspapers
had aroused strong anti-Semitic feeling. The sentence of Dreyfus,
by court-martial, to life imprisonment on Devil's Island was
therefore popular. At his public military degradation Dreyfus

[45] Veblen, *Imperial Germany,* p. 210.

had shouted his innocence so defiantly that some wondered, but
the crowds roared against him. Two years passed before Colonel
Georges Picquart, in the Secret Intelligence Department, by
slow degrees unearthed evidence that the real traitor was a certain Major Esterhazy, a nondescript international adventurer.
But the Army officers universally refused to believe that a mistake had occurred. The hated Jew could not be innocent and besides it would never do to admit that an unjust blunder had been
made. The royalists and clericals rallied strongly to the defense
of the Army, in the hope of discrediting and ending the Republic. A court-martial of Esterhazy had to be held, but it was
conducted secretly in order to keep Picquart's information from
being made public, and the culprit was acquitted in due form.
Picquart was moved about France and finally sent to Tunis.

Zola's famous letter, explicitly accusing a long roster of military
men of guilt in the case, was published in Clemenceau's paper
L'Aurore, on January 13, 1898. It threw Paris into an uproar
which was increased by Zola's trial for libel before an openly
prejudiced judge. Though Zola's conviction was reversed by the
Court of Cassation, he concluded that a second trial would result
in his imprisonment and fled to England. All France was then
placarded with a new official demonstration of Dreyfus' guilt,
written by the Minister of War on the basis of documents forged
by Colonel Henry, chief of the Secret Intelligence Department.
Henry, exposed, killed himself. Esterhazy fled from France and
admitted his guilt. Notwithstanding all this a new Minister of
War resigned rather than sanction a reopening of the Dreyfus
case.

A new court-martial of Dreyfus was nevertheless forced in
1899, and he was again convicted. By this time his innocence
was so manifest that President Emile Loubet gave him a pardon,
which he reluctantly accepted. In 1906 the Court of Cassation
finally gave Dreyfus a complete exoneration. He was reinstated
in the Army with as much ceremony as he had been degraded

and promoted in rank.[46] Picquart, who had also at length been imprisoned for his defense of innocence, presently became Minister of War.

THE ARMY REPUBLICANIZED   In 1902, the French people voted on the Dreyfus affair and the liberal, republican forces won 350 seats, the reactionary elements emerging with only 220. The Radicals then proceeded to weed out the heavy preponderance of army officers who were royalists at heart and to put the armed forces in charge of men who would loyally serve the Republic. In 1905 the term for conscripts was reduced to two years and the sons of all classes were obliged to do their turn.

EDUCATION MADE PUBLIC   The "Bloc Republican" then turned its attention to reducing the power of the Church, particularly over education. The religious orders had grown rapidly until they numbered 190,000 monks, 75,000 nuns, possessed great wealth and taught most of the children of France. More opposed to the Republic than the regular clergy, the orders were so powerful as to be difficult of control by the bishops. The "very specimens of their pupils' efficiency which they submitted to the jury at the Paris Exhibition of 1900 showed that they were rearing them to hate and oppose the Republic."[47]

A law of 1901 provided that only "authorized" orders could teach. All others must disband. Few were authorized and in the spring of 1903 the bulk of the monks and nuns were expelled from France. The Concordat of 1801, made with the Church by Napoleon I, was also abrogated. In 1904 another statute provided that all religious instruction should cease entirely within ten years. By 1914 more than 80 percent of the children of France were taught in public schools.

CHURCH AND STATE SEPARATED   In 1905 a law separating the Church from the State was passed, which removed the clergy from the public pay roll and restored to the Church full control

---

[46] Vizetelly, *Republican France, 1870–1912*, Boston, 1912, pp. 411, 428–31, 454–55.

[47] Vizetelly, p. 456.

of its own internal organization. A two-year deadlock over the use of the churches followed. During that period the anti-clerical bloc won a national election by a more sweeping majority than in 1902. The election of 1906 returned 420 members of the Bloc Republican, leaving but 174 seats to its opponents.

NATIONAL RESURGENT These struggles with the aristocratic and clerical forces accounted in part for the somewhat tardy advance of France in social legislation. Other explanations were that the majority of Frenchmen still lived in agrarian communes and that France was highly prosperous from 1908 to 1914. The ruling Radicals being faithful to the peasants and small-business men, the industrial workers turned to socialism. Their great leader, Jaurès, was one of the most earnest and constructive pacifists to be found anywhere. But French chauvinism also increased rapidly and after the disintegration of the Bloc Republican on social issues, the strongly nationalist Raymond Poincaré became Premier in 1912 and President in 1913. After a bitter battle the conservative-nationalist forces which he led secured a three-year Army service law in 1913, a step which caused the election in 1914 of the most radical chamber in the Republic's history. From his key position in the presidency Poincaré nevertheless held out for the three-year Army service law until he found a cabinet which would accept it.

The stage was set for a momentous struggle between conservative nationalism and liberal humanitarianism when the crime of Sarajevo intervened. Nowhere in France was there any serious challenge to the right of the people to settle all national issues by democratic means.

The Sweep of Liberal Reforms in Great Britain

In Great Britain the decade before the war was a period of great social reform and of important constitutional change. In 1906 a long period of rule by the Conservatives came to a close.

Their inefficiency in conducting the Boer War and even the fact that the war had been fought counted against them. The Taff Vale decision of the House of Lords, making labor unions liable to the employers for losses resulting from strikes, alienated labor. Joseph Chamberlain's espousal of tariff protection split the Tories, and the election of 1906 gave a landslide to the Liberals. They came in with a majority of 356 seats in the House of Commons, the largest margin which any party had had since the passage of the Reform Bill in 1832.[48]

HOUSE OF LORDS VETO REVIVED   The Liberals at once passed a Trades Dispute Act which reversed the Taff Vale decision, legalized picketing and gave immunity to union funds. A Workman's Compensation Act extended protection to low income laborers. Then in swift succession the House of Lords rejected three reform measures: an education bill, a bill to abolish plural voting, and a licensing bill, regulating liquor selling. The Prime Minister, Sir Henry Campbell-Bannerman, charged that the Conservative Leader, Balfour, was controlling the fate of bills in the Lords and warned that representative government no longer existed if a party overwhelmingly defeated at the polls was to remain "in supreme control of legislation."[49] The Tories replied that an attack on the House of Lords would postpone all social reform indefinitely. To this Asquith retorted that such reform was already blocked by the determination of the Lords to protect the vested interests from progressive social reform. Early in 1907 a resolution that the Lords should not delay the action of the House of Commons beyond the life of a single parliament carried, 432 to 147.

OLD AGE PENSIONS   While this fight simmered, an Old Age Pension Bill was passed in 1908 and a measure attacking bad housing conditions, in 1909. Old age pensions had been endorsed by Chamberlain years before and had long been considered. The maximum pension allowed, to persons over seventy, was

[48] *Whitaker's Almanac*, 1938, p. 288.
[49] *Hansard*, 4 S.H.C., 1907, Vol. 169, pp. 78–89.

$1.25 a week to those having incomes less than $3 a week.
Yet Lord Lansdowne denounced the granting of this pittance
to the last days of the desperately poor as "one which will
weaken the moral fiber of the nation and diminish the self-
respect of our people."[50]

While expressing such sentiments, the Tories promoted by all
means available to them the famous naval panic of 1909. They
expected either to convict the Liberals of leaving the country
undefended or to force them to spend so much money on
battleships that little could be found for social services, without
bringing taxation which would defeat the government.

THE LLOYD GEORGE BUDGET The Liberals were extricated
from this dangerous dilemma by the genius of Lloyd George,
the non-conformist Welshman who was Chancellor of the Ex-
chequer. His celebrated budget of 1909 was deliberately framed:
(1) to provoke a conflict with the House of Lords which would
break its power; (2) to provide the money for both battleships
and social reform; and (3) to reduce by taxation, as drastically
as possible, the privileged position of the landlords.

The social situation in Great Britain was one of great extremes
of wealth and poverty. Britain was a very wealthy nation, but
half of the national income went to 12 percent of the people.
Millions lived constantly on the edge of starvation. Less than
1 percent of the people owned as much as an acre of land.
Almost half of the arable land in England belonged to 2250
aristocrats and in Scotland 90 percent of the land was held by
some 1700 persons.[51]

To strike at these glaring inequalities, Lloyd George proposed
two kinds of taxes: (1) steep increases in income and inheritance
taxes on higher brackets, with an additional levy on unearned

[50] Thomas C. Meech, *This Generation*, London, 1927, pp. 149, 154.

[51] Benns, *European History Since 1870*, pp. 205-6. As late as 1927, two-
thirds of the wealth of the United Kingdom was held by just under 400,000
people, or less than one per cent of the population, and one-third by 36,000
people, or less than one in a 1000.—A. M. Carr-Saunders and D. C. Jones,
The Social Structure of England and Wales, London, 1927, pp. 113-14.

income; and (2) a series of land taxes aimed at the unearned increment of land values and at undeveloped land, i.e., the huge areas in game parks, lawns, etc. Lloyd George frankly hoped that the taxes would "have the effect eventually of destroying the selfish and stupid monopoly which now so egregiously mismanages the land."[52]

In his budget speech Lloyd George declared that it was a war budget. It was a budget "for waging implacable warfare against poverty and squalidness." He cited the many hundreds of thousands of people who endured stern hardships "due to circumstances over which they have not the slightest command" and asked if it was "fair to subject multitudes to these miseries until nations had learned to stop spending their means on armaments." Winston Churchill also warned that unless social conditions improved Britain would be "exposed to fatal dangers against which fleets and armies are of no avail."

THE TORIES REVOLT   The landlords could see nothing but the "unfairness" of taxes aimed at them. They were especially furious about the budget strokes at "unearned" increment and "unearned" income. If the aristocrats were once labeled by law as parasitic, would they not logically be exterminated by later legislation? Unable to understand how Britain could continue unless ruled by her landed lords, the Earl of Rosebery declared that "the budget threatens to poison the very sources of our national supremacy." Lord Willoughby de Broke charged that the budget was both revolution and socialism, and from Land's End to Inverness the Tories loudly echoed this double damnation. Lord Mil-

---

[52] Charles W. Pipkin, *The Idea of Social Justice*, New York, 1927, Vol. I, p. 238. So far as his land taxes were concerned Lloyd George was to be disappointed, since they were repealed in 1919. The steeper income and inheritance taxes, however, especially the latter, threatened to accomplish his purpose. In 1938 the "National Trust" was planning to take over many of the great estates, free them of all taxes, including death duties, and permit their titled owners to reside in them perpetually—all on the theory that it would be far better for the great houses to be thrown open to public visit occasionally than to be used as schools and hospitals.—The *Daily Telegraph and Morning Post*, October 8, 1938.

ner, at Glasgow, urged the Peers to reject the budget and to "damn the consequences."

THE FIRST CAMPAIGN OF 1910 The House of Lords accepted this advice with abandon and refused their assent by a resounding majority of 350 to 75. For the first time in generations the Lords had ventured to defeat a money bill. The challenge was promptly accepted by the government. Parliament was dissolved and in the campaign which followed the Liberal leaders dealt with the landlords in the plainest language. "To have to take the eldest son, whether he is able or not," said Lloyd George at Edinburgh, "is a bad system for everybody." Snobbery, he continued, was an impossible foundation for a democratic constitution. "It helped to destroy Spain for they would not trust their great enterprises to the men of ability and power among them, but chose some representative of a great house." He denied the qualifications of the Peers to legislate, on the ground that sympathy based on knowledge was essential to legislation and the Lords had neither. At Newcastle, referring to the House of Lords in a sentence which struck home, he asked "whether five hundred men, ordinary men chosen accidentally from among the unemployed, shall override the judgment of millions of people who are engaged in the industry which makes the wealth of the country?" And again, "Who ordained that a few should have the land of Britain as a prerequisite? Who made 10,000 people owners of the soil, and the rest of us trespassers in the land of our birth."[53]

Dissecting the belief of those who possessed the nation's wealth that taxes should come from the people, Prime Minister Asquith said pungently that after reading the Lords' debates he "came to the conclusion that there was not a single one of our proposed new taxes, except perhaps the duty on motor spirit, in which the keen scent of one or another of the Tory spokesmen

[53] J. H. Edwards, *David Lloyd George, the Man and the Statesman*, New York, 1929, pp. 317–18; 338–39.

could not detect the fatal and poisonous taint of Socialism."[54]

All the Government parties joined in turning back upon the House of Lords the charge of revolution. The Labor leader, Arthur Henderson, pointed out that the action of the Lords on the Budget Bill had established an uncontrolled force, antagonistic to democratic thought and tendency. They were "not prepared to aid and abet revolution"; they were "actually daring to precipitate it." It was not the "unemployed into whose souls the iron of want and suffering had eaten" that had initiated this revolution. It was the representatives of privilege and vested interests.[55]

Yet the fiercely raised cry of socialism alarmed enough of the middle classes greatly to increase the strength of the Conservatives in the election of January 1910. They won 273 seats to the Liberals' 275. The 122 votes of the Irish Nationalist and Labor parties were necessary to give the government a safe majority. It was, therefore, all the more essential to push on with the curbing of the Lords, since the minor parties knew that the uncontrolled Lords were an impassable barrier to their desires, notwithstanding the Lords' reluctant acceptance of the Lloyd George Budget in April 1911. A general election could not be risked and won as an accompaniment of all important legislation.

CURBING OF THE LORDS MOVED   Before the Peers bowed to the "Peoples Budget," the Government had already moved, March 21, 1910, a resolution which soon grew into the Parliament Act of 1911. This bill provided: (1) that the Lords could no longer veto a money bill, or delay one more than a month; (2) that any other measure would become law in spite of the Lords, if it had been passed by the Commons in three sessions extending over a two-year period; and (3) that the maximum life of a Parliament be reduced from seven to five years.

These proposals still left the Lords the power to call inertia

---

[54] Pipkin, p. 245.
[55] Pipkin, pp. 245–46. *Parliamentary Debates*, 5S. 1909, 13 H.C., 574.

and amendment and delay to their aid in such a fashion as to make it very difficult to overrule them on any non-money bill. Still, when the nation was strongly determined it would be possible to do so.

Even this limitation upon the aristocratic chamber was totally unacceptable to the landlords and their allies. During the mourning for King Edward VII a bi-party commission met fruitlessly twenty-one times in an effort to reach an agreement. Parliament was accordingly dissolved again, November 28, 1910, specifically upon the issue of curbing the Lords. In this contest the Tories held their strength, except for two seats, but could gain nothing. Twice within the year the nation had voted decisively for removing the obstruction of the Lords to social reform. The House of Commons accordingly passed the Parliament Bill on February 22, 1911, by a vote of 362 to 241, and sent it on to the Lords.

During the four years of the Parliament of 1906 the complete extent to which the hereditary Lords had become an adjunct of the Tory party had been fully demonstrated. During this period no single bill against which the Tories had voted on third reading in the House of Commons had passed the House of Lords. The Tories thus possessed an unbeatable combination. When they could control the Commons, all power was theirs; when they lost control of the Commons they could still block in the House of Lords any Liberal measures which displeased them. Furthermore, the Tories did not intend to surrender this veto over all reform. For five months the noble gentry vented their anger on the Parliament Bill in the House of Lords and in midsummer there was no sign of their subsidence. At long last the Cabinet secured a promise from King George V to create enough new Peers to overwhelm the embattled Tory lords.

THE CREATION OF PEERS INVOKED This news was conveyed to the Conservative leaders in a letter from the Prime Minister on July 22, 1911. When the gentlemen who felt that Great Britain belonged to them in perpetuity, through the divine touch of a king's accolade, heard that their veto over the nation's affairs was to be weakened by the appointment of perhaps four hundred brand-new Peers—without any centuries, or decades even, of sanctified birth behind them—all the deep wells of inherited and alarmed pride overflowed. The thought of having their social primacy in the realm watered down by the creation of a small horde of new nobles, and of losing at the same time their power to veto the expropriation of their great possessions, was unbearable. When the Prime Minister rose in the House of Commons, on July 24, "the concentrated fury of feuds ancient and modern entered into the souls of his opponents." Traitor! Traitor! shouted Lord Hugh Cecil, and the cry was taken up by other sons of Peers and their allies. To them high treason was synonymous with the impairment of their privileged position. White with passion, the young Tories incited their elders, as the Prime Minister repeatedly tried to speak. Not one of his words could be heard. The Speaker appealed for order in vain.

Finally, the Prime Minister gave up and Mr. Balfour arose to reply to the speech which had never been delivered, and with visible embarrassment at the orderly hearing accorded him he refuted the arguments he presumed the Premier would have made.

THE PARLIAMENT ACT PASSED   The final scene occurred in the House of Lords on August 10, 1911. Hour after hour the battle raged between the die-hards and a section of the Tories who argued for submission. In reply to repeated taunts that the government was bluffing, Lord Morley warned them in measured syllables which pierced every corner of the building that the necessary Peers would be created promptly. Lord Rosebery, for the cooler-headed Tories, also counseled surrender, quoting the example of the Duke of Wellington on the last comparable occasion, in 1832. Surely no one could doubt Wellington's courage; but the enraged majority was still unconvinced. Perhaps it was Lord Curzon's graphic portrayal of the arrival in the House of Lords of the four hundred new Peers which settled the issue. In any event, a block of Conservatives voted with the small group of Liberal Lords and the majority of the Tories simply disappeared, thus giving the Government a margin of 131 to 114.[56]

SOCIAL INSURANCE EXTENDED   With the obstructive power of the Lords definitely limited, the government then moved forward to complete the great National Insurance Act of 1911, aimed at sickness and unemployment. These ameliorations of industrial poverty, long successfully applied in Germany, were savagely attacked by the Conservatives in by-elections. The requirement of contributions from the employees, along with others from the employers and the State, was assailed as "compulsion," naturally to be resented by all true Britons. Domestic servants were encouraged by their mistresses to write in protest against the small contribution required of them as unjust abstractions from their wages. The main purpose of the scheme, it was alleged, was to create an army of bureaucrats. But the most formidable opposition came from "the stubborn and organized opposition of the medical profession, who were openly threatening to refuse to carry out the provisions of the Act unless more favorable terms were conceded to them."[57]

FURTHER REFORMS ADOPTED   Though chiefly noted for the enactment of the National Insurance Act, the year 1911 also saw the Anglican Church disestablished in Wales, where most of the people were dissenters. The House of Lords refused to pass the measure but under the terms of the new Parliament Act it became law in 1914. Labor was rewarded for its loyalty by a law providing a salary of £400 a year for members of the House of Commons. This long delayed measure of justice to men

[56] Meech, *This Generation*, pp. 203–13. When the division bell sounded Lord Willoughby de Broke headed off two of the escaping Lords (diehards up until then), but one noble duke, whose hat and coat Willoughby had thoughtfully hid, eluded him and fled hatless and coatless. Eight other die-hards changed sides at the last moment, giving the government its majority.

[57] J. H. Edwards, *David Lloyd George, The Man and the Statesman,* pp. 353–54.

without fortunes was made imperative by the Osborne Judgment of the House of Lords in 1909, which declared it was illegal to use trade union funds to pay members of Parliament. In March 1912 a great strike of miners was settled by a law meeting the miners' demands for a minimum wage, but in 1914 the labor situation was again very alarming to many.

THE IRISH HOME RULE CRISIS Nothing, however, approached in gravity the crisis which resulted from the effort of the Liberals to conclude the campaign begun by Gladstone in 1886 to give Ireland home rule. The Third Home Rule Bill, introduced in the Commons in April 1912, did not leave that body until January 1913, when it was promptly rejected by the Lords. Approved by the Commons again in 1913, it came up for its final passage in that body in 1914. Then the Conservatives (the official name of their party was still Unionist, *i.e.*, based on the Irish controversy) now resolved to overthrow the Government and its "socialistic" measures by a last-ditch resistance to home rule for Ireland. The old cry that Protestant "Ulster will fight and Ulster will be right!" was revived and the new Tory leader, Bonar Law, declared in July 1912 that "There are things stronger than parliamentary majorities. I can imagine no length of resistance to which Ulster people will go in which I shall not be ready to support them."[58]

THE CONSERVATIVES BACK REBELLION This open invitation to rebellion and civil war, made not by the untutored proletariat but by the official leaders of the aristocratic and conservative classes, was immediately backed up by the drilling of 100,000 Ulster volunteers, supplied with arms and munitions imported from Germany, and by the taking over of governmental functions in North Ireland by the Ulster rebels. Though the Government failed to deal drastically with the treason which had developed, it did secure the passage of the Home Rule Bill in the Commons for the third and final time in May 1914. High Army officers resigned when asked to proceed to Ulster; armies gathered in

[58] Swain, *Beginning the Twentieth Century*, p. 53.

both ends of Ireland; and feeling rose toward the breaking point throughout Britain.

The eyes of the whole people, and of the Government, were riveted so strongly on the danger of civil war that there was little attention to spare to the crime of Sarajevo and the Austrian diplomatic campaign which followed it. The confidence of German diplomats that the British were so occupied and divided by the Irish struggle that they could not intervene in a distant Balkan conflict was indeed well founded.

Democracy on the March

When Western civilization suddenly collapsed in the summer of 1914, the struggles of the peoples of the old world for liberty and democracy were far from completed, as indeed they never can be. But from China to Ireland the people of every nation were evincing a powerful determination to throw off the rule of the groups which exploited them—whether dynastic, aristocratic, clerical, or imperialistic. In every country, also, the control of the privileged groups was being ended, curtailed, or undermined. In some places, especially Russia, the achievement of free institutions appeared to be still remote, but the trend toward them was strong and universal.

II. The Hegemony of Germany, 1871–1890

Democracy was truly on the march in the first years of the twentieth century. In both the United States and Europe great social reforms were under way which would improve the lot of the common man and add to his economic security.

The first fourteen years of the century were a period of great ferment and reform in the United States. The agrarian Populists and the urban Socialists united with ordinary American liberals in demanding such radical reforms as suffrage for women, unemployment insurance and workmen's compensation laws, minimum wage laws and penalties for child labor, direct primaries and direct election of Senators, graduated income and inheritance taxes. This was the period when a half dozen great reform governors, led by Woodrow Wilson, made sweeping changes in leading states. It was the time of the vital, Republican-led Progressive movement and of Wilson's New Freedom, which put a long series of reform laws of unprecedented importance into force before the war broke in 1914.

Unfortunately, this whole upward movement of civilization was at the mercy of the fundamental anarchy which persisted among the national states. Great gains might be made within the several nations, but in the course of a single day the selfish action of the leaders of one nation could stop all advance and destroy most of the advances made by many nations.

Today there is a minority of people in every civilized nation which recognizes that it is no longer possible for the world to contain more than a hundred "sovereign" nations. Science and invention have destroyed forever the conditions under which so many unfettered national wills could operate without disaster. The very idea of scores of nations which are dependent on one another for their very existence imposing their supreme wills upon each other is an absurdity. In 1914 only a few people were aware that national progress could not proceed much further without far-reaching international organization. The great majority of people could not think beyond the national state. Indeed the passage of a long period without catastrophic wars had made it seem unnecessary even for the Europeans to face the issue upon which their continued existence depended. As for the Americans, they did not dream that the world had become a unit, of which they were an inseparable part.

In 1898, as we emerged into world politics through the Spanish-American War, the world did seem to be a place in which at least the powerful nations could manage their own existence, at the expense of weaker peoples perhaps, but without serious risk to the strong. The Great Powers had not yet lined up into two jealously hostile camps; the deadly acceleration of the arms race had not yet begun. The world still seemed to be a place in which agriculture was the rock of existence and space a protection against the evil intentions of other powers. Yet, on November 9, 1897, an old and very conservative British statesman uttered a warning which should have reverberated in every European home, high and humble, leading to anxious counsel and a universal determination to control the impending course of events. Said Lord Salisbury at the Lord Mayor's banquet:

Remember this—that the federation of Europe is the only possible structure of Europe which can save civilization from the desolating effects of a disastrous war. You notice that on all sides the instruments of destruction, the piling up of arms are becoming larger and larger, the powers of concentration are becoming greater, the instruments of death more active and more numerous and are improved with every year, and each nation is bound for its own safety's sake to take part in this competition.

These are the things which are done, so to speak, on the side of war. The one hope that we have to prevent this competition from ending in a terrible effort of mutual destruction which will be fatal to Christian civilization, the one hope we have is that the Powers may be gradually brought together to act together in a friendly spirit on all questions of difference which may arise until at last they shall be welded in some international constitution which shall give to the world as a result of their great strength a long spell of unfettered and prosperous trade and continued peace.[1]

That Salisbury's warning disturbed few can be safely assumed. In 1897 Western Europe was emerging from a quarter century of peace imposed by the military power of Germany. It was only recently that Germany had begun to hunger for a place in the sun. For decades Bismarck had been concerned only in holding what he had won.

His gains had been great. By means of three carefully planned wars he had maneuvered into one imperial domain many German states that did not want very much to be unified. First, in 1866, mighty Austria had been persuaded to join powerful Prussia in ending the suzerainty of Lilliputian Denmark over the provinces of Schleswig and Holstein. Then, in 1867, an easy quarrel with Austria over the disposal of the provinces taken from Denmark had ended in the overthrow of Austria at Sadowa and her expulsion from Germany. This result accomplished, Bismarck's remaining terms were most moderate: no annexations; no indemnities; not even the occupation of Vienna. Bismarck desired to have Austria's friendship and support in the future, but most of all he wished to avoid her enmity in arms when he came to his greatest undertaking, the defeat of France.

---

[1] *The London Times,* November 10, 1897.

Bismarck's Early Primacy

PEACE TERMS, 1871   When he had easily punctured the hollow shell of the French Empire of Napoleon III, with the reckless assistance of that monarch's futile ministers and generals, Bismarck's terms were far different. After Sedan, in October 1870, the French Minister of Foreign Affairs proposed to Bismarck, at Ferrières, a firm and intimate alliance between France and Prussia, a proposal which would have solved France's problems and Europe's, if loyally executed. But Bismarck rebuffed this bid for easy peace terms.[2] This time the enemy should pay. The Iron Chancellor did not set his face against his generals and public opinion. Five billions of francs were assessed, to be paid in five years, and German troops occupied Northern France, at the expense of France, until the indemnity was collected.

THE FRENCH PAY   The indemnity was large. It seemed a huge amount at that time, and probably France would be long in raising the full sum. The effort involved was enormous, and in the disorganization of defeat and its aftermath of civil war painful enough. Yet Bismarck would not hear to even a week's postponement of the early installments. He was rigid about the kind of notes and bills required.[3] The German army was kept ready for instant attack. On one occasion a German advance was prevented only by swift compliance with an ultimatum, after French troops operating against the Paris Commune had overstepped a little the line laid down for them.

Then, after the second fall of Paris, the French people made an immense effort to redeem their soil and paid so rapidly that they were able to ask for permission to pay the last installment on September 5, 1873, six months before the first possible date of emancipation specified in the treaty of peace. Consent to make

[2] R. B. Mowat, *The Concert of Europe,* New York, 1930, pp. 6–7.
[3] *Ibid.,* pp. 13, 24.

this final payment was given by Bismarck with mixed emotions. The indemnity which he had thought would keep France weak for a long period had but revealed her strength and courage. Moreover, while the German industrial boom which the indemnity would finance germinated, the payment of the millards seemed to have benefited France more than Germany.

BISMARCK'S IRREPARABLE ERROR But a still more important calculation of Bismarck's had miscarried. Believing himself justified in dealing harshly with an ancient enemy, he had taken Alsace and most of Lorraine. Had they not been German two centuries before? And did not the Alsatians speak German still? And would not the French, by their own confession, have taken territory if they had won?

These questions seemed to answer themselves. Yet in taking Alsace-Lorraine Bismarck was turning back the clock of history further than it could be reversed. When the provinces had last changed hands, one of the many jealous German states was affected, but no German national feeling had been outraged, for none existed. But nearly a hundred years before 1871 the French Revolution and the Napoleonic era completed the process of making the people of France into a nation. The great French trinity of revolutionary ideals, though imperfectly realized, still lived. The little Corsican had bled France and Europe white, but he had unified more than the laws of France.

That the Alsatians still spoke German did not mean that they were German, or that they could be turned from freedom-loving Frenchmen into Germans by Prussian methods. Yet if Bismarck had taken Alsace alone his empire might have endured. After Sedan some loss of territory was expected. But when Bismarck went further and took French Metz and nearly all of Lorraine, sharpening the preliminary terms of peace always to France's disadvantage, he made a wound in the national body and spirit of France which would not heal. The demand of the generals for a strong military frontier was plausible, but "the Rhine was as good a boundary as the Vosges."[4] The supposed need of a buffer between French resentment and the none too enthusiastically unified South Germans was even less valid, for the forcible alienation of the people of Alsace and Lorraine, without any consultation of their wishes or heed to their protests, was the worst way of establishing peace on the Franco-German frontier.[5] Instead of acting as a non-conductor, the alienated people remained a constant irritant to both Germany and France. Henceforth the conquered provinces had to be held by a big army, always on the *qui vive,* preserving a constant subdued war atmosphere. Bismarck had "created a Germany defiantly holding on to an advance post in the enemy's territory."[6] "Necessity" now reinforced the Prussian tradition of a great army, with its inevitable arrogance and offensive spirit.

THE FIRST SECRET TREATIES, 1873 The great master of *Realpolitik* had committed an irreparable blunder, one which dogged him through the rest of his days, a blunder which led from one involvement to another until Europe was split into two warring camps, one centering around the despoiler of 1870, the other about the despoiled. No sooner was the Treaty of Frankfurt signed than Bismarck began to dread the renewal

---

[4] S. B. Fay, *The Origins of the World War,* New York, 1930, Vol. I, p. 52.

[5] Bismarck's disregard of the wishes of conquered peoples was further illustrated by his suppression, with Austria's consent, of the promise in the Austro-Prussian treaty of peace that a plebiscite should be held among the Danes of North Schleswig.

[6] Mowat, *The Concert of Europe,* p. 17. The full responsibility for the annexation was Bismarck's. He refused the plea of the Prussian Crown Prince that Metz be left to the French, and ignored the warning of the *Kolonische Zeitung* that "we shall arouse all Europe against us and lead to a coalition for which France would wait in vain." Some socialists and the editor of *Zukunft,* who protested against the annexation, were jailed.—Carroll, p. 80.

Mansergh's comment is that Germany had committed "a political blunder of the magnitude that brings about an empire's downfall, though it is fair to record that Bismarck realized something of the risks involved."—Nicholas Mansergh, *The Coming of the First World War,* London, 1949, p. 19.

of the old anti-Prussian coalition of the days of Frederick the Great—Austria, France, and Russia. The new German Emperor was sent at once, in August 1871, to visit the Emperor Francis Joseph. The next year a return visit of the Hapsburg monarch was managed in such a way that the Tsar became lonely and asked to be invited.[7] In 1873, the first secret treaty of the new era bound Russia and Germany to send 200,000 troops to the aid of the other in case either should be attacked, and a close agreement between Austria, Russia, and Germany was concluded, October 22, 1873.

Thus did the reactionary rulers of the three mighty empires of Europe draw together for protection—against what? To the Eastern Emperors there was comfort in standing together against liberalism, radicalism, socialism. To Bismarck the isolation of France was the great end, the France which had had a radical revolt in her capital after the German hosts quit it, and then had adopted a disreputable Republican form of government. This pariah must be kept isolated and without allies. Already, on October 3, 1872, the German Ambassador to France, Count Arnim, had reported to Bismarck that not 100,000 Frenchmen were willing to regard the loss of the two provinces as anything but temporary, and when that luckless diplomat favored the French Royalists, as any loyal servant of His Imperial Majesty might, he was condemned and disgraced by Bismarck. If France became Royal again the fears of the three august Emperors, or of two of them, would be allayed.[8]

THE FIRST WAR SCARE, 1875. The rapid recovery of France and the swift payment of her ransom frightened Bismarck.[9] Throughout most of 1873 he was in his blackest mood. In October he instructed Count Arnim to tell the French President that "the world of affairs in Germany" regarded the outbreak

---

[7] J. A. Spender, *Fifty Years of Europe, A Study of Pre-War Documents,* New York, 1933, pp. 21-2.

[8] Spender, *Fifty Years of Europe,* p. 24.

[9] R. J. Sontag, *European Diplomatic History, 1871–1932,* New York, 1933.

of war "as a lesser evil than being endlessly under the threat of it."[10]

Yet the threat which disturbed the great Chancellor's sleep continued to grow until in March 1875 the French had the temerity to begin the reorganization of their army on the Prussian model, a flattery which was too sincere for Bismarck's appreciation. When it was even rumored that France had ordered 10,000 good German horses, a decree was at once issued that the horses must stay at home, and on April 9 the *Berliner Post* carried its famous article, "Is War in Sight?" The Emperor William indignantly condemned "the editors," probably knowing where the chips of his criticism would fall, while the master of Europe gave the first demonstration of that technique of Imperial German diplomacy which was to alarm Europe repeatedly in future years. "Bismarck preserved an ominous silence."[11]

But Europe became voluble. Queen Victoria wrote a personal letter to Emperor William I. Cautionary hints arrived from Rome and Vienna. The Tsar, on a visit to Berlin, added his restraining voice, and the announcement of his minister, Gorchakov, that "now peace is assured," left Bismarck energetically denying that any preventive war had been intended. His bluff had been called. The first great war scare was over. Thereafter, the French Government, which had perhaps not been quite as alarmed as it pretended, knew that it could not be kept in subjection merely by threats of another war. Realizing also that his dictatorship of Europe could not be stretched that far, Bismarck redoubled his admonitions to the German Ambassador that France must be kept from becoming eligible for alliance.

AUSTRO-RUSSIAN RIVALRY IN THE BALKANS   After 1875 Bismarck was compelled to give increasing attention to the East, for it was there that the probable ally of France lay. France had always sought allies in the East. When Austria was the foe

[10] *Die Grosse Politik*, Vol. 1, p. 221.
[11] Sontag, *European Diplomatic History, 1871–1932*, p. 10.

she came to terms with Turkey, then Sweden and Brandenburg; later she had combined with Austria against Frederick the Great. Russia, too, in the time of Peter the Great and many of his successors, notably Catherine II, had turned to France for assistance.[12] In the East also was the perpetual problem created by the brutal misgovernment by the Turks of the Balkan Christians, largely Orthodox Slavs. The gradual decline of Turkish power also created problems of the greatest importance for the other Eastern Empires, Hapsburg and Romanov. The Russian intelligentsia, especially the all powerful Orthodox clergy, naturally felt sympathy with their brethren in the Balkans who were under the heel of the infidel Turk. There was the double tie of race and religion. But more important was the conviction of all Russian leaders that the control of the Turkish Straits ought to be in their hands. Constantinople was "the key to our house" and it should be possessed. These two interests were so deep seated that even the destruction of the Orthodox Empire in Russia could not permanently remove them.

On the other hand, the interest of the Hapsburgs in the Balkan Slavs was, from their viewpoint, equally fundamental, for if a strong Balkan state arose it would be certain to exercise a fatal attraction to the millions of South Slavs and Rumanians of the Monarchy, whom the Magyar leaders were determined to keep in a servile condition. The Hapsburgs must therefore prevent the rise of any Balkan state of which they could not make a vassal. This "necessity" also made it essential that the influence and power of Russia, the great Slav state, should not increase in the Balkans, particularly at the Straits.

It was in the midst of this clashing of imperialistic rivalries that the most fundamental force of all had to operate, the urge of the Balkan peoples, divided and brutalized by centuries of misrule as they had been, to independent nationhood. Both

[12] Charles Seymour, *The Diplomatic Background of the War*, New Haven, 1916, pp. 39–40.

Austrian and Russian pretensions were a danger to them, as the Russian recovery of the Rumanian part of Bessarabia in 1878 showed, but the Austrian threat was the more to be feared. It was a permanent negation of nationalism in the Balkans, especially of Serbian nationalism, while Russia once in control of the Straits might be content, or at all events absorbed in Asiatic Turkey, until the Balkan people could establish themselves.

In 1875 Bismarck had to give his attention to the Near East. In July another rebellion broke out in the Turkish-ruled province of Bosnia-Herzegovina, and continued for many months, spreading eventually to the Balkans. For some time Count Julius Andrássy, the elder, the Magyar Minister of Foreign Affairs for Austria-Hungary, resisted the temptation to annex the two provinces, fearing the inclusion of more Slavs in the Monarchy. But the desire to prevent Serbia from securing an outlet on the Adriatic led him to conclude with Russia the Reichstadt agreement of July 8, 1876, whereby Austria was to acquire Bosnia-Herzegovina, if the current revolts should crumble the Turkish power as then seemed probable.

When the Turks recovered and repeatedly defeated the insurgents, a new agreement was made, January 15, 1877, which permitted Russia to begin war on Turkey in April and to conclude the peace of San Stefano at the outskirts of Constantinople on March 3, 1878. The chief feature of the treaty, a large Bulgaria with frontage on the Aegean, alarmed Austria and also brought the Conservative British Prime Minister, Benjamin Disraeli, on the scene.

TURKISH RULE OVER THE BALKANS RESTORED   During the Turkish massacres of the Bulgarians, in 1876, the Liberal leader Gladstone had paralyzed Disraeli's hand by stirring popular feeling against the Turks. But when the Turks became the underdog the old anti-Russian feeling of Crimean War days revived, supported by concern for the new Suez Canal of which

Disraeli had just acquired part control. Hence a British fleet was sent to the Dardanelles to defy Russia, and Disraeli joined in the pressure on the Tsar to submit his victorious treaty to revision by the powers in conference. The Tsar Alexander had had to be driven by Russian Pan Slav sentiment to attack Turkey, but now he was still more reluctant to be hailed before the bar of Europe like a criminal.[13] However, with his country exhausted by the war he was compelled to submit to the carving of his proposed Bulgaria into three parts, two to be autonomous provinces of Turkey, and the third a part of a wholly Turkish strip that stretched from Constantinople to the Adriatic. Bosnia and Herzegovina were duly delivered to Austria, but remained nominally under Turkish sovereignty.

"PEACE WITH HONOR," 1878 These and other arrangements were ratified in 1878 by the Congress of Berlin which Bismarck had reluctantly permitted to meet in his capital, and Disraeli returned to England proclaiming triumphantly: "I bring you Peace with Honour." In 1938 another Conservative Premier was to return from Germany to London with the same claim, and with far less basis for it. At Berlin in 1878 Disraeli condemned the South Balkan peoples to thirty-four years more of slavery, and Europe to that fatal series of convulsions which attended the final liberation of the Balkans and ended in World War I. It is difficult to believe that the excision of that chronic abscess could have been as damaging to the world in 1878 as it was in later years. Certainly, Disraeli's utter callousness about the fate of small peoples was not good practical politics.[14]

[13] Bismarck had also prodded Russia to war by references to her honor, the probable decline in the morale of her army and the danger to the monarchical principle in a weak conclusion of the crisis.—Carroll, p. 137.

[14] Within a few years Disraeli's successor as leader of the Conservatives, Lord Salisbury, admitted that Britain had backed the wrong horse in 1878 and that the defense of Turkey in the Crimean War had been equally unwise.—Sontag, *European Diplomatic History, 1871–1932*, p. 17; *Die Grosse Politik*, Vol. X, p. 10.

The Building of Bismarck's System of Alliances

THE AUSTRO-GERMAN ALLIANCE, 1879   For Bismarck the Treaty of Berlin was a near calamity. In spite of all his efforts to play the "honest broker" he could not send the Russian Minister Gorchakov home with any but the bitterest feelings. The Tsar felt that his benevolent neutrality in the Franco-Prussian War had been almost as basely rewarded as his suppression of the Hungarian revolt in 1848 had been by the Hapsburgs during the Crimean War. Then when the German members of the commission set up to execute the Treaty of Berlin sided generally with Austria, the Tsar wrote a letter to the Kaiser complaining that the consequences "might be disastrous to both our countries."[15]

The letter disturbed Bismarck. With Russia really angry, the dreaded drawing together of France and Russia might occur. The best way to prevent it, he decided, was to make an alliance with Austria. That would alarm the Tsar and bring him to heel. The Emperor William, however, took no stock in these tactics. All through the month of September 1879 he fought stubbornly against the proposal and was only dragged step by step into it. First he was compelled to give his reluctant consent to a purely exploratory visit of Bismarck to Vienna. Then whole batteries of official and military opinion were mobilized against him, supported by Bismarck's best arguments. The idea of the alliance was simple, Bismarck maintained. Germany and Austria bound themselves to defend each other if attacked by Russia, or by Russia and another power. Every alliance, said Bismarck, was composed of a horse and rider. Germany must be the rider, as she easily could be with Austria, whereas Russia could always coerce German support by threat-

---

[15] *Die Grosse Politik*, Vol. III, p. 14.

ening to go over to France. Austria had no place else to go and, moreover, her *status quo* stand in the Balkans was backed by England.

It sounded like a good argument, but the Kaiser was not convinced. He took turns with Bismarck in threatening to resign, until finally the Emperor gave way, "but not before he had fought every inch of the ground and been reduced to a state of physical prostration which alarmed his entourage."[16] The Kaiser had struggled hard to have the treaty at least communicated to the Tsar, but the best he could secure was the sending of a conciliatory memorandum about the pacific purposes of Germany and Austria, which did not reveal that the treaty was definitely directed against a Russian attack.

THE THREE EMPERORS' UNION RENEWED, 1881 Soon Bismarck's tactics were rewarded. The Russo-Turkish War had sharply increased the revolutionary opposition to the Tsarist autocracy. The thought of being separated from his autocratic brethren so alarmed Alexander II that he began negotiations for a renewal of the *Drei Kaiser Bund.* Then Alexander himself was assassinated, and to Alexander III, who supported an intensification of reaction, monarchical solidarity was even more desirable. Hence, on June 18, 1881, the representatives of the three Emperors signed a most secret treaty which was so carefully guarded that its terms did not escape until 1918. Its chief articles closed the Straits against the British Fleet and provided that should one of the parties be attacked by a Great Power the others would remain neutral.

THE TRIPLE ALLIANCE CREATED, 1882 Two days before the signature of this treaty, another was signed between Austria and Serbia which made the latter an Austrian vassal. Negotiations had also been under way since October 1880 for the adhesion of Italy to the Austro-German Alliance. These parleys assumed an urgent tone after the French annexation of Tunis,

[16] Spender, *Fifty Years of Europe,* p. 48.

in 1881, had sharply angered Italy. Since 1878, Bismarck had been urging France to colonial ventures—in Annam and Tonquin, in Morocco, to which he "repeatedly" pointed "as a suitable field for her colonial activity," and in Tunis which he held up to her as "the ripe Tunisian pear."[17] That the seizure of Tunis would catapult Italy into the circle of German allies was not Bismarck's main concern. He desired most of all to divert France from Alsace-Lorraine, and for several years he succeeded. That was a more solid gain than the support of the Italians, with their "restless, arrogant jackal policy" as he termed it. Italy's promise would "have no value if it is not in her interest to keep it." Nevertheless, it was worth something to have Italy pledged to attack France in case of a Franco-German war, and not to attack Austria in the event of an Austro-Russian war.

RUMANIA ADDED, 1883   The very secret Triple Alliance Treaty of May 20, 1882, was "a complicated system of heterogeneous liability," signed for a term of five years.[18] It was soon followed by an Austro-Rumanian treaty of alliance, signed October 30, 1883, at Bismarck's instance. This pact capitalized Rumania's resentment at the loss of Bessarabia, and was directed against Russia, though she was not mentioned by name. It was signed at once by Germany, by Italy in 1889, and remained the most secret of all the secret treaties. In Rumania, each succeeding Prime Minister swore his successor not to mention it to a soul and the secret was so well kept that the Rumanian people finally went to war on the side of Russia, without ever knowing that they were bound by solemn treaty, renewed February 5, 1913, to fight against her.

BISMARCK'S NETWORK OF ALLIANCES COMPLETE   Bismarck's great structure of secret treaties had now reached its ultimate dimensions. After 1882 the Three Emperors' League, the Austro-German Alliance, with its flanking Serbian and Rumanian

---

[17] Erich Brandenburg, *From Bismarck to the World War*, London, 1927, p. 10.

[18] Brandenburg, p. 16.

supports, constituted a "network of secret, conflicting and almost unintelligible obligations of which no one could foresee the value, or even the interpretation, if they came into operation."[19] The isolation of France had indeed become a highly complicated business.

Recent historians rightly emphasize the strictly defensive nature of the Bismarckian alliances and his great skill in holding his "horses" to their defensive role. Bismarck was undoubtedly one of the greatest of all defenders of the *status quo*. Having swiftly and easily conquered an empire, he was determined to hold it by balance of power politics as long as possible. Keeping others from fighting, if possible; holding a tight rein on the Austrian horse, yet insuring her preservation; restraining Russia by keeping some diplomatic hold on her; diverting France to Africa and threatening her by turns; building up a system of secret alliances which would preserve for himself the decisive voice in all European questions; no diversion of energy and antagonizing of Britain by colonial adventures—in Bismarck's belief the juggling of all of these wise principles should preserve for Germany her empire and the hegemony of Europe.

FORCE THE ARBITER   Yet, says one of the foremost German historians of the period, "Bismarck was absolutely certain that all his prudential measures were not sufficient to prevent permanently and adequately the great conflict which he feared."[20] Therefore Germany must be armed as she never had been, armed for a war which would make that of 1870 "but child's play." "Not one voice in France," thundered the great man, "has renounced Alsace-Lorraine; at any moment a government may be established which will declare war." And when it came "on both sides an effort will be made to finish the adversary, to bleed him white, that the vanquished may not be able to

[19] Spender, p. 55. See Count Julius Andrássy's analysis of the many intricate obligations created in his *Bismarck, Andrássy and their Successors,* pp. 93–4.

[20] Brandenburg, *From Bismarck to the World War,* p. 15.

rise again, and may never for thirty years dare even to think of the possibility of turning conqueror."[21]

This was the best which Bismarck had to offer—one war of conquest after another, each fought with the object of grinding the enemy into the earth so that there might be an interval of armed peace until he, or some other challenger of the established "order" rose again; secret alliances, eternal suspicion and the feverish accumulation of arms which would make the next conflict certain—this was the Bismarckian ideal. The great apostle of blood and iron accepted the international anarchy as he found it. He wasted no time in trying to establish a state of affairs in which confidence and the assumption of continued civilized existence could grow; he merely sought to restrain the anarchy for a time until Germany could become strong enough to triumph again. Instead of trying for an organization of Europe which might ward off the progressively more destructive wars which he correctly foresaw, he put his great talents to the task of building around Germany in the center of Europe a system of "defensive" alliances which would ensure another victory. That his "success" in this intricate endeavor would make certain the rise of a counter combination that could overwhelm his own shaky structure did not deter him. Europe was so disorganized and his own skill was so great that no other diplomatic architects would be able to surpass him. He would always have the balance of power on his side. He was too shrewd to suppose that a balance of power could be achieved between two groups of powers equal in strength, a delicate equilibrium that would stay balanced. "All politics reduces itself to this formula," he insisted repeatedly: "Try to be *à trois* as long as the world is governed by the unstable equilibrium of

[21] *American Historical Review*, January, 1918, p. 331. In 1890 the elder Moltke predicted that "If the war which has hung over our heads . . . for more than ten years past" ever broke out it would not be ended in one or two campaigns. A Seven or a Thirty Years War was more probable and "woe to him who first sets fire to Europe."—Sontag, p. 16.

five powers."[22] Just as in his own alliances there must be horses for Germany to ride, so he was uninterested in any balance of power that was not overbalanced in his own favor.

Thus Bismarck constructed his diplomatic house of cards and cemented it together with his own fear and self-confidence, with Austria's weakness and subservience, with Russia's apprehension of the rise of her oppressed people, with Italy's pique and restless megalomania, with Rumania's very secret resentment against Russia, and with Serbia's abject vassalage.

RENEWAL OF COMPLICATIONS, 1887   Then the very complexity of the structure brought perpetual troubles. All of his secret treaties were made for definite, short terms, and one or another of them was always running out. An expiration, too, almost invariably brought a prolonged period of strain and exasperation to the great manipulator, for his horses were always demanding either an easier load or some guaranteed free pasture of their own. It was highly inconsiderate of them to be getting these offensive thoughts into their heads, but they would do it; and since there must be horses for the German rider, their acquisitive propensities had to be humored.

The gradual turning of the alliances away from their original purpose of safeguarding Alsace-Lorraine was especially evident in the renewal of the Triple Alliance in 1887. Both Austria and Italy made objections. Austria was fearful of a Franco-German war; Italy demanded protection of her "just claims" in Tripoli and Morocco against France. Otherwise Italy would go over to France, unless her allies guaranteed the existing situation on the coasts and islands of the Mediterranean. Austria wanted the interior of the Balkans guaranteed, but was not interested in the coasts and islands. Accordingly, the renewal of 1887 added greatly to the already notable complexity of the original treaty of 1883. Another section was now included, binding only on Austria and Italy; a third bound only Germany and Italy

[22] *Nineteenth Century,* December, 1917, p. 1119.

and a fourth avowed that everything was in accordance with the spirit of 1882, "because today, as then, the three monarchies are aiming essentially at the maintenance of peace."

When treaties of alliance become energetic about preserving peace and the *status quo* then the allies are really blocking out expected gains. Thus, long paragraphs in the Austrian-Italian treaty of 1887 provided for the division of Balkan spoils and plainly contemplated war, even if it be not "provoked" by another power. Likewise, even more specific paragraphs in the German-Italian treaty of that year said that if France did anything to extend her North African possessions Italy might go to war with her, on all fronts, and Germany would support her. This surprising twist of a purely "defensive" alliance was, of course, explained by Bismarck to his own satisfaction. The origin of a war between France and Italy would be "of no consequence," he declared, "for Germany could not permit Italy to be annihilated or reduced to a state of dependence by France." Bismarck therefore went the whole road and promised in the fourth article, that if the war came Germany would "in a measure compatible with circumstances," help Italy to seize French territories. Bismarck's purpose, of course, as he explained later, was to "bind Italy to the Central Powers by means of gifts, such as could be made in the shape of Nice, Corsica, Albania and territories on the North African coast,"[23] language strangely similar to that which was heard so stridently from the Rome-Berlin Axis in 1938–1939.

MEDITERRANEAN AGREEMENTS CHECKMATE RUSSIA But not even the greatest of diplomatic equestrians could keep so many horses moving in teamwork. In 1885 a revolt of the Rumelian Bulgarians reopened the Balkan question, with Russian and British roles reversed. The Tsar having found the Bulgarians

[23] G. Lowes Dickinson, *The International Anarchy, 1904–1914*, New York, 1926, pp. 86–90; A. F. Pribram, *The Secret Treaties of Austria-Hungary, 1879–1914*, Oxford, 1920, Vol. II, p. 80.

independent, was angry with them. For the same reason the British forsook the upholding of sacred treaties in Turkey's behalf and espoused the rights of small nations. To check the Tsar's designs Salisbury unbent from his splendid isolation enough to make an agreement with Italy and Austria promising, with due circumspection, to cooperate in opposing any change in the status of Bulgaria, the two autonomous parts of which had just united. These agreements were made in February and March 1887, and coinciding with the renewal of the Triple Alliance they made Bismarck's triumph momentarily complete. Now Russia could not interfere with the new Bulgaria, nor make any other important move in the Near East.

Austria, however, had encouraged the Serbs to attack the Bulgarians during the crisis and had soon to shield her protégé from the consequences of defeat. The Tsar's wrath was then turned against Austria for attempting to encroach on his hoped-for preserve, and he refused to agree to the second renewal of the Three Emperors' Alliance which came due in 1887. He would team with Austria no longer.

REINSURANCE, 1887   At the same time, he still dreaded relying on turbulent Republican France and, with some lingering hopes of dividing Germany from Austria, proposed a separate Russo-German treaty. To clear the ground and increase the Tsar's sense of isolation, Bismarck promptly communicated to him the text of the Austro-German Alliance of 1879, which he had promised Austria to keep secret. Finding that this treaty barred a Russian attack on Austria, the Tsar's government accepted a treaty with Germany which bound Germany to neutrality in case Austria attacked Russia and also gave Germany's consent to a forcible solution of the Straits issue by Russia. Bismarck could count on England, Austria and Italy to block that, and in case of a Russo-Austrian war he could define for himself the term "attack" and "defense." He had candidly stated during the negotiations that "the question what is an aggressive war cannot

be defined in a treaty."[24] On the other hand, he secured a
Russian promise of neutrality if France should "attack" Germany. To make these new vows more surely binding he also
agreed to keep them strictly secret from Austria. By the Reinsurance Treaty of June 18, 1887, Bismarck added to the insurance of his southern frontier, in case of war with France, a
"reinsurance" of his Eastern marches. "Now," says Fay, "he was
reinsured against any danger on his Eastern frontier."[25]

Rising Resistance to Bismarck's Rule

Nevertheless, the remainder of the year was charged with danger. The increasing pressure of Russian troops upon Galicia
produced a panic in Vienna and, while steadily talking in
favor of Russia, Bismarck began to act in Austria's behalf.
Though he would not aid the German prince Ferdinand of
Coburg to become the ruler of Bulgaria he would not forbid it.
He pressed "cautiously but steadily," too, where Russia was
weakest—on her finances, until finally her bonds were excluded
from the Berlin stock exchange. On December 18, 1887, the Tsar
surrendered and accepted the new Bulgarian dispensation.[26]

The pressure on Russia's finances was effective, for the corrupt Russian autocracy had continually to be supported by
foreign money. But instead of hastening to bind up Russia's
wounds when she had been sufficiently chastised, as he had
always done before, Bismarck kept the Berlin loan market
closed to Russia until she turned to the Paris Bourse, irrevocably as events proved. As the old conjurer lost his cunning
his irascibility increased.

After the flight of Boulanger in France had reduced a really
alarming threat of révanche, Bismarck's son, Ambassador in

[24] *Die Grosse Politik*, Vol. V., p. 248.
[25] Fay, *The Origins of the World War*, p. 78.
[26] Sontag, pp. 44–5.

Paris, continued to threaten France ill-temperedly over small incidents.[27] Bismarckian manners "counted for much in the ultimate breakdown of his policy. Nations which might have submitted to his will, if he had spared their feelings, felt wounded in their self-respect when he used his advantage to browbeat and bully, or practiced a calculated incivility in place of the politeness which had been a tradition of even the deadliest diplomacy."[28] Resentments were being stored up which steadily deepened the feeling in Paris and St. Petersburg that the hegemony of Germany and Austria must be challenged unitedly.

At the moment when Bismarck still dominated Europe, so completely that none dared to quarrel with him, he was forced to admit that his policy had failed. On January 1, 1888, the *Neue Freie Press* spoke dolefully of "the cracking of the walls of an unsound house which usually precedes a catastrophe." What was "driving Europe toward catastrophe" was the endeavor to overthrow the European "legal system" of 1870, "which Germany had created, protected and firmly imposed on the recalcitrant."

After seventeen years of incessant effort to keep France isolated, and Germany surrounded by an intricate web of alliances, security was as far off as ever. Although almost every statesman in Europe, friend or foe, nursed some bruise from the German big stick or sullenly resented some discovered duplicity, Alsace-Lorraine was still a dangerous hostage in the German camp. Bismarck's hour was nearly over and he had but one resource left, to put new layers of armor upon the German mailed fist.

BISMARCK'S FAILURE CONFESSED   In preparation for his appeal to the final arbiter among the nations, he had published in the newspapers, on February 3, 1888, the Austro-German treaty of

[27] See his dispatch of May 1888 to his father.—*Die Grosse Politik*, Vol. VI, No. 1282.

[28] Spender, *Fifty Years of Europe*, pp. 106–7.

1879, as a warning to the Pan Slavists and as evidence to the German people, and others, of Germany's purely defensive policy. Three days later he appeared in the Reichstag to demand the addition of more than 700,000 men to the German army reserves.[29] "God," he thundered, "has given us on our flank the French, who are the most warlike and turbulent nation that exists, and He has permitted the development in Russia of warlike propensities which until lately did not manifest themselves to the same extent." A war with France would not necessarily bring Russia in, he said, without revealing that his still secret Reinsurance Treaty with Russia "guaranteed" Russian neutrality should France attack. But a war with Russia would be certain to bring France in, "since no French government would be strong enough to prevent it, even if it desired to do so." Germany must therefore have "a million good soldiers for the defense of each of our frontiers" and another million in reserve. It was madness to suppose that Germany would use this immense army for a preventive war, but, he concluded: "We Germans fear God, but nothing else in the World."

In these resounding words did the great Chancellor make public confession that his policy had failed. He had spun a maze of secret alliances which had indeed given his new Germany a chance to grow strong, but nothing could really be depended on except blood and iron. The sovereignty of one state over the many "sovereign" powers of Europe could be maintained ultimately by force alone. Germany would have that force.

Bismarck's game was played out. No one else could have kept it running so long. In his hands the playing of power politics had been relatively safe, because he sought only to hold his gains. Yet the narrowness of his vision defeated him. "His idea of security never went beyond a grouping of forces for the benefit of Germany and the disablement of France."[30] The attempt to find security for one nation in the permanent out-

29 Spender, p. 112.
30 Spender, p. 126.

lawry of another only increased the feelings in France which Bismarck feared, and at the same time drew world opinion to her side.

HIS POLICIES REVERSED When the young Kaiser William II dismissed Bismarck, on March 18, 1890, his policies were rapidly reversed. His successors proclaimed that they could not operate his complicated policy and in truth their abilities were not sufficient. They began by refusing to renew the Reinsurance Treaty with Russia. Aided by the jealousy of Holstein and a memorandum of Under Secretary Berchens which predicted all sorts of Balkan complications, the new Chancellor, Caprivi, and Secretary of State, Marschall, decided that the Reinsurance Treaty was incompatible with the Austrian Alliance and would cause infinite damage to it, if the secret should leak out either from Russia or from Bismarck. That the two treaties did not formally conflict appears to be clear, but that in the case of an Austro-Russian clash each power would expect to receive support from its pact with Germany was as certain. Perhaps a final choice by Germany between Austria and Russia could not have been postponed for long, but Bismarck's successors eventually inverted every one of his basic rules. They challenged England on the sea; they quarreled with France in the colonial field; let Austria become the rider in the Austro-German Alliance; and gained the opposition of both Russia and Britain.

THE GERMAN GOVERNMENT LEFT UNWORKABLE It is commonly said that it was Germany's misfortune that she did not produce any great statesman from Bismarck to the World War. It is not so frequently added that Bismarck was largely responsible for the non-appearance of any other statesmen. Willingly accepting the Prussian dictum that the German was not a political animal, that he must be ordered about and provided for by his Junker superiors, Bismarck erected the constitution and government of his Empire around himself. Both executive and legislative powers were heavily centered in the Chancellorship, responsible only to the Emperor whom Bismarck knew he could control. Then for twenty years Bismarck was substantially the government. He managed everything; he overawed or intimidated everyone else. He was too busy pulling the strings of international politics to have time or desire to coach his subordinates, to stimulate initiative in them and give them the wisdom of experience, or to share his power with the German people, training them in self government and self control. Thus, far from leaving behind him anyone to take his place, he left a people disturbed by "a restless, unsure spirit. Arrogant boastfulness and nervous fear, criticism and flattery of other nations—gusts of contradictory feeling swept over the German scene, arousing bewilderment, alarm and anger in neighboring peoples."[31] Unfortunately, too, these tendencies happened to be raised to a pathological degree in the new Emperor, William II, who brushed the mighty Bismarck aside and saw to it that all future Chancellors should be either mediocre servants or clever flatterers.

Even more important for the future of Germany and Europe was the conservative, authoritarian character of the society Bismarck had welded on the Germans. They alone among the peoples of the West accepted their modern state from the old ruling groups, instead of taking it by pressure from below, so that all institutions—even "the schools, the universities, the established Protestant churches and not least the armed forces" —defended the predominance of the conservative elements and the interests of the expanding industrial and commercial classes.[32]

[31] Sontag, p. 47.
[32] Fritz Fischer, *Germany's Aims in the First World War*, New York, 1967, p. 3.

III. The Formation of the Triple Entente, 1891–1907

———◈———

There are many who defended Bismarck's diplomatic handiwork, but few who will deny that the elaborate system of secret alliances which he built up was almost certain to evoke a counter grouping. When the defense of Bismarck is boiled down it reduces itself to the claim that he postponed the Franco-Russian Alliance as long as he did, aided by other major factors: French weakness and instability, Russian reaction and abhorrence of liberal ideals. Though the foundations of the Franco-Russian Alliance were securely laid in Bismarck's time, it required another four years to overcome the Tsar's fears of republicanism enough to ripen the first negotiations of the French and Russian military authorities into the full-fledged alliance of January 4, 1894.

The Franco-Russian Alliance, 1894

This agreement, like all of Bismarck's pacts, "was in its origin essentially defensive in purpose."[1] The preamble solemnly precluded any "other aim than to prepare for the necessities of a defensive war." It was only if France or Russia should be "attacked" by Germany, or by one of her allies "supported" by Germany that the new allies should converge on her "with

[1] Sidney B. Fay, *The Origins of the World War*, New York, 1930, Vol. I, p. 119.

all speed." To avoid the difficulty of securing the approval of the French Parliament, the alliance was effected merely by an exchange of diplomatic notes which gave effect to the military convention of August 17, 1892. The terms of the latter, including the duty to mobilize at once if one of the Central Powers did, were kept secret until after World War I. The French Minister of War had the text in his pocket when the Chamber of Deputies assented to war with Germany in 1914, but nobody compelled him to produce it.

A LOOPHOLE REMOVED, 1899 In France the alliance of 1894 was hailed with joy by the conservatives. An anti-parliamentary campaign began at once to take shape. Hopes of regaining the lost provinces were exploited in the interest of internal reaction. The word was assiduously spread that there must be no radical measures, no reform proposals that might upset the Tsar, who was accepted by some as "virtually our ruler." And, though the elements of the Right eventually had to accept reform in France, they were always able to prevent any French pressure for reform upon the Tsar's government. Many liberals joined the historian Antonin Debidour in protesting against alliance with "an ignoble government whose barbarism and corruption stank in the nostrils of the civilized world," but the propertied classes persistently ignored the fact that budgetary deficits in Russia were perpetual.[2]

In 1899 it occurred to French Foreign Minister Théophile Delcassé that the always expected break up of Austria-Hungary would also dissolve the Franco-Russian Alliance, since the military convention was to have the same duration as the Triple Alliance. Without the knowledge of Parliament, or of most of the Cabinet, he hurried to St. Petersburg and secured a new exchange of letters, dated July 28 and August 9, which promised that the

[2] Georges Michon, *The Franco-Russian Alliance, 1897–1917*, New York, 1929, pp. 74–79. After the alliance had been in operation several years, Tolstoy declared that the Russian people had not the slightest idea that it existed. If they did it would be "in the highest degree distasteful to them." —p. 108.

military convention should remain in force as long as the diplomatic agreement. If the Triple Alliance should be dissolved, and Germany left entirely isolated, the Franco-Russian Alliance would still continue.[8]

GERMANY UNPERTURBED The Germans were slow to believe that the alliance existed, and for some years were not alarmed by it. They knew that their strength was still superior. For a time, too, there was something like a feeling of mutual respect among the continental powers. A balance of power had been created. Each of the Great Powers on the Continent now felt supported and either somewhat more secure or a little less so. The balance of forces was not close enough to upset suddenly the German hegemony and throw the German powers into a malaise of nervous apprehension. The balance was not even close enough to put both sides in fear of an imminent attack. The Germans, moreover, had history on their side. Had there not been bitter rivalry and never-ending suspicion between Russia and Britain for many decades? British fears for India seemed a permanent guarantee of British hostility to Russia, and had the French and British not been incessant rivals for centuries? No national antagonism was older or had been consecrated in as many wars. That Britain would never join the Franco-Russian group seemed a safe calculation, especially since she had favored the Triple Alliance for decades.

No conclusion appeared to be better founded. But the Germans forgot that in the international anarchy "friendship" is based upon enmity and that the greater enmity governs. Thus the Fashoda crisis on the Upper Nile seemed to be but one more embitterment of the relations between France and Britain. For France, too, the humiliation was bitter and complete, so intense that it forced Delcassé and his countrymen to decide

[8] After Delcassé's return from Russia, full of pride at his accomplishment, Henry Berenger asked: "Would any honest man conceive the idea of protecting himself against a robber by joining forces, on terms of equality, with a murderer and calling him friend and ally?"—Michon, p. 112.

which *was* the greater enemy, Britain or Germany, and though the decision was painful its result was foreordained. Germany was the greater enemy and there was no gain or safety in continuing to quarrel with both the lesser enemy and the greater. Then instead of bending every energy to win Great Britain's casting vote, Germany tenaciously pushed her naval threat against British sea supremacy until the British reluctantly came to the conclusion that Germany was their greatest potential enemy.

Britain's Search for Allies, 1898–1904

ANGLO-GERMAN ALLIANCE NEGOTIATIONS, 1898–1901 For many years Germany had sought an alliance with Britain. On three different occasions Bismarck tried to open negotiations for an alliance, but London was uninterested. After 1890, also, William and his ministers were continually putting out feelers in London, without success.[4] It was not until 1895 that Britain indicated a change in policy through Salisbury's abortive but statesmanlike proposal to Germany that Turkey be partitioned and Russian control of the Straits balanced by the creation of strong Balkan nations. When nothing came of this, the British waited three more years, during which difficulties multiplied in every direction. The Fashoda crisis was developing; the British legal position in Egypt was untenable; Russia was advancing in the East; and the Kaiser's Kruger telegram had shown that a conflict with the Boers might be dangerous.

Convinced that their isolation was now perilous, the British first turned to Russia, January 19, 1898, only to have their offer of a general entente regarded as a suspicious maneuver or a sign of weakness. Joseph Chamberlain, British Colonial Secretary, thereupon made his first offer of an alliance to Germany, March

[4] Erich Brandenburg, *From Bismarck to the World War*, London, 1927, pp. 97, 103.

29, 1898. The German Ambassador, Herman von Hatzfeldt, was scandalized by having all Britain's cards placed before him at once. In Berlin, Bülow at once feared that if the treaty should fail through lack of approval by the British Parliament, Germany would be fatally compromised with Russia. He also asked colonial concessions first and the Kaiser suddenly broke the pledges of secrecy and wrote to the Tsar, May 30, 1898, mentioning enormous offers from England and asking what Russia would offer him. For once the Tsar countered cleverly and mentioned the recent British offer of a general entente with Russia. This convinced the Kaiser of England's perfidy and Holstein backed him with an opinion that any agreement with Britain or Russia would damage Germany with the other. Bülow then advised a non-committal attitude with Britain that would keep His Majesty *arbiter mundi*.

The Germans now believed that they stood in a strategic central position between the Franco-Russian Alliance and Great Britain. They thought they held the decisive voice and would need to be consulted on everything. Moreover, they were determined to be consulted. With a constantly expanding industry, trade and population, they resolved to become the same kind of world power that Britain was. Some thought that Germany's economic future really depended on acquiring great colonies, but the really unanswerable argument was that Germany's power and glory required world recognition. On both counts the British found at every turn of the long negotiations with the Germans that they were asking some bit of land or a harbor as an evidence of Britain's good faith. Hence, also, the Anglo-German treaty of August 30, 1898, whereby the two agreed to divide Portugal's colonies between them, if Portugal had to borrow money giving them as security. Then when Portugal managed to get money otherwise the Germans were aggrieved that Britain had not prevented it, and more deeply offended when they observed Britain, under the stress of the Boer War, renewing her ancient alliance with Portugal. The unexpected American seizure of the Philippines was no more acceptable and when Admiral Dietrichs failed to find any way of sharing in this spoil Germany bought the Micronesian Islands from Spain.[5] She carried the dispute over the Samoan Islands almost to a rupture of relations with Britain, before an exchange of territories left these islands to be shared by Germany and the United States.

Nevertheless, Chamberlain pressed his alliance proposal upon the Kaiser and Bülow, during their visit to Windsor in November 1899, saying that Russia must be checked and that France was declining. Shortly after, encouraged by Bülow, he proposed the alliance in a public speech, but Bülow replied coldly in the Reichstag on December 11 and capitalized on the unfavorable reaction in Germany to advance the Naval Law of 1900.

By this time the public opinion of all continental nations was strongly hostile to England because of the Boer War. On March 3, 1900, the Tsar proposed that Russia, Germany, and France jointly intervene. Germany, perhaps correctly, scented a trap to cause a complete break between her and Britain and countered by proposing again, as in the Kaiser's letter of May 30, 1898 to the Tsar, a continental league with a mutual guarantee of possessions. Since that would involve a French renunciation of Alsace-Lorraine the proposal came to nothing. But the continental league idea continually stirred the Kaiser's dreams. Again and again it crops out in German diplomacy, and always it foundered on the rock of Alsace-Lorraine. Such a union would have left Germany permanently the greatest military power, dominating a grand alliance which could deal with Britain on colonial matters as it chose. This dream was the nearest approach to a vision of world organization based on peaceful development for all the nations that was even considered in Europe prior to 1914. But it was still to be an alliance to promote German aims. The hope of it, too, tended to lure Germany into a double-dealing policy.

[5] Brandenburg, p. 124.

Though often rebuffed, Chamberlain clung obstinately to his efforts to make Germany an ally. The death of Queen Victoria, January 22, 1901, afforded him another opportunity to press the Germans. But Holstein had cast Britain for a death struggle with the Dual Alliance and he scoffed at the British threat to draw near to France and Russia.[6] Bülow also feverishly telegraphed in the same vein to the Kaiser at Windsor, who was inclined to close with the British. By waiting, Germany could get much more. Yet in spite of Germany's coyness Lord Lansdowne eventually asked the Germans four definite questions, March 23, 1901, and was told in reply that England must join the Triple Alliance and secure the public approval of the House of Commons, conditions which the British Cabinet, never united on a German alliance, would not accept. They were convinced not only that the Austro-Hungarian empire could not outlast Francis Joseph, but that to support Austria meant to back her policy of preventing the break up of the Turkish Empire, which was even more certain to come. On their part the Germans thought that unless they were given guarantees for Austria they could not be compensated for guaranteeing British possessions in all parts of the globe. Ruled by Prussian bureaucratic traditions, they could not get down on paper a complex of Bismarckian formulas which would make the bargain a certain one for Germany. They could not understand the British desire for a loose understanding, not too precise, the kind which later proved to be stronger than the all-written variety.

Through it all suspicion of "perfidious Albion" persisted, the suspicions inherent in the secret diplomacy whereby the "sovereign" states tried to prevail over one another. These suspicions were personified in the sinister, morbid figure of Friedrich von Holstein, a tool of Bismarck's, whose hatred of his master enabled him to stay on in the German Foreign Office and to poison German diplomacy for sixteen years. Ambitious and crafty, "a creature of the dark, afraid of publicity," fearful of

[6] *Die Grosse Politik*, Vol. 17, p. 16.

responsibility, jealous and vindictive, he continued to guide German policy because the men who succeeded Bismarck did not know how. They listened to Holstein "with fear and respect" as the great magician's disciple. They needed some revelation of his witchcraft, the more because the morose old man, still the idol of the German people, was constantly criticizing their puny efforts through the columns of the *Hamburger Nachrichten*, and otherwise. "Nowhere else in Europe could a man like Baron Holstein have influenced policy" so long.[7]

ITALY'S "ON THE FENCE" TREATIES, 1901–1902 While Germany was refusing England's hand, Italy was beginning to leave the Triple Alliance. In December 1900 a secret Franco-Italian accord was made by an exchange of notes in which the pretensions of Italy in Tripoli and of France in Morocco were mutually recognized. At once the new intimacy was publicly cultivated by exchanges of decorations and fleet visits. On December 14, 1901, the agreement was alluded to in the Italian Chamber and on November 1, 1902, another exchange of notes placed Italy wholly atop the fence between the two alliances. It was agreed that should either party be the object of "a direct or indirect aggression" the other would be neutral. Neutrality was promised also if, "as the result of direct provocation" either should find herself compelled, in defense of honor or security to take the initiative of a declaration of war. Prior notice would enable the other party to judge whether "indirect aggression" was sufficiently provocative to justify war. These elastic promises were, of course, fitted minutely into the interstices of Italy's obligations to Austria and Germany, in such a way as not to clash verbally with the terms of the Triple Alliance, but Italy's disloyalty was nevertheless completely clear.

AN ANGLO-JAPANESE ALLIANCE, 1902 When the Anglo-German negotiations finally expired, the German leaders were not uneasy, even when Chamberlain made an anti-German speech, in Octo-

[7] R. J. Sontag, *European Diplomatic History, 1871–1932*, New York, 1933, p. 48.

ber 1901. They knew, too, that the way to handle England was to treat her roughly, even brutally, until she came to terms. At the close of the year 1901 a violent press conflict over the Boer War raised German hatred of Britain to new heights. Then suddenly there came a sharp indication that Britain was turning elsewhere.

Failing to secure German support, the British concluded that Japan might be used to restrain Russia's advance in China. An alliance with Japan would be sufficient to halt Russia, it was hoped. Having learned all the tricks of diplomacy, as well as those of the drill field, Japan negotiated simultaneously with both London and St. Petersburg, in the latter case to see if combination with the enemy might not be the better policy. At length the decision went to Britain, in spite of Marquis Ito's urgent objection. An Anglo-Japanese Alliance was signed in January 1902, providing that if either signatory found itself at war with two powers over Korea or China the other would come to its aid.

When the treaty was published in February 1902, on the insistence of Japan, there was a great diplomatic commotion, partly because no one had suspected its negotiation. Berlin was delighted, on the theory that England and Russia would now be permanently alienated. Bülow was sure that the British would by degrees come to recognize their need of Germany.[8] Russia was alarmed, but could rouse no support in Germany. The best she could get was a joint Franco-Russian statement saying that in the event of a China war both would take counsel together "on the means of safeguarding" their interests in the Far East. This development disturbed the British, who had hoped the treaty would warn off both Russia and France. When it seemed likely to do neither, and Japan plunged ahead toward a break, alarm grew in London, as well it might had they foreseen that forty years later Japan would be trying to take over all of China and East Asia.

[8] *Die Grosse Politik*, Vol. 17, p. 156.

THE ANGLO-FRENCH ENTENTE, 1904 By the end of 1902 the wisdom of making a Franco-British agreement which might prevent a Russo-Japanese war from spreading was apparent to London. The uneasiness caused by two sore spots in North Africa also counseled action. Britain was physically master of Egypt, but her occupation was on the sufferance of an international agreement which tied up Egypt's revenues intolerably. Any one of several powers could make trouble for Britain in Egypt at any time, and they perennially did. A British puppet Sultan also held a steady weakening grip over Morocco. The Moroccan pear was nearly ripe and France would desire to pluck it. Would it not be better for Britain to yield Morocco in return for the withdrawal of her chief rival from Egypt?

These conclusions having been arrived at, it was discovered that both the ancient hostility of the French and British and their current Fashoda and Boer feuds could be overcome. During 1903, Sir Thomas Barclay shepherded the Chambers of Commerce over the Channel. Parliamentary delegations also ferried to and fro. King Edward VII visited Paris and President Loubet sojourned in London, July 6, 1903. It was actually discovered that such a visionary excursion as the signing of an arbitration treaty could be accomplished, October 14, 1903, excluding, of course, questions of "national honor" and "vital interests."

On April 8, 1904, several Franco-British treaties were signed, settling long standing disputes in almost every part of the world. The key pact was the Egypt-Morocco deal. This bargain was framed in the usual two parts, one public, the other secret. The published treaty had the conventional disclaimer, "no intention of altering the political status of Morocco," though it "appertained" to France to keep order, and provide all "administrative, economic, financial and military reforms." The secret articles divided Morocco between France and Spain, when the Sultan should "cease to exercise authority." A similar pair of Franco-Spanish treaties, signed October 3, 1904, quieted Spain.

Within a year's time it had developed that there was nothing immutable about Anglo-French rivalries and hatreds. Centuries of strife, but recently brought to boiling point, ceased in a moment when fear pointed the way. Fear of isolation and of entanglement in the Far East, fear of the German army and navy and dread of quarreling in the presence of Germany made possible a sweeping agreement such as reason and common sense might have arranged long before.

The First Morocco Crisis, 1905

In London there was immense relief that Britain had escaped from an intolerable position, one in which every Great Power was free to put the diplomatic screws upon England. In Berlin, Bülow, now Chancellor, pretended to be gratified that his neighbors were composing their difficulties, but in reality Germany at once began to fear encirclement. "There is not a shred of evidence that Landsdowne and his colleagues wished to form a coalition against Germany."[9] They were too intent upon escaping from their own besiegement by a ring of hostile powers. But in the world of secret alliances one nation's safety must be another nation's danger. Therefore, it was necessary for Germany to do something, but what? Holstein advised the smashing of the Entente, by force if necessary. The Kaiser again urged the continental league. Bülow decided to take Holstein's line, though not to the point of war, highly favorable as the moment was with Russia defeated in Manchuria and paralyzed in Europe. Germany had commercial rights and interests in Morocco under the multilateral treaty of 1884, assets which would probably disappear if France took over Morocco and applied her closed-door colonial policy. But since France was careful to ignore Germany, and the process of "peaceful penetration" was advancing rapidly, Bülow would not recognize the logic of the Anglo-British Entente by asking for guarantees of

[9] Sontag, *European Diplomatic History, 1871–1932*, p. 93.

German commercial opportunity in Morocco. He adopted instead the policy of keeping ostentatiously silent while secretly supporting the Sultan to resist French pressure.

THE KAISER AT TANGIER This procedure made the French distinctly uneasy, but when it did not get results, Bülow decided to have the Kaiser stop at Tangier on his way to the Mediterranean and give a sharp warning. His Majesty had deprecated any stir over Morocco and had to be plied with glowing accounts of the discomfiture the French would suffer before he gave his reluctant consent. Bülow then hastily cut off his escape by a public announcement and overcame, by telegraph, another retreat of the Kaiser after he was at sea. When Tangier was reached, March 31, 1905, the roadstead was so rough that a German officer coming from shore had a narrow escape and William vowed that he would not land. Finally he did, and rode into town on a white Arab horse which nearly threw him when the celebrating Arabs fired their guns promiscuously. That the Sultan had threatened to exterminate all Spanish anarchists if anything happened, did not comfort the Kaiser greatly. But he came through it, to his own immense relief and that of Berlin. Holstein was so agitated during the ordeal that he had a hemorrhage of the stomach. When the news arrived that the flustered Emperor was safely aboard his ship again, Bülow sat weeping at his desk, uttering thanksgivings to Heaven.[10] "But why did you send me there?" demanded the Kaiser. "It's all incomprehensible to me." "It was necessary for my policy," replied Bülow. "Through Your Majesty I threw down the gauntlet in challenge to the French to see whether they would mobilize."[11]

DELCASSÉ FORCED TO RESIGN France did not mobilize, but she did feel both menaced and mystified. The German Ambassador spoke ominously and the German press took a high line, yet Germany disclaimed any desire for compensations. This was a

[10] Bernhard von Bülow, *Memoirs, 1903–1909*, New York, 1931, p. 107; Nowak, *Germany's Road to Ruin*, New York, 1932, p. 298.

[11] J. A. Spender, *Fifty Years of Europe, A Study of Pre-War Documents*, New York, 1933, p. 243.

new phenomenon. Germany only demanded a conference of the signatories of the Morocco Treaty of 1884. Did she mean to drag France before Europe as a criminal? Did she intend war? Or was she really out to disrupt the Entente with Britain? In reality, German policy had been complicated by the Kaiser's declaration to King Alfonso at Vigo, in March 1904, that Germany had no territorial designs in Morocco. This had led to support of the Sultan and this in turn to another declaration of territorial disinterestedness by the Kaiser at Tangier. Reluctantly bound by these pledges, Bülow's actual plan was to impede the French occupation of Morocco as much as possible until at some later time heavy compensation could be exacted.[12]

In the meantime the conference idea promised two gains: the overthrow of Delcassé as Foreign Minister of France; and the disruption of the Franco-British Entente, by convincing France that opposition to Germany was too dangerous and British support too uncertain and ineffective. France should be bludgeoned into friendship. For a time, too, success beckoned. The French people began to wonder if Britain was pushing them into a conflict with Germany. Opposition to Delcassé mounted and after Bülow had repeatedly urged dismissal, Premier Pierre Rouvier forced him out, June 4, 1905. The next day the Kaiser made Bülow a prince and all Germany glowed with pride.[13] The Chancellor had already refused to make a general settlement of colonial questions with Rouvier and he now refused to state terms on Morocco. Let the conference assemble.

BJÖRKO INTERLUDE   It was while the agenda of the Algeciras Conference was being thrashed out that the Kaiser was given the opportunity to undertake a diplomatic voyage of his own

---

[12] Brandenburg, pp. 201, 223; Die Grosse Politik, Vol. 20, pp. 346–52.

[13] "Trusting in my skill and strength to force Delcassé's fall without resorting to extreme measures, I did not hesitate to confront France with the danger of war."—Bülow, Memoirs, Vol. II, p. 108.

Bülow's last two demands for Delcassé's head were delivered on May 30, three days after the destruction of the Russian fleet at Tsushima.

and to make a real trial for his continental league. On July 24, at Björko in the Baltic Sea, William had his famous séance with the Tsar in which, buoyed up by prayer and the spirits of his ancestors, he induced Nicholas to sign a treaty which promised: (a) that in case one of the two Empires should be "attacked by a European power" its ally would aid it "in Europe" with all its forces; and (b) that Russia should bring France into the alliance, though the Kaiser insisted that the French must not know about the treaty until it was in force. To tell them earlier would be "absolutely dangerous," said William.

Yet when William came home with this astonishing diplomatic achievement in his pocket his ecstacy was dashed by Bülow's disciplinary threat to resign. The Kaiser had himself inserted "in Europe" into the treaty, which, said Bülow, removed its value as a threat to India and therefore as a check upon England. Nicholas, too, heard from his ministers that the pact was in conflict with the Franco-Russian alliance, and the Kaiser's dream of inducing France to renounce Alsace-Lorraine and put him at the head of a European coalition faded out once more.

THE ALGECIRAS CONFERENCE Six months later, on January 16, 1906, the Morocco Conference met at Algeciras. France had submitted to the German demand for a conference, partly because of the vigorous effort of President Theodore Roosevelt to persuade France to accept it. Roosevelt had just mediated successfully between Japan and Russia and had actively assisted them in concluding a treaty of peace at Portsmouth, New Hampshire, September 3, 1905. Deterred by no idea that international politics was not a game for Americans to play, Roosevelt now took a vigorous part in the Algeciras Conference, putting strong pressure on Germany to induce her to accept the terms favored by the French.[14] Germany's expectations of win-

[14] J. B. Bishop, *Theodore Roosevelt and His Times*, New York, 1920, Vol. I, pp. 467–505; Allan Nevins, *Henry White*, New York, 1930, pp. 261–83.

ning away Russia, Italy and Spain proved vain. Only Austria stood by her. Britain gave France all the support she desired. Her new Liberal Foreign Minister, Sir Edward Grey, would not formally pledge armed support, but, on January 31, 1906, he gave France his full moral backing. Faced with the undoubted necessity of European controlled police in Morocco, if European traders were to operate there, Germany could not prevent the assignment of the police to France and Spain.

HOLSTEIN DROPPED   After months of jockeying, Germany finally had the choice of surrendering or of disrupting the conference. Holstein advised the latter course, and when his advice was disregarded offered his resignation. To his surprise it was accepted. Heretofore, the men who were outwardly responsible to the nation had invariably acquiesced in his decisions.[15] At last his tortuous policy of playing off the Powers against each other, constantly trying to snatch some coaling station or comparatively worthless bit of territory from one or another, had brought Germany to the brink of war.

Now that Holstein was out, would his "policy" of planless opportunism be abandoned?

THE ENTENTE TIGHTENED   Events would determine. But much of Holstein's work would persist. French nationalist sentiment had been wounded and roused to a determination to defy future German browbeating. The Franco-British Entente had been tried and welded by a major ordeal. Henceforth, both the French and British peoples would be on the alert to repel what they thought to be Germany's bludgeoning tactics.

This determination was expressed in the famous memorandum of Sir Eyre Crowe, Under Secretary in the British Foreign Office, written in the autumn of 1906. Toward Germany there should be "unvarying courtesy and consideration in all matters of common concern, but also a prompt and firm refusal to enter into any one-sided bargains or arrangements, and the most unbending determination to uphold British rights and interests in every

[15] Brandenburg, p. 207.

quarter of the globe."[16] This policy was easily defensible but it
would have been wiser to have made greater allowance for the
restless acquisitiveness of a great people come late upon the
world scene. Nothing was more likely than that Germany would
make demands when France began to absorb Morocco. Hence
instead of ignoring her, as Delcassé openly did, it would have
been better to smooth her feelings and offer her something. But
the game of power politics is seldom played in that manner.

TSARISM RESTORED AND FINANCED   Instead of propitiating Germany, French nationalist leaders turned away from the Algeciras
Conference, in March 1906, and exerted themselves to bolster up
the finances of the bloodstained autocracy of their Tsarist ally.
The Socialist leader, Jean Léon Jaurès, wrote on January 23,
1905, the day after Bloody Sunday in Russia, that "a river of
blood flows henceforth between the Tsar and his people. From
this time forth, the Tsar and the regime he represents are the
outlaws of human society." But the leading French newspapers
maintained complete equanimity. While all other nations rang
with protests, the Paris press asserted that what was occurring
in Russia was a question of domestic politics, of no concern
to foreigners, and Delcassé defended the St. Petersburg massacre
in the Chamber, vehemently rebuking two Senators for "the
disgraceful language" of their protests. Le Temps, on February
22, was even alarmed at the Tsar's weakness, when he announced
the calling of an "Assembly of Notables."[17]

Throughout the year 1905 the Russian autocracy was at the
mercy of France. Bankrupt, defeated abroad, disowned by its
own people, it could not survive without great financial aid

[16] G. P. Gooch, "European Diplomacy Before the War," *International
Affairs*, January 1939, Vol. 18, No. 1, p. 83. While Crowe was not another
Holstein, he was a strong personality, he was anti-German and he was an
influential official in the Foreign Office until after 1914.

[17] Michon, pp. 133–42. Anatole France spoke witheringly of the "monstrous alliance." It was "both hateful and senseless that Democratic France
should be bound by a secret treaty to the murderous autocrat." Clemenceau
also wrote that "nothing could excuse M. Delcassé for having attempted to
justify the massacre in the face of humanity's world wide condemnation."

from France, assistance which could have been a powerful lever in liberalizing and democratizing the Russian government, thus safeguarding France's already immense loans to Russia. But, although France never hesitated to arrange that the loans be used for military preparations, her leaders never tried to mitigate the brutality and benightedness of the Tsarist regime. On the contrary, appeals were made for support of the 1906 loan as a means of helping the Tsar to restore order! The leading French papers actually kept up a running fire against the Duma, *Le Temps* alleging that the Russian people were not ripe for any democratic reforms, and the *Journal des Débats* joining it in approving Stolypin's arrest of members and dissolution of the Second Duma, though their correspondents in Russia supported the Duma.[18] Frightful Jewish pogroms in Russia were minimized and Bourgeois, the Foreign Minister, repeatedly persuaded Steeg, the leader of the Radical Party, to postpone presenting a resolution of greeting from the Chamber of Deputies to the Duma until the last day of the session. Then when Steeg still met objections and the Socialists were about to press for action, Clemenceau himself hastily adjourned the Chamber. He, along with Bourgeois and Briand, had acquiesced when Poincaré, as Finance Minister, approved a loan of 2,250,000,000 francs to Russia, without any conditions attached to it, the largest international loan ever issued up to that time. With this money Tsarism was able to crush the revolution, dissolve the Duma and avoid any real reform.

When the great loan was consummated, in the spring of 1906, Maxim Gorky wrote: "See, this is what thou hast done, France, Mother of Liberty! Thy hand stretched out in greed hath closed the path of independence for a whole nation." In France, the leaders, including the three noted liberals named above, could think of nothing except to buttress the power in Russia which had made an alliance with France against Germany, a feeling which the Morocco crisis doubtless accentuated. There

[18] Michon, pp. 172–73.

were many warnings, from Frenchmen and Russians, that both the ally and the "investments" would be lost unless the Russian people were made partners in the alliance, but to no avail. Gorky pleaded that the struggle in Russia would be neither long nor painful if Europe ceased to give the Russian Government "money to enable it to perpetuate these massacres and executions." But, he warned, "if the state of tension in which the nation is living goes on much longer, there will be such an accumulation of hatred and cruelty in the Russian soul that, when the inevitable explosion comes, the outpouring of these pent-up forces will horrify the whole world."[19]

This accurate prediction of what was to occur in 1917 had no effect on French policy. French funds kept on pouring into Russia, to the great indirect benefit of Germany. The large conversion loans of 1889–1894 went principally for purchases in Germany. Later, as the French loans continued, German exports to Russia rose from 224,714,000 rubles in 1904 to 440,957,000 rubles in 1910, and Russian imports from Britain from 332,230,-000 rubles to 467,547,000, while French sales to Russia never exceeded 100,000,000 rubles. Nevertheless, the great mass of small investors in France kept the stream of money running to Russia, until in 1913 the total reached seventeen billion francs, 10,616,000,000 of which had gone directly to the Russian government.[20] For twenty-five years the decaying Russian autocracy was bolstered by political loans from the land of The Revolution, the home of free peasant proprietors and liberty-loving shopowners.

[19] Michon, pp. 154, 160–61. In *Humanité* on July 22, 1906, Jaurès also prophesied "a terrible cataclysm" in Russia, from which freedom would emerge victorious "but rabid and bloodstained."

The Viborg Manifesto, issued by the outlawed members of the Duma, warned that fresh loans made without the consent of the Russian nation would not be repaid.

[20] Michon, pp. 146–47, 174. The bankers absorbed in commissions 17 percent of the large loan of 1909. At least they profited.

Anglo-Russian Entente, 1907

After the Morocco crisis, too, the Liberal government of Great Britain moved further away from the "natural alliance" with Germany, which recurrently appeals to highly placed Englishmen, and toward an understanding with repressive Russia. Sir Charles Hardinge and Sir Arthur Nicolson, successively Ambassadors to Russia, and high officials in the Foreign Office, agreed in urging that Britain push on to a general entente with Russia. This course encountered strong resistance among the Liberals, who disliked the internal tyranny of the Russian autocracy as heartily as its unscrupulous aggressions abroad. But fear of Germany and the advantages of another *détente* with a great rival impelled British Foreign Secretary Sir Edward Grey to proceed as fast as Foreign Minister Isvolski could drag the Russians. They detested English Liberalism heartily, particularly since they were still occupied in the bloody repression of their own people's effort to achieve free institutions. However, Russia was exhausted and unprecedented English sympathy with her ambitions in the Straits was most welcome.

A British condition was fulfilled in the signing of a Russo-Japanese treaty of July 30, 1907, with the customary open and secret articles, whereby the parties agreed to divide Manchuria between them and to exclude everyone else. The Anglo-Russian Entente, signed August 31, 1907, dealt with sources of friction between the two empires in the Middle East, Japan having pushed Russia back in the Far East while London had become reconciled to Russian control of the Straits. Both agreed to leave Tibet alone. Russia recognized Afghanistan and Southern Persia as British spheres of influence. These agreements protected all the approaches to India, relieving one of the major concerns of Great Britain.

PERSIA PARTITIONED   Yet the new entente centered in Persia. Russia had been steadily encroaching on Northern Persia, the valuable agricultural part. This area was now turned over to her and a neutral zone established between the Russian and British spheres, all without any reference to the rights of the Persians. The agreement once made, the Russians pushed steadily ahead, defeating by armed force where necessary, every effort of the Persian nationalists to save their country. The latter could drive out the Shah, but not the Russians. This sordid business was a continual vexation to Grey and his Liberal following, but they could do little to restrain the process they had set in motion.[21] The Persians had to wait until the Powers exhausted themselves in the Great War before they could recover control of their country.

Nevertheless, the treaty of 1907, which for once contained no secret articles, ended another ancient and hereditary national rivalry, temporarily at least. The bear and the lion suddenly discovered that there had been no real reason for their generations of enmity and they could just as well be friends, especially since they had a common dread of the great power of Germany. If, also, Russia had remained a capitalistic autocracy after the World War, the new friendship might well have endured as long as the Franco-British liaison did. There was no material reason why the British and Russians should become enemies again.

POWER BALANCED   In 1907 the effort to organize peace and national security by defensive alliances came to full flower. Though the British ententes with France and Russia were not "alliances," and never legally became so, the Triple Entente was a reality. Now the Triple Alliance was balanced by a combination which in a few years would have superior military power. Much more than Bismarck had ever feared, or his successors

[21] When the Government announced, June 4, 1908, that the King had accepted an invitation to visit the Tsar, there was such a storm in the House of Commons that Grey had to fight for his political life.—G. P. Gooch, *Before the War*, Oxford, 1938, Vol. II, p. 30.

thought credible, had come to pass. Yet the development achieved in 1907 was as inevitable as anything can be said to be. When one great power began to make "defensive" alliances the process had to continue until a temporary equilibrium had been reached. In a world of predatory states all seeking to prevail over one another by jungle tactics, no nation could rely for safety upon its own arms. Throughout this period diplomacy was always on a war basis. The threat of war was always in reserve, and frequently trundled out into the foreground. In the international anarchy, membership in rival leagues of imperialistic nations was much better than belonging to no international organization at all.

Anglo-German Naval Rivalry

The formation of the two grand alliances made wholly certain a deep intensification of the arms race. Germany would strain every nerve to retain the supremacy on land; Britain would make sure that she kept control of the sea. It was now more than ever "a matter of life and death" to both.

Up to 1904 Germany's naval ambitions do not seem to have been the leading factor in ending Britain's isolation. Originally, the British had regarded the German Navy "as a harmless hobby of the Kaiser's."[22] It remained to be proved that it was an obsession with him. The Kaiser's envy of the assured ways of the English and of their greater possessions went back to his childhood. Then as a little boy he had seen the British fleet at Portsmouth and Plymouth and had dreamed of having many great ships himself some day, a dream which never left him.[23] Yet for ten years after he became Emperor he argued with the Reichstag in vain. The Germans had never had a navy and had no desire for one. Besides, retaining the military supremacy of

[22] Brandenburg, p. 271.
[23] Bülow, *Memoirs, 1903–1909*, p. 30.

Europe was expensive enough. It was not until 1896 that William was given some support. His Kruger telegram, the first overwhelmingly popular thing he ever did, and perhaps the last, was promptly answered by a denial from Lord Salisbury that Germany had any right to interfere in behalf of the Boers, and by the mobilization of a squadron in the English Channel. Some Germans could now see that they could not stand up to England without a navy.

TIRPITZ' NAVAL LAWS, 1898–1900 At this juncture William found a man capable of spreading this realization. In 1897 Admiral Alfred von Tirpitz became the head of the small German Navy. Tirpitz was everything that his sailor Emperor could have desired. He was mature, vigorous, a great administrator, a superior propagandist, and he had an inflexible will which would keep even the Kaiser himself from weakening. Soon Tirpitz had a Naval League going and a many sided propaganda. In 1898 he put his first building program through, providing for nineteen battleships and some fifty cruisers. Early in 1900 he secured another law doubling the number of battleships to be provided and laying down a building program up to 1920. This time he said openly that the fleet must be equal to its greatest task, "a battle in the North Sea against England."[24] Tirpitz was astute in getting a long-range program enacted, for thereafter the Kaiser could always declare that it was the law and could not be altered. Every rebuff of a German claim, each incident overseas, could also be used as a justification for the program and for its acceleration, and German capitalists could go ahead with the immense task of developing shipyards and supporting industries.

Yet this paper navy did not arouse concern in England until it began to ride upon the sea. It was never once mentioned during the long negotiations for a British-German alliance.[25] Up to this time antagonism had been greater in Germany than

[24] Tirpitz, *My Memoirs*, New York, 1919, pp. 122–23.
[25] Brandenburg, p. 271.

in Britain, though the British had not approved of Bismarck's tactics in creating the German Empire and since then had expected calculated brutality and guile to come out of Germany. By 1903 feeling in Britain against Germany was so strong that it compelled the government to abandon its intention of aiding the German Baghdad Railway project. In 1904 a new home fleet was formed and a base made for it at Rosyth in Scotland, facing Germany.

THE DREADNOUGHT, 1906   Unquestionably the Morocco crisis of 1905-6 sharpened feeling on both sides and provided fresh fuel for Tirpitz' propaganda. In November 1905, a supplementary law was announced in Germany, providing for new vessels and a large increase in the size and cost of future battleships. A month earlier there had been laid down in Portsmouth dockyard the keel of the greatest battleship designed up to that time. A year and ten days later, also, the *Dreadnought* began her sea trials. No great warship had ever been built so quickly. It was soon said, too, that this one ship could sink the entire German navy. But this would mean that one German Dreadnought could make obsolete the immense preponderance of pre-*Dreadnought* battleships which the British possessed. By building a far more powerful ship than any nation had, it is usually said that Britain foolishly gave away her sure supremacy of the sea and made it possible for Germany to start a new race on even terms. Certain it was that a more costly and dangerous building contest had been started.

Yet close examination of the question suggests that the *Dreadnought* was a development sure to come in any prolonged naval competition between two great industrial nations.[26] She was not greatly larger or more expensive than her immediate predecessors. She was far more powerful because she was faster and had ten 12-inch guns, instead of four, and batteries of smaller weapons. She was thus equal to two of her predecessors on

[26] See the study by E. L. Woodward, *Great Britain and the German Navy*, Oxford, 1935, Chapter 5.

broadside or to three firing ahead. She was not laid down, either, until after the most anxious debate by British naval chiefs. They knew that naval science could now provide such a ship and that the "all big gun ship" was being discussed in several other countries. Should they depreciate their great battle fleet by making the break? It was risky, but suppose that Germany should build three or four such ships before Britain began? Would she not have decisive control of the sea? And if Britain took the lead would she not still have the advantage of surprise and a lead that could not be overcome? Could they afford to wait? Given a serious, perhaps desperate, naval race, could any Admiralty long resist the temptation to compete qualitatively as well as quantitatively? While national survival depends upon nothing better than possessing the best and most mobile weapons, it is up to the fighting men to provide them.[27]

THE MULLINER PANIC, 1909 The completion of the *Dreadnought* was an unfortunate thing for the new Liberal government in London, which wanted to spend on social services some of the money then going into unproductive floating fortresses. Spurred by unrest in Parliament, the Government decided, in July 1906, to cut its naval program from four large ships to three, and to postpone one of the three until after the Second Hague Conference. Germany steadily resisted the discussion of arms limitation at this conference, and the question was staved off without serious debate. Germany thought it an attempt by Britain to win a cheap naval supremacy. By this time the membership of the German Navy League exceeded 900,000, and the fleet was a thing upon which German nationalist opinion would not compromise. On February 16, 1908, the Kaiser wrote to Lord Tweedmouth, First Lord of the Admiralty, asking the British to kindly leave Germany out of their naval discussions. He execrated Metternich, his Ambassador in London, for sending him correct reports of English opinion

[27] German calculations were so upset that no battleship was launched for a year. The great strategic value of the Kiel Canal was also destroyed until it could be widened, a very long and costly undertaking.

and finally recalled him. Early in 1908 another amendment to the German Navy Law provided for four dreadnoughts each year until 1911, instead of three.

Since the British had laid down three ships in 1907 and only two in 1908, they were losing their lead. After Sir Charles Hardinge was sharply rebuffed by the Kaiser at Berlin, in August 1908, English leaders, in and out of the government, concluded that the German menace had to be met. The country must be aroused. This opinion was particularly strong in the mind of Mr. H. H. Mulliner, an employee of a battleship building firm which was without orders and in financial difficulties. He had been bombarding the government since May 1906 with news that five or six great machines for gun turntables were being built in Germany for Krupps. He and a colleague had seen "parts" of these machines.

Mr. Mulliner's information was very slow in catching hold, but in 1909 it became the basis of a great naval panic.[28] The fear spread that Germany was stealthily about to build enough dreadnoughts to seize suddenly the control of the sea. The time for the completion of hulls was steadily dropping, along with a constant increase in the size of guns. The making of these complicated monsters, with their turntables and turrets, was the limiting factor. Now if the armament could be secretly assembled in advance, hulls might be rushed to completion and a whole fleet hurried out to destroy British sea supremacy. This probability may seem to the reader not very great, but in an arms race no contingency is too far fetched to be overlooked, or believed.

On January 4, 1909, Grey complained to Metternich that material was being assembled in advance for four German ships. On February 3, Metternich replied that this was true, but that construction would not be accelerated. On March 17 he also admitted that contracts for two ships had been given in

[28] For a full account of the Mulliner Panic see Philip Noel-Baker, *The Private Manufacture of Armaments*, New York, 1937, pp. 449–510.

advance of the normal date, to save money, but again denied acceleration. The British government decided to recommend four ships for the coming year, and the Admiralty asked for six. The Conservatives won by-elections on the cry "We want eight and we won't wait!" Their leader, Mr. Balfour, but lately Prime Minister, gave the country a fright on March 16, 1909, by solemnly maintaining that Germany would have thirteen dreadnoughts on April 1, 1911, to Britain's twelve. The Admiralty thought that the Germans would not complete the thirteen until August 1, 1911, but that was cold comfort to alarmed citizens. The government took authority to build the eight ships, and in July announced that they would be constructed. When May 1911 arrived the Germans actually had five ships completed and in March 1912 nine, instead of the twenty-one which Balfour had so ominously predicted. There was no acceleration of the published German program.

GERMAN BUILDING CONTINUED   But in Germany fear and suspicion was as great as in England, from the Kaiser down to the general public. William was early convinced that Germany was being "encircled" by his uncle, King Edward, and by 1908 one of Edward's visits to another country was enough to give rise to something like a panic in Germany. The situation was so acute that Bülow finally became convinced that it was necessary to call a halt to the naval race. On June 3, 1909, he held a secret meeting with the military and naval chiefs, which was attended by Metternich, Ambassador to Britain, at which the civilians strongly urged limitation. But Tirpitz blocked compromise at every point.

TIRPITZ' "RISK" THEORIES   Tirpitz had started out on the platform that national commerce, industry, intercourse, colonies, and "to a certain extent fishing on the high seas are impossible without a fleet capable of taking the offensive."[29] He was thus a firm believer in the international anarchy. No nation could carry on any important activity overseas without a huge navy.

[29] Woodward, p. 19.

Such doctrines, too, won ready assent in most countries. It was commonly assumed that any nation with a merchant marine needed a big navy to protect it. The claim was false, for a few small cruisers are sufficient for that. Great navies can have only two purposes: to win victory in war and to back up diplomacy to the point of war.[30] Nor can there be two navies strong enough to control the sea in any given part of the world.

To get around this obvious truth, Tirpitz early invented the "risk" theory—and clung to it until his enormously expensive dreadnoughts disappeared beneath the waves of Scapa Flow in 1918. Germany must have a navy, not as large as Britain's, but strong enough to make a conflict on the sea a dangerous risk to Britain. This would make her yield in diplomatic encounters, and thus enable Germany to get colonies and other advantages. It might not be necessary to approach the size of the British fleet very closely, Tirpitz argued in the early years. All that was necessary was to have sufficient ships to weaken the British in battle enough to permit their other rivals to combine their fleets and achieve sea supremacy. The formation of the Anglo-French Entente in 1904 and the sinking of Russia's navy at Tsushima practically destroyed this version of the theory, and the Anglo-Russian Entente of 1907 completed its demolition. There were no navies left to combine against a victorious but depleted British Navy, though curiously enough the Germans persistently cast the United States for that role.[31] From 1905 on, if any naval threat was to make English statesmen tractable Germany alone had to provide it. This Tirpitz and his growing following meant to do.

[30] See the clear analysis of Lieutenant Commander Melvin F. Talbot, "The Navy America Needs," *Current History*, April 1933, pp. 1–8.

[31] Their belief that nations must always be preparing to fight each other, and that old enmities must continue, was raised to a certainty by the incivilities exchanged by President Cleveland and Lord Salisbury over Venezuela in 1895. Confidence in an inevitable conflict between Britain and the United States became "an article of faith among German statesmen in these years." Spender, p. 165.

AN ELUSIVE "DANGER ZONE"   That their risk navy would create a risk for Germany they readily agreed, but they miscalculated again as to what the risk was. Instead of foreseeing the creation of a diplomatic combination which would gradually curtail Germany's power to demand concessions anywhere, the Tirpitz school thought that if they could prevent England from launching a preventive war for a certain period they would be safe. There would be a "danger zone," during which the temptation would be great for the British to attack, but they would never quite summon courage to do so, or find the proper occasion. Then the German Navy would be strong enough to make the "risk" too great and it could move steadily on to supremacy. Tirpitz believed that he had two winning cards, cheaper construction costs and conscript sailor labor for his ships. With these Germany could stand the financial strain longer than England could.[32] That German imperialists could believe that Germany was able to pay for both the world's greatest army and navy, overcoming the concentration of the British on their navy alone, is evidence of the immense confidence which the Germans had in their wealth and power.

With his mind fixed on passing "the danger zone" safely, Tirpitz pressed on, impervious to all evidence that the danger zone was constantly extended. The diplomatic situation steadily worsened for Germany, largely because of the naval race. The British met every increase in the German Navy with a greater one. Yet Tirpitz held firm and prevented any weakening by the Kaiser. The latter task was not difficult, since the Navy was William's passion. It was to be the great achievement of his reign, the thing which would make him outstanding in Hohenzollern dynastic history. His forebears had been great on land; he would be great on the sea as well. Every suggestion that Germany ought to slow up naval construction stirred his anger. Germany had as good a right to a navy as any power did. Her ships were built against no one. It was a high offense

[32] Fay, Vol. I, pp. 236–37.

against German dignity and honor to try to limit her Navy. He would stop building only if England gave Germany a firm agreement to be neutral in future wars.[33]

ABORTIVE NEGOTIATIONS, 1909   This was the demand which Bethmann Hollweg, who became Chancellor on July 14, 1909, was required to support in the Anglo-German negotiations of August–November 1909. Beginning by easy stages, the British were brought by degrees to see that they must give an explicit, written promise to remain neutral, if Germany fought more than one power. This was equivalent to giving Germany a free hand in Europe. It was requiring more than England had conceded to France and Russia. Germany would halt the naval race on no other terms, and then she could promise no more than a slowing of the tempo of her naval program which would at the same time be carried out as laid down by law, an apparent defiance of the laws of arithmetic.[34]

Arms Limitation Rejected

THE FIRST HAGUE CONFERENCE, 1899   The Hague Conferences of 1899 and 1907 illustrated excellently both the brusqueness of German diplomacy and the total abandon with which the nations pursued the struggle for power. Though couched in attractive phrases, the Tsar's invitation of August 24, 1898, was motivated by nothing higher than the recurrent bankruptcy of his treasury. To keep up with Germany he required new artillery for his army, especially if Austria re-equipped her

[33] Throughout these years the German navalists uttered the belief that force alone counted. "Force is the decisive factor in the world; nations maintain themselves by strength of combat and unity of purpose, not by superiority of civilization." And again: "Eternal peace, of which there has recently been much talk, contradicts the ancient and still valid generalization that change and not quiet, war and not peace, are part of the nature of things and of life itself." *Nauticus*, 1910, p. 24; 1911, p. 53.

[34] *British Documents*, Vol. 6, pp. 293–302, 510, 513; *Die Gross Politik*, Vol. 28, pp. 239–43.

forces. It would never do to make a limitation proposal to Austria, but perhaps a general agreement could be reached.[35]

In all the foreign offices the Tsar's proposal produced the greatest astonishment and perplexity. Everyone rightly suspected that the proposed agreement not to exceed the budgetary provisions for arms in 1898–1899 was a scheme to serve Russian ends. But what to do? The Kaiser margined that the Tsar had chosen "a very peculiar way" of showing how peaceful he was. Lord Salisbury was sure that no power would consent to arbitrate questions of "honor" and "vital interests."[36] Baron Holstein knew that "The establishment of the so-called Arbitration Court can have no other result than by defining the various interests to facilitate the formation of groups for war or for subjecting weaker parties."[37] Everyone in authority was aghast at the Tsar's foolish proposals. But public opinion, especially in Britain, Italy, the United States and the small nations, supported the outlandish Russian ideas.[38] The Tsar, too, was the most august of autocrats. Hence the governments all had to send delegates.

The French delegates went to "spare the Tsar and to seek a formula to circumvent the question."[39] The instructions to the German delegates were identical. They were to be ready with reservations that would rob any proposals made of unfavorable tendencies.[40] Even the American delegates arrived instructed that the limitation of armed forces was "so inapplicable to the

[35] E. J. Dillon, *The Eclipse of Russia,* London, 1918, pp. 277–78.

[36] Spender, pp. 172–74.

[37] *Die Grosse Politik,* Vol. 15, p. 188. To his credit it must be recorded that in germinating the conference idea Count Witte was thinking of "my old pet idea of a league of pacific nations vying with each other in trade, industry, science, arts and inventions." Such visionary ideas did not trouble the contemporary statesmen of Witte's time. They were all too occupied in making threats of war, or in parrying them. Dillon, *op. cit.*

[38] Brandenburg, p. 130.

[39] Count Munster to Chancellor Hohenlohe, April 21, 1899, *Die Grosse Politik,* Vol. 15, p. 186.

[40] Brandenburg, p. 130.

United States at present" that all initiatives were to be left to others. The "expediency of restraining the inventive genius of our people" in devising means of defense was also doubtful and all measures to control the use of weapons in war likely to be illusory.[41] Captain Alfred T. Mahan stated that the United States government would "on no account even discuss the question of any limitation of naval armaments." He explained that American vital interests now lay East and West, instead of North and South. The United States needed a large navy with which to take part in the struggle for Chinese markets."[42]

The German delegates had intended to remain in the background, but when a standstill agreement on armaments for five years was actually proposed the German delegates had to veto it, and their position on the proposed arbitration of disputes was similarly negative. Holstein wrote that impartial decision was impossible since all citizens of Great Powers were bound to regard the State "itself as an end, not as a means toward the attainment of higher aims." Therefore the proposed court could only be a Russian scheme for forming combinations of powers against one power or another.[43] Germany would only agree to the creation of a harmless panel of possible arbitrators, to whom resort should be wholly voluntary. "Most of the other states wished to go further, or at least made a pretense of doing so, but yielded to make the resolution unanimous."[44]

THE SECOND HAGUE CONFERENCE, 1907   Again in 1907 when the Second Hague Conference met on the initiative of the United States, though by invitation of Russia, Germany took the odium of preventing any advance either toward arbitration or arms limitation, when other powers would have assumed the responsibility had they been compelled. This time Great Britain alone wanted arms limited, to check the German naval threat. Russia, defeated by Japan and fortified by large French and

[41] Andrew D. White, *Autobiography*, London, 1905, Vol. II, p. 253.
[42] *British Documents*, Vol. I, pp. 229–31.
[43] *Die Grosse Politik*, Vol. 15, pp. 188–89.
[44] Brandenburg, p. 131.

British loans for rearmament, was now as adverse to stopping arms competition as anyone. Russian leaders joined all the others in pouring scorn upon such a utopian idea.[45] In February 1907, Germany refused to agree to the discussion either of arms limitation or obligatory arbitration. She was finally persuaded not to bolt when the British did propose, August 17, 1907, that "the Governments should undertake the serious examination of this question," a resolution which was adopted without a second vote,[46] but the creation of some slight presumptions in favor of arbitration was blocked by Germany and Austria.[47]

"Public opinion was either indifferent or unorganized throughout the world, and the diplomats had the game in their own hands."[48]

[45] The deprecatory utterances of a dozen "statesmen," including some English leaders, are quoted in G. Lowes Dickinson, *The International Anarchy, 1904–1914*, New York, 1926, p. 355.

[46] James Brown Scott, *The Reports of the Hague Conferences of 1899 and 1907*, Oxford, 1917, pp. 892–97.

[47] Brandenburg, p. 277.

[48] Dickinson, p. 357. The conference did discuss seriously the right of capture at sea, to the discomfiture of the British. When the results finally reached Parliament, in the Declaration of London, the House of Lords refused ratification.

IV. The Rivalry of the Armed Leagues, 1908-1914

———◆———

The Annexation of Bosnia, 1908-1909

In between the Second Hague Conference and the naval scare of 1909 there developed the first trial of strength between the Triple Alliance and the Triple Entente. The completion of the latter had tended to shift the center of gravity in the Triple Alliance from Berlin to Vienna, since Germany felt more than ever dependent upon her "one reliable ally."

AEHRENTHAL'S POSITIVE POLICY After 1906, also, there was in the Vienna foreign office a determined statesman, the first in many years, who was resolved to relieve the internal strains in the Monarchy by a vigorous foreign policy. Intending also to convince Europe that the Monarchy could still act, Count Lexa von Aehrenthal revealed to Marschall von Bieberstein, German Ambassador to Turkey, in December 1907, that he was aiming at an annexation of Bosnia-Herzegovina, already administered by Austria-Hungary since 1878, and at a railway through the Sanjak which would isolate Serbia from Montenegro, Albania, and the Adriatic.[1] Nine months later, in September 1908, Aehrenthal visited Schön, the German Secretary of State, at Berchtesgaden, and somewhat vaguely discussed the annexation of Bosnia "in time." He was contemplating "the clearing

[1] Erich Brandenburg, *From Bismarck to the World War*, London, 1927, p. 307.

out of the Serbian revolutionary nest." Serbia, he suggested, might be given to Bulgaria.[2] Schön promised support.

THE BUCHLAU BARGAIN   The Russian Foreign Minister, Isvolski, had already been informed by Aehrenthal of the proposed annexation, and on September 16 he arrived at Buchlau Castle in Austria to make a bargain whereby in return for his consent the Straits would be opened to Russia. Isvolski then proceeded to Germany and Italy on his way to Paris and London to secure agreement to his part of the deal, but had barely reached Paris when the annexation was announced. On September 23, Prince Ferdinand of Bulgaria had come to Budapest to find out when the annexation would occur. Ferdinand then hurried home to proclaim the independence of Bulgaria from Turkey. The result was that both Bulgaria and Austria published their proclamations on the same day, October 5, 1908. Each had desired to forestall the other. Partly for this reason Isvolski was caught emptyhanded and he now found both France and Britain cold to the opening of the Straits, while Russian opinion compelled him to remember the future of the South Slavs.

GERMANY BACKS AUSTRIA: RUSSIA, THE SERBS   Serbia at once appealed to Russia, by every way open to her, and under Pan-Slav pressure the Tsar promised his support. Though Bülow must have had information from Schön in advance of notice from Austria on September 26, the Kaiser did not. He was highly indignant at Austria's act of "piracy" against his Turkish protégé. He was "personally wounded in (his) deepest feeling." But his advisers all agreed that Austria must be supported.[3] According to Schön, Bülow "was not averse to letting things take their course to a climax and to a trial of strength

[2] Schön's note on the interview, September 5.

[3] Aehrenthal had told his Council of Ministers, on August 19, that he was "absolutely sure of Germany." The Kaiser had joyfully sent the news of his rebuff to Hardinge on the naval issue, thereby convincing Aehrenthal that he had Germany in his pocket. Spender, p. 315.

between the Central Powers bloc and the Triple Entente, which was not yet firmly established."[4] The military chiefs of staff in both Germany and Austria agreed that now was the time to attack Serbia, and Bülow himself spurred Vienna on against the Serbs. On December 16 he told the Austrian Ambassador Szögyény that the moment would never be more favorable and added that "it would be highly desirable if a sign of life should be manifested again in international politics."[5] But Aehrenthal, influenced perhaps by a sharp letter from the Tsar to Francis Joseph, gradually turned against this solution as too expensive and dangerous. The expansion of Bulgaria at Serbia's expense could easily be arranged later.

Meanwhile, it became clear that none of the Triple Entente was ready to fight over Austria's unilateral abrogation of parts of the Treaty of Berlin. Grey deeply resented the infringement and objected to the affront to the Young Turks, who had just come to power and were supposed to be liberals, but when Austria purchased their acquiescence with approximately $12,500,000, the issue with Russia and Serbia became more acute.

GERMANY's "ULTIMATUM" At length it developed that Isvolski though beaten was so embittered that he would not surrender, while Serb and Austrian troops faced one another in large numbers and the war party in Vienna was gaining the upper hand. Finally the crisis was broken by Germany. On March 22, 1909, Isvolski was asked to give his promise that if

[4] Freiherr von Schön, *The Memoirs of an Ambassador,* London, 1922, p. 83; Viscount Grey, *Twenty-Five Years, 1892–1916,* London, 1925, Vol. I, p. 191. Partly to keep Turkey from leaving the German camp, the German press protested almost unanimously that Germany had not been consulted about the annexation. The liberal papers condemned Austria's coup and the nationalist press resented it as likely to involve Germany in a war from which she could get nothing for herself. There was a note of reserve in the few newspapers which supported the move. When the press began to show fear that leadership was passing from Berlin to Vienna, Bülow hushed this tendency.—E. M. Carroll, *Germany and the Great Powers, 1866–1914,* New York, 1938, pp. 592–93.

[5] Ö.-U.A., Vol. I, p. 607.

requested by Austria to consent to the repeal of Article 25 of the Treaty of Berlin, he would do so. A Yes or No answer was required and if there was any evasion, "We would then draw aside and allow matters to take their course," that is, at Serbia's expense. The Tsar had already telegraphed his thanks to the Kaiser for an earlier proposal and begged him to restrain Austria; the next day Isvolski also capitulated unconditionally, without waiting to consult the French and British Ambassadors.[6]

THE EFFECTS OF THE CRISIS   The long and dangerous crisis was ended, by wise action on Germany's part, say some historians; by a mail-fisted ultimatum, others reply. The state of Russia's armaments permitted her no choice but to yield to the "advice" given by Germany, and when a year later the Kaiser boasted in Vienna of having stood by his ally in "shining armor" any doubts in the minds of Russian nationalists as to what had happened were removed. Russia had been humiliated, they argued, and it must not happen again. Serbia also was embittered and aroused as she had never been before.

The Triple Entente, too, had suffered a sharp check the year after it was formed. In his talks with Aehrenthal before the annexation, Isvolski had insisted that the annexation must be approved by a European conference. In this he was supported by Britain throughout, but Germany and Austria would not consent to the same demand which Germany had successfully enforced at Algeciras. If the public law of Europe was to be upheld, the demand for a conference was reasonable. But know-

[6] Isvolski was doubly compromised. In his Buchlau bargaining he had had little regard for the future of the South Slavs, thinking only of the Straits. Yet Russian nationalist opinion had been "strangely indifferent to the Straits" but "stirred to the depths by the Serbian cause."—Bernadotte Schmitt, *The Annexation of Bosnia*, Cambridge, 1937, pp. 244, 248. This monograph is the most complete and exhaustive account in English of the crisis of 1908–1909.

The German "ultimatum" to Russia was written by Kiderlen-Wächter, who was as ready personally to back it up with force as he was in the later Morocco crisis of 1911.

ing that she and Austria would again stand alone, Germany now took the position of France in 1905, and of Russia in 1878, that a Great Power should not be haled before a conference like a criminal.

For a time "the German and Austrian diplomats actually believed they had broken up the Entente."[7] Yet, adds Count Montgelas, this victory "firmly cemented the Triple Entente." For the fourth time in fifty-five years Russia had been compelled to give way to the despised Danubian Monarchy. France and England were convinced that the Triple Entente must be tightened up. The South Slavs, both inside and outside the Monarchy, were stirred strongly against it. Russia was largely committed to support Serbia in the future. And after a long and very expensive mobilization, Austria had nothing except a legal title to the provinces, extorted by illegal action and superior force. Her physical and moral hold on the provinces was no stronger than it had been for forty years. Indeed, her difficulties in the provinces increased sharply, instead of diminishing.[8]

On Germany's side, she might maintain that she had held her one ally, yet she had aggressively covered Austria's rear "without asking if she were in the right," and with very short notice of the grave decision that had been taken.[9] Of great importance to Germany, too, was the large armament program

[7] Count Max Montgelas, *The Case for the Central Powers*, New York, 1925, p. 36; Count Julius Andrassy, *Diplomacy and the War*, London, 1921, p. 39.

[8] Count Julius Andrassy, one-time Foreign Minister of Austria-Hungary, commenting in 1921 on the Bosnian annexation as a cause of the Great War, said: "We had committed a definitely illegal action, and we had given an example to Italy which she hastened to imitate." Not a man or a penny was gained and money was sent to Turkey "for what belonged to us already." Russia was angered, but not weakened, and Serbian hatred increased. Both armed and planned revenge. Russia made agreements with Italy and Japan, and prepared to advance solution of the Straits question. Andrassy, *Diplomacy and the War*, pp. 39–40.

[9] Brandenburg, p. 334.

which Russia immediately undertook, with the object of avoiding a similar humiliation in the future.[10]

The Bosnia crisis of 1908–1909 was the most important of all the successive crises which finally culminated in World War I, because it was an almost complete rehearsal for the 1914 crisis.

The Hapsburg Monarchy was doomed to extinction because its dualistic form gave the Hungarian landlords the power to block all self-government for their large Rumanian minority, and a considerable part of the South Slavs, in the Monarchy. Yet its very life was menaced by the attraction of the independent Serbs and Montenegrins upon their racial and religious kinsmen in both halves of the Monarchy.

The only real solution for it was a policy so liberal and attractive that all of the South Slavs might be unified as a kingdom inside the Monarchy. This meant that Serbia must be induced or compelled to come inside, a difficult operation at best and one rendered impossible of achievement by the adamant opposition of the Hungarian magnates to the inclusion of additional Slavs, and even more important their total refusal to grant political, economic and social rights to their subject races. The monumental work by Albertini, *The Origins of the War of 1914*, makes very clear in many places that this was the rock upon which the Monarchy foundered. Since the trialistic solution, the union of the South Slavs under the Hapsburgs, could not be carried out, the only alternative left was to crush the flaming nationalism of the South Slavs and to dispose of Serbia by breaking her up, dividing her territories mainly between the Monarchy and Bulgaria.[11]

[10] Schmitt, p. 126.

[11] Luigi Albertini, *The Origins of the War of 1914*, Vols. I, II and III. Oxford University Press, New York, 1952, 1953. As the editor of the most famous Italian newspaper during the 1914 period, the *Corriere della Sera* of Milan, Senator Albertini had in a sense been one of the actors in the 1914 tragedy. His public position and reputation also gave him access to virtually all of the living actors in the drama, whom he interviewed personally or by letter. He also mastered all the previous works on the origins

When Aehrenthal determined to annex Bosnia-Herzegovina formally, thus closing the door to a union of the South Slavs under Serb leadership, he originally thought of a trialistic solution, but was soon deflected by Magyar opposition to thinking of creating a "Big Bulgaria at the expense of Serbia" and of "laying hands on what remains of Serbia as soon as a propitious star is in the ascendant in Europe." This theme recurs again and again, and was Aehrenthal's legacy to Berchtold, who tried in 1914 to carry it through. The Germans also endorsed it heartily, the Kaiser saying on October 16, 1908, to Count Hoyos: "You can throw Serbia to the Bulgars and so rid yourselves once and for all of your tiresome neighbor."[12]

Austrian official circles were quite ready for this drastic solution. *Danzer's Armee-Zeitung* published on January 7, 1909, a long article maintaining that war was now "inevitable" because Russia, Italy, Serbia, and Turkey all "drive us" to war and that "we shall now lay hand on Serbia." It concluded "Our blood throbs in our veins, we strain at the leash. Sire! Give us the signal!"[13]

However, Aehrenthal changed his mind, deciding to leave this event to his successors, but not before the character of

of World War I and the vast mass of documents published by the governments, after the overthrow of the great European monarchies opened their archives and forced the Entente governments to do likewise, if in lesser measure.

No one else has made as full use of these documents, quoting them with a sure familiarity and often repeating the same quotation profitably in the different contexts of several chapters. When the considerable mass of his own new documentary evidence is added, the result is a work so impressive, so cogent, fair and convincing that it is likely to be the really definitive work on this highly controversial period.

The labor involved was so enormous that Albertini did not finish the second volume before his death. However, it was competently completed by Luciano Magrini, and the extensive materials which Albertini had collected appeared in a third volume.

[12] Albertini, Vol. I, pp. 192, 200, 205, 230, 231.

[13] *Ibid.*, pp. 264–65.

the Austro-German alliance had been changed into an offensive combination essentially in the control of the weaker partner, Austria-Hungary. "From 1909 onwards the foreign policy of Germany was harnessed to that of the Dual Monarchy," though this was not fully understood in London and Paris.[14] This change was accomplished principally in an extensive exchange of letters between the two Chiefs of Staff, Moltke and Conrad, in which Moltke agreed that the "longanimity of the Monarchy in the face of Serb provocation will come to an end. Then nothing would remain but for her to enter Serbia," and "the moment Russia mobilizes, Germany will also mobilize." This would probably mean the spread of war "over the whole continent."

This was a far cry from Bismarck's stern admonition that German forces must not be used "for the benefit of Hungarian and Catholic ambitions in the Balkans" and his conclusion that "For us, Balkan questions can in no case be a motive for war."[15]

At the conclusion of the crisis Moltke wrote to Conrad his "deepest regret that a chance has been let slip which will not so soon offer itself again in favorable conditions." He was sure that they would have been successful in localizing the war.[16]

A few days later Tommaso Tittoni, the Italian Foreign Minister, signed a treaty with Austria and Germany, long under negotiation, which flatly contradicted the Balkan section of the Racconigi Pact and led the Teutonic allies to think they had Italy tied in again. Actually, Russian assurance that Italy could go ahead in Tripoli was the significant result of this new doubledealing.

RUSSO-GERMAN AGREEMENTS, 1910 The year 1910 brought a

[14] Nicholas Mansergh, *The Coming of the First World War*, London, 1949, p. 132. Thereafter the peace of Europe was in danger because Austria was "bound to pursue adventure in order to delay disintegration."

[15] Albertini, Vol. I, pp. 268–73.

[16] *Ibid.*, p. 296.

lull in which there was actually no diplomatic crisis. The visit of the Tsar and his ministers to Potsdam, on November 4 and 5, led to a Russo-German treaty on Persia and the Baghdad Railway. The visit caused much uneasiness in the other chancelleries, but it turned out that the subsequent efforts of the Russians and Germans to draw each other into political commitments which would damage the other with its allies, failed. However, the armament factories and naval ship building yards were bursting with activity throughout the year.

The Second Morocco Crisis, 1911

GERMANY "ENCIRCLED" During 1911 another Morocco crisis developed. On assuming office Bethmann Hollweg and his Foreign Secretary, Alfred von Kiderlen-Wächter, were confronted with a diplomatic encirclement which reduced to small proportions Germany's hopes of getting a world empire, and which might involve her in the most dangerous kind of a war for her existence. The three great colonial empires were banded together in agreements which automatically put up "Keep Out" signs almost everywhere. Only in Asiatic Turkey did the Germans have a comparatively clear field for imperialistic expansion, and here their Baghdad Railway was going forward only against the concerted delaying tactics of the Entente powers. The arms race with the same powers, on both land and sea, was also a highly explosive factor.

The determination to localize an Austro-Serb war was thus born long before 1914 and the consequences were faced if this effort should fail. It was certain, also, that another attempt would be far less likely to succeed, since Russia was left sorely bruised and determined not to submit so tamely again. The other members of the Triple Entente also felt that Germany had achieved a showy diplomatic triumph, after defeating the long continued efforts of the Entente powers, plus Italy, to regularize the annexation of Bosnia in a European conference, which would have at least preserved some semblance of treaty law and of the European Concert.

Aehrenthal had also taken an action in withdrawing Austrian garrisons from the Sanjak of Novibazar, between Serbia and Montenegro, which was to facilitate greatly Serb triumph in the First Balkan War. His professed motive had been to win the Turks to acceptance of the destruction of their nominal sovereignty over Bosnia, and to convince Europe of his reasonableness, though Brandenburg states that his real purpose was to prevent Italy from claiming compensation.[17]

RENEWED ITALIAN EQUIVOCATION, 1909   For three years longer the predominance of Germany in Europe seemed to be valid. In fact the defection of Italy from the Triple Alliance, already probable enough, was hastened by the Bosnia crisis.

The Tsar visited King Victor Emmanuel at Racconigi, October 23, 1909, and a new secret treaty was concluded, providing that neither government would make any future agreements concerning the Near East without mutual consultation. The *status quo* was to be preserved in the Balkans. Each power was to "regard with benevolence" the interests of the other in Tripoli and the Straits.

Imperialists Dominant in Germany

To escape from their dangerous isolation with moribund Austria and their doubtful partner Italy, the Germans had two alternatives: to come to terms with Russia, giving up their preponderance in Turkey, turning over the Straits and control of the Balkans to her; or to stop the naval race with Britain.

[17] Brandenburg, p. 316.

British friendship would in all probability restrain French and Russian provocation, and even keep Italy loyal.

IMPERIALISTS DOMINANT   Both Bethmann and Kiderlen favored coming to terms with Britain. But they were frustrated by two conditions: one was the anarchy of independent and warring elements inside the German government, striving around the person of the Kaiser; the other was the ascendancy of the imperialistic elements. "Admiral von Tirpitz, the Navy League, the Defense League, the Conservatives, National Liberals, and the rest of the Pan-Germans, the participating heavy industries and their allies of the Press"—all were unwilling to reduce the naval program "by a single battleship for the sake of friendship with Britain."[18] Moreover, the same elements backed the "profiteer industrialists" and promoters, who came to think that the government existed to draw its shining sword in their behalf, whenever they desired. Leading among these were the Mannesmann Brothers Firm, which dealt in concessions in Morocco and disputed endlessly with French groups.

ABORTIVE AGREEMENT, 1909   A Franco-German Treaty of February 8, 1909, had provided for "economic equality" for German interests in Morocco, but the monopolistic tendencies of the French were not exorcised thereby. Instead, they interpreted the new treaty as nullifying the sections of the Algeciras Treaty which had called for public bidding by *all* nationalities for public works in Morocco, while the Germans construed the 1909 treaty as assuring to them half of all contracts. The chief effect of the treaty was to stimulate French penetration of Morocco and arouse the inevitable trouble with the natives, for the "order" which the French desired was sure to look to the Moroccan leaders as something like slavery; therefore trouble and military occupation.

[18] Theodor Wolff, *The Eve of 1914*, London, 1935, p. 28. The determination of William II to have his pedestal in history as the bold creator of a fleet was the "altogether critical influence on the course of policy."

FEZ OCCUPIED The sending of French troops to Fez, on May 21, 1911, came soon after the collapse of a Franco-German consortium for developing the Congo, due to French nationalist opposition. France having openly contravened the sovereignty of the Sultan, guaranteed by the Act of Algeciras, the situation was ripe for another Franco-German clash. It followed closely, moreover, the course of the 1905 struggle. Bethmann and Kiderlen had reviewed the course of Bülow and Holstein in the earlier conflict and pronounced it very bad, yet when their turn came they behaved in much the same way. They decided to bow to the inevitable in Morocco, but to compel France to yield heavy compensation in the Congo before doing so.

THE "PANTHER'S SPRING" Without giving their Ambassador in London any information about the plan, Kiderlen gave warning to France that the destruction of the treaties gave Germany complete freedom of action. Then he relapsed into ominous silence, while the Pan-German press talked both of compensation and the partition of Morocco. Again, too, the Kaiser played the same role. His judgment was wholly against quarreling over Morocco; he had not ceased to regard it as an unprofitable game. Doubtless remembering his enforced exploit at Tangier, he had written promptly, when he heard of the alleged "massacre" in Fez: "Please take prompt steps to prevent any shouting for warships." Yet he ended by approving Kiderlen's plan to send a warship to Agadir, as notice that Germany must have something substantial. Kiderlen was aiming at the whole of the French Congo, and after the *Panther* had appeared in the Agadir harbor, on July 1, he came to the point on July 15.

BRITISH WARNING But already the *Panther* had aroused strong apprehension in London that Germany meant to seize a zone in West Morocco. When England was trying to secure Germany as an ally, ports in this same region had been offered her, but now that Germany was the enemy her possession of a strategic harbor on the Cape route could not be contemplated.

On July 4 Grey told Metternich that Britain must be consulted
about any new Moroccan settlement and when two weeks had
elapsed without any reply, he authorized Lloyd George to give
Germany a public warning in his Mansion House speech of
July 21, 1911. The sentences of this utterance had a strange
ring later, during the period when Britain appeased Nazi Germany. Said Lloyd George:

> I believe it is essential in the highest interests, not merely of
> this country, but of the world, that Great Britain should in all
> hazards maintain her prestige among the Great Powers of the
> world. Her potent influence has many a time in the past, and
> may yet be in the future, invaluable to the cause of human
> liberty. . . . But if a situation were to be forced upon us in
> which peace could only be preserved by the surrender of the
> great and beneficent position Britain has won by centuries of
> heroism and achievement, by allowing Britain to be treated,
> where her interests were vitally affected, as if she were of no
> account in the Cabinet of nations, then I say emphatically that
> peace at that price would be a humiliation intolerable for a
> great country like ours to endure.

This pronouncement aroused great wrath in Germany, not so
much because of its content, as because it was made at all.
"Hands off!" cried the *Lokal Anzeiger* on July 26, voicing the
almost unanimous protest of the German press against Britain's
"meddling in a question which did not concern her."[19] Though
the government now promptly told Grey what Germany was
after, they shared the resentment of the German public that
Britain should have interfered in their quarrel with France and
helped to reduce the settlement price in the Franco-German
agreement of November 4 down to 170,000 square miles of
French Congo territory, most of which was worthless and a
burden to administer, though important river outlets were obtained. The disappointment of German nationalist opinion left

[19] Carroll, p. 669.

no room for doubt that Kiderlen had been defeated. The manner of his reach for central Africa had also increased dislike and suspicion of Germany throughout the world, at the same time it revealed the weakness of the Triple Alliance. Italy had again been very lukewarm and the Austrian semi-official press had repaid Germany's "shining armour" support of her in 1909 by generally warning Berlin, even before the French occupation of Fez, against another Moroccan adventure.[20] The German feeling that Austria would fight in a general war only if her own interests were deeply concerned, was strengthened.

THE ENTENTE CONSOLIDATED The net effect of the crisis upon the Triple Entente was to strengthen it. Though the Tsar had, like Austria, strongly urged on his French ally the avoidance of a conflict in a region where he was uninterested, his advice was clinched by the observation "You know our preparations are not complete."[21] Whether Russia was lukewarm or unready, it was plain that by ignoring completely the existence of the Franco-British Entente, framed originally around Morocco, Kiderlen drove those two countries still closer together, promoted the military understandings between them and deepened the feeling that mysterious thrusts must always be expected from Germany. On July 25, after Kiderlen's very stiff reply to Lloyd George's Mansion House speech, Grey had at once warned the Admiralty that the Fleet might be attacked at any moment, and tunnels and bridges were guarded for weeks thereafter. Both in 1905 and in 1911 Germany had imposed terms upon a French Cabinet, which was disposed to minimize the conflict between the two nations, and had roused strongly the French nationalist spirit. In both crises English Liberals joined the opposition to Germany. In both years, also, the close of the dramatic Moroccan crisis was followed by a coup in the East.

[20] Carroll, pp. 651, 698.
[21] Sidney B. Fay, *The Origins of the World War*, New York, 1930, Vol. I, p. 292.

The Tripoli War, 1911–1912

This time it was Italy which struck out, leaving Germany again to make the best of it. The recognition of the French protectorate in Morocco made Italy wonder if France might turn to Tripoli next. She feared also a break up of European Turkey in which Austria might gain territory and then point to Tripoli as Italy's "compensation." Trusting no one, and having all the Powers signed up to let her have Tripoli, Italy proceeded to attack Tripoli, in September 1911, and began a war which she could not finish. The ultimatum delivered to Turkey was, in Prime Minister Giolitti's own words, "Couched in such a way as not to leave any possibility of evasion open, and so as to avoid lengthy discussions, which were to be avoided at any cost."

In Austria, Conrad pressed again for a preventive war against Italy, but was overruled. In Germany, the Kaiser was indignant that Italy should attack his Turkish protégé, but soon subsided.

The Balkan Wars, 1912–1913

At once the Balkan states saw that their time had come. The first treaty of alliance was signed between Serbia and Bulgaria in March 1912, with the indefatigable assistance of the Russian ministers at Sofia and Belgrade. It contained a provision that Russia would be consulted before war with Turkey was begun. A treaty between Bulgaria and Greece followed and by August all the representatives of the Powers in the Balkans were sending home ominous messages. The Powers became alarmed. Even Sergei Sazonov, the Russian Foreign Minister, appears to have tried to hold back his protégés, fearing their defeat and Russia's unpreparedness for a general war. At least on a visit to

England he convinced the British of his genuine alarm.[22] But just when the Powers were ready to make a joint *démarche,* Montenegro declared war on Turkey, October 8, and the other three Balkan states mobilized and attacked. When the Powers solemnly warned the allies that they would not be allowed to make any territorial gains, the four Balkan kings, on October 13, as solemnly proclaimed lofty motives and scorned the idea of territorial conquests. Then, to the astonishment of everyone, the Turks were rapidly defeated and almost driven from Europe.

At once Austria and Italy drew together in a common determination to prevent the Serbs from retaining a sea port on the Adriatic. Though no ambition could be more natural or legitimate for any people so close to blue water, Austria was resolved not to permit the Serbs either a commercial or a military window on the sea, while Italy wanted the Albanian coast herself if anyone was to get it. By the end of November an impasse had been reached. Russia and Austria were heavily mobilized against each other and the situation was both expensive and dangerous.

Again, too, Kiderlen wrote wise resolutions during September and October, on the necessity of preventing Vienna from seizing control of policy again. Yet by November 28 he was advising that "if Austria has to fight for her position as a Great Power, no matter for what reason, we must range ourselves at her side." No suggestion must be made that Austria accept any humiliation. Bethmann also declared, on December 2, that "if our allies at the moment when they are asserting their rights" (that is to bar the Serbs from the sea) should be attacked, Germany must fight. Once again, the Kaiser after condemning Austria's dictatorial attitude roundly and protesting against war over any Albanian port, acquiesced in a "strong" policy.[23]

---

[22] G. P. Gooch, *Before the War,* Oxford, 1938, Vol. II, p. 97. Poincaré had been informed of the existence of the Serb-Bulgar treaty earlier, but he did not see the text until he went to St. Petersburg in August. He at once pronounced it *"une convention de guerre!"* He, too, thought the Russians were then trying to put on the brakes. Fay, Vol. I, p. 433.

[23] Wolff, pp. 150–56.

A STANDING CONFERENCE AT LONDON But since none of the Powers wanted war Sazonov proposed a conference of the six Great Powers to compose matters. The Ambassadors of the Powers in London were designated to serve, and from December 17, 1912, to July 25, 1913, they met sixty-three times and wrangled interminably over the boundaries of Albania. Throughout this period the question of a port for Serbia was the chief bone of contention, especially since Montenegro besieged Skutari for months, in defiance of the Powers, finally captured it and for a time refused to give it up. Since Austria had entered the conference only on condition that Serbia be excluded from the sea, the possibility of her being circumvented by a union of Serbia and Montenegro kept the danger of general war acute, especially after the barring of Serbia from Albania had led to the demand of Serbia for a larger share of Macedonia.

This disturbance of the agreements between Serbia and Bulgaria ended in the Second Balkan War and the complete defeat of Bulgaria, after which Serbia, now twice triumphant and larger than ever, resented still more hotly her exclusion from the sea. But Russia, preoccupied with the fate of Constantinople, again advised the Serbs to trust to the future and told them that they would have to be satisfied with a railway to an Albanian port, to which Austria had agreed.

In the London Conference Germany worked loyally for the peaceful settlement of all of the successive squabbles over Albanian towns and each crisis was weathered. The probable defeat of Bulgaria by her allies, plus Rumania, had made the Austrians desire drastic action again, especially since Austria had urged Bulgaria to fight Serbia, but on July 6, 1913, Bethmann supported Rumania's claims to "compensation" and "insistently" warned "against the idea of wanting to gobble up Serbia." Italy also refused her consent to Austrian intervention.[24]

AUSTRIAN ULTIMATUM TO SERBIA, OCTOBER 1913 However, owing to the slowness of the boundary commissions in fixing the

[24] *Die Grosse Politik*, Vol. 35, pp. 122–24, 129.

boundaries of Albania, fighting broke out and Serbia occupied several Albanian villages, in retaliation for Albanian raids. Indications of Greek intransigence also helped to alarm Vienna anew. The Austrians feared that the fragile walls of their barrier between Serbia and the sea might gradually be pushed down and that Europe would accept another *fait accompli.* Two long ministerial councils were held, on October 3 and 13, at which Conrad as usual urged war. Finally, on October 18, after receiving assurances of Germany's moral support, Berchtold suddenly dispatched an eight-day ultimatum to Serbia, demanding the withdrawal of her troops. All Europe was surprised, feeling that the grievance alleged was comparatively minor, and though the Entente powers and Italy disapproved of the abrupt Austrian step, warnings poured into Belgrade from all quarters. For the third time Russia advised the Serbs to wait, and on October 20 they capitulated.

Russia was now more than ever committed to support Serbia in the future. When Premier Nikola Pashitch went to St. Petersburg in February 1914, begging 120,000 rifles and a few cannon, especially howitzers, the Tsar replied: "For Serbia we shall do everything."

AUSTRIA GUARANTEED STRONG FUTURE SUPPORT When without warning to her ally Austria had suddenly issued a challenge to Serbia the German Foreign Office was instructed that "His Majesty has received with great satisfaction the news that Austria was to be told that she might be perfectly sure of our support." Both William and Bethmann appear to have held out until August 1913 against the "constant pressure of the two general staffs declaring that the sands were running out for Austria against Serbia and for Germany against Russia." Early in September the Kaiser was contemplating the "coming struggle between East and West."[25] Shortly after the Austrian ultimatum to Serbia, Count Leopold Berchtold, the Austrian Foreign

[25] J. A. Spender, *Fifty Years of Europe, A Study of Pre-War Documents,* New York, 1933, p. 361.

Minister, had a long talk with William in which the latter expressed the firm opinion that "The Slavs were born to serve, and not to rule, and this must be brought home to them; and if they thought that salvation was to be expected from Belgrade, they must be undeceived." The Serbian army must be placed under the Emperor Francis Joseph and, if Serbia refused, "Belgrade must be bombarded and occupied until his will is fulfilled. And rest assured that I am behind you, and am ready to draw the sword whenever your action requires." Throughout the entire conversation, reported Berchtold, "His Majesty ostentatiously used the occasion to assure me that we could count absolutely and completely upon him. This was the red thread which ran through the utterances of the illustrious Sovereign, and when I laid stress on this on taking my departure and thanked him as I left, his Majesty did me the honour to say that whatever came from the Vienna Foreign Office was a command for him."[26]

On October 18 the Kaiser had expressed similar sentiments to Conrad von Hötzendorf at Leipzig, at the culmination of a yearlong celebration of the centenary of the War of Liberation against Napoleon, a series of martial festivities which made no mention of Stein and Scharnhorst, but gave the impression that it was the Hohenzollerns who had gotten rid of Napoleon. In this interview William told Conrad emphatically that "the measure is full," recommended energetic action against Serbia and declared: "You may count upon my support. The others are not ready and will make no effort to prevent your action. You must be in Belgrade in a couple of days." This momentous advice was followed, in November 1913, by an admonition to Conrad that Austria's value as an ally would diminish if she had not the strength of mind to undertake bold action.[27]

[26] *Austrian Documents,* Vol. 8, pp. 512–15.

[27] Conrad von Hötzendorf, *Aus meiner Dienstzeit,* Vienna, 1922–1925, Vol. III, pp. 469–70, 486; Wolff, pp. 330–33.

It is Albertini's conclusion that throughout the First Balkan War the

Thus in two of the most important utterances made by any statesman in the pre-war years the Kaiser laid the basis for the final clash of the grand alliances, and fixed upon Serbia as the immediate objective of the Teutonic armies. The Austrian and Hungarian governing classes and races were more insecure than ever, and with them the Austro-German Alliance. There must now be radical action that would halt the decline of power, both for the Monarchy and for the Alliance.

THE TRIPLE ENTENTE TIGHTENED   In the Entente countries, also, the strain had increased, and with it a tightening of the cooperation between them. France supported Russia's moves during the Balkan Wars with many misgivings until the Balkan allies had won, whereupon Poincaré congratulated them for disregarding the warning which he had joined in giving them as the war began. Though French interests were little involved, and though Russia had let it be emphatically known in Paris during the 1911 Morocco crisis that she would not fight over a matter of "compensation" for Germany in the Congo region, the French attitude was that Russia must not feel that France was lukewarm. This had been the feeling in St. Petersburg after the 1909 Bosnia crisis, and it had been followed by the 1910 Potsdam flirtation of Russia with Germany. During his visit to the Russian capital during August 1912 Poincaré had discovered no popular enthusiasm for the Franco-Russian alliance. He "went about everywhere almost unnoticed" and concluded that there was "more indifference toward the Alliance among the population of St. Petersburg than in the most lethargic of French provincial towns."[28]

Therefore Poincaré tried constantly both to keep a firm hold on Russia's policy and to give her confidence of armed support,

---

Austrian Government not only never had the courage to act but that it never made a plan or tried to influence the action either of its foes or its allies, a state of mind which must have impressed the Germans.—Albertini, Vol. I, pp. 380, 397–402.

[28] Poincaré, *In the Service of France*, Paris, 1926, Vol. II, p. 106.

should her interests ultimately require it. Thus as Premier, on March 13, 1912, he acknowledged a Russian promise not to take any step in the East without giving France notice, with the rejoinder: "But it is not enough that you give us notice; we must give our consent." Again as President he urged Russia not to take any action likely to provoke a war over Balkan questions without a prior exchange of views. At the same time, Isvolski was able to report of Poincaré, apparently with complete truth, that "he never forgets for a moment that the day may come when France must afford Russia armed support."[29]

In the latter part of the First Balkan War French opinion was distinctly surprised and restless when Austria mobilized and Russia did not, the latter even indicating that if Austria attacked Serbia, Russia would not intervene. This unrest was reported by Isvolski to St. Petersburg along with distinctly stronger utterances from Poincaré.[30]

In spite of all Poincaré's vigilance and loyalty, France was not the master of her policy. It was in the control of Russia, for without the support of her hordes of brutalized peasant conscripts France could not contend with Germany on any basis of equality, or with any hope of victory. With Russia all things might be possible. Stephen Lauzanne could even describe her as "a colossus which could shatter this terrestrial globe with its fist."[31]

FURTHER CONFERENCES RULED OUT   On both sides the lines had hardened during the Balkan Wars, in spite of the fact that the Powers had prevented war between themselves by cooperating

---

[29] Gooch, Vol. II, pp. 172, 191; Fay, Vol. I, p. 316. The recall of the circumspect, if recluse, Ambassador George Louis from St. Petersburg, at Russia's instance, and his replacement by the anti-German Delcassé, was another toll paid to the alliance.

The secret naval convention of July 16, 1912, united the French and Russian fleets for concerted action and inaugurated regular conversations between the naval staffs.

[30] Albertini, Vol. I, pp. 402–18.

[31] George Michon, *The Franco-Russian Alliance, 1891–1917*, New York, 1929, p. 264.

through the London Conference of Ambassadors. This long protracted effort was a first rudimentary approach to a league of nations strong enough to wrestle continuously with international disturbances as they occur. But the very success of the conference doomed a similar effort in 1914, for the business of finding formulas that all would accept was most wearisome and vexatious. When after the Second Balkan War the Austrian statesmen and the generals became aroused they found themselves restrained by the London Conference, and when at last the conference simply ceased to be, without any formal adjournment, they were glad to be free to impose their fiat upon Serbia as soon as the opportunity offered. Their ultimatum of October 18, 1913, showed how to get things done, and when the crisis of July 1914 arrived, the one thing that the Austrians were most certain of was that they would not be dragged into conference again.

Unresolved Issues in the Balkans

THE SANDERS AFFAIR: GERMANY VS. RUSSIA AT THE STRAITS The ending of the long series of Balkan crises brought a relief from tension, as well as from the heavy financial strain upon Austria and Russia of long continued military mobilizations on a large scale. But on November 2, 1913, a new crisis arose over the appointment of a German general, Liman von Sanders, to command the army corps at Constantinople. Russia at once saw her hopes of controlling the Straits dwindle, and much negotiation ensued before a compromise was announced, January 15, 1914, which allowed Sanders to reorganize the Turkish army without personal command at the Straits. With an English naval mission controlling the Turkish navy, the Germans argued that no great outcry should be made if German generals accepted invitations to reorganize the army of the Turks. The maintenance of their primacy at Constantinople seemed vital to them, since upon it depended the continued success of their great project, the commercial drive down through Asia Minor.

DID RUSSIA CHOOSE WAR? At the Straits the main thrust of Germany's imperialistic ambition crossed that of Russia. The Sanders dispute focussed this clash so sharply that two Special Conferences were held by the Russian ministers to determine whether the forcible seizure of the Straits was practicable. At the first conference, on January 13, 1914, it was decided that no measures of compulsion must be adopted without the support of France and England. At the second session, February 21, 1914, the conclusion was reached that the Straits could only be seized as an incident in a general European war, and at its conclusion.[32]

From these decisions it is sometimes said that Russia worked for war thereafter, in order to get the Straits. If so, it was the most legitimate object at which the Romanovs had ever strained. The greatest land mass on the globe did not possess a single deep sea harbor that was not frozen several months in the year. Moreover, her principal egress to the sea was in alien hands and, as the Italian-Turkish war had lately demonstrated, subject to closure against her. In a world in which prestige and security were closely associated, this situation was naturally felt to be both humiliating and dangerous.

As to whether the ruling classes in Russia planned war, it is difficult to think they had so far forgotten the Revolution of 1905, the result of the Russo-Japanese War, as to believe a greater conflict would not be more dangerous to the regime. Yet the Russian autocracy was not likely to profit by experience, and the evidence is convincing that the noisy Pan-Slav section of the Russian intelligentsia was a power to be reckoned with.[33]

[32] Fay, Vol. I, pp. 532–41.

[33] See the reports of Pourtalès, the German Ambassador in St. Petersburg, Die Grosse Politik, Vol. 38, pp. 253, 269, 293; Vol. 39, pp. 540–89. Pourtalès thought as early as February 6, 1913, that if Austria invaded Serbia the Tsar would be compelled to attack. Gooch speaks of "the mighty

If the Pan-Slavists could be controlled, and another revolution warded off, time was on Russia's side. Her military power was growing rapidly and the Hapsburg Empire was visibly disintegrating. In all parts of Europe its collapse was expected at the death of Francis Joseph, who was now eighty-four. Brandenburg believes that this was the moment Russia had in mind when she so often told the Serbs to wait. He concludes that Russia meant to back the Serbs then, but "not to force the pace by artificial means."[34]

AUSTRIA VS. SLAV NATIONALISM   Indeed there was no need to force it. On November 18, 1912, German Ambassador Tschirschky had sent a long report to Berlin in which he described the decay of the Monarchy. Only in the provinces which were German to the core did conditions continue more or less normal. Everywhere the idea of a unified realm was fading away. If a war came it would be impossible to put the Slav regiments in the first line.[35] In 1913, 193,000 young men of the non-German races evaded military service. Regular channels for their escape across the frontier were organized. In 1914, as riots and prosecutions mounted, along with hatred below and alarm above, Tschirschky reported again, on May 22, 1914, "I often ask myself if it really pays to attach ourselves firmly to this ramshackle State and continue the toilsome task of carrying it along with us. But I see no other political combination which we could substitute for it."

Bismarck's policy of gaining security by secret alliances had now come to full fruit. Germany was bound to a state which the force of nationalism was shattering before her eyes. Force

Pan-Slav sentiment in Russia."—*Before the War*, Vol. II, p. 418. Wolff adds: "To all who stood for Russian national prestige any evasion of an issue, any fresh withdrawal in face of a threat was felt to be out of the question."—*The Eve of 1914*, p. 250. Other writers speak of danger to the Tsar's throne if he yielded to Austria again.

[34] Brandenburg, p. 475.

[35] Wolff, p. 190.

alone could preserve it. As an ally Austria was now both a burden and a danger to the existence of Germany herself. In opposition to the strongest urge of the age, and of all ages, the urge of men of the same race and language to govern themselves, "she linked up her fresh and vigorous national strength with the corrupt remnant of a decaying empire doomed to destruction."[36] Yet the dissolution of the Monarchy without disaster to Germany and without a European conflagration, was made impossible by the German policy of refusing all agreement with England on the naval issue.

The Final Arms Race

HALDANE NEGOTIATIONS   The last chance of accommodation in this direction was removed by the failure of the mission of Lord Haldane, the British Minister of War, to Berlin in February 1912. Again the Germans demanded a strict agreement for British neutrality in a European war. The British offered to "make no unprovoked attack upon Germany and pursue no aggressive policy toward her." They would pledge that "aggression upon Germany is not the subject and forms no part of any Treaty, understanding or combination to which England is now a party, nor will she become a party to anything that has such an object."[37] But Germany would not accept this formula unless neutrality was specified in it. Haldane returned convinced that Germany's drive for hegemony would have to be resisted. He thought from his "study of the German General Staff, that once the German war party had got into the saddle, it would be war not only for the overthrow of France or Russia but for the domination of the world."[38]

[36] Brandenburg, p. 523.
[37] Gooch, Vol. II, pp. 83–84.
[38] Barbara W. Tuchman, *The Guns of August*, Macmillan, New York, 1962, p. 53.

The naval race must now go on to its logical conclusion, the Germans maintaining that their dignity, empire and commerce required a navy as large as they cared to build; the British arguing that they must retain control of the sea, since naval defeat would mean annihiliation for them. Both contentions were valid, in the sovereign anarchy which existed. But it must be concluded that the necessity of Britain was the greater.

DID GERMAN TRADE RIVALRY DRIVE BRITAIN TO WAR? This theory was a natural offshoot of blood-and-power politics, but the evidence to support it is unsubstantial. That the phenomenal rise of industrial Germany caused acute feeling and repeated sensational press outbursts in Britain is undoubted. That once military war began the British did ruthlessly destroy German trade is equally incontestable. That their navy eventually starved Germany into submission is likewise a matter of record. But it does not follow that Britain would ever have precipitated a war in order to throttle German competition. The worst of the British alarm on this score was over before the naval race began. The British had discovered that they could compete with Germany, that the world was big enough for both, and that Germany herself had become a very great market for British goods. Though they did not enjoy the German rivalry, and though they did object to German protectionist methods which permitted "dumping" abroad, they were used to the trade competition by 1900. The best evidence that the German threat was not considered deadly is that free trade was not abandoned in Britain, though it is alleged that the campaign for protection in England and the beginnings of imperial preference in the Empire convinced the Germans that only their naval threat could prevent ruin to Germany by this route. Yet if Britain had adopted protectionist reprisals, this action would have given Germany no legitimate reason for war. She had begun to use protectionist weapons first.

A very complete study of Anglo-German trade rivalry by Hoffman inclines to the conclusion that there was a very strong relation between German trade success and Britain's drift into war with Germany. The same study, however, is emphatic in concluding that "no evidence whatever has been unearthed to indicate or even to excite a rational suspicion of a conspiracy of interests in Britain to reduce Germany for purposes of economic gain." There is not a sign of such a motive in the published documents "nor is there any evidence that the violently anti-German press was the voice of British economic interests that stood to gain by Germany's ruin."[39] Important trade journals rebuked the "fire brands" and condemned the idea of an inevitable war with Germany. That the "yellow press," and sometimes more reputable journals, used the German trade and shipping gains to stir up feeling against Germany, after 1906, is clearly shown in Hoffman's concluding chapter. But this campaign was an inseparable accompaniment of the naval race, the result of it, not the cause. Had Germany agreed to put away the naval challenge, had she allied herself with Britain, the press thunders would have been directed against the wicked French and the impossible Russians.

After 1900 the German Ambassadors to Britain strove almost invariably to induce Berlin to stop the naval race. At no time did they ever report commercial rivalry as a cause for war or enmity in British minds, and they often reported the contrary.[40]

[39] R. J. S. Hoffman, *Great Britain and the German Trade Rivalry, 1875–1914*, Philadelphia, 1933, pp. 277–78.

[40] Hatzfeldt denied, October 28, 1896, that there was any intention of attacking German colonies. Metternich wrote, February 17, 1900, that England had no desire to destroy the German navy or German commerce. "English capital is too strongly interested in Germany to want any diminution of German prosperity, and England would not think it worth while to take upon herself the undying enmity of Germany." On April 16, 1904, the *Chargé d'Affaires* wrote that "the building of the German fleet and not the economic competition of Germany was the main cause of English ill-feeling." During 1907 the Kaiser himself agreed that the English commercial classes wanted peace. Stumm reported in 1908 that English distrust of Germany was due almost entirely to the expansion of the German fleet. Eckardstein and Kühlmann made similar reports. In December 1908 Metternich contradicted the Tirpitz thesis as follows: "To attribute to London financial circles any desire for war would be absurd. They tremble with

But in Berlin Tirpitz and the Kaiser refused to budge, and at the same time continually advertised their claim that the German Navy was essential as an instrument of diplomatic blackmail. This role of the German Fleet was substantiated in every diplomatic exchange by demands for a free hand in Europe, until no doubt remained in British minds that Germany was determined to achieve world supremacy, on both sea and land.

The British knew that a great navy could not exist unless founded on a large merchant marine. But the reverse did not follow. They could not object to the Germans having some fine ships to parade in foreign ports, for prestige purposes, but British control of the sea was a fact. For a century this control had not interfered with the growth of any nation's merchant marine. In time of peace, German trade was in no more danger than American commerce; in time of war nothing but a superior navy could save either German trade or colonies. Therefore Britain refused either to surrender her sea supremacy or to pay tribute for the privilege of retaining it.

WAS GERMAN IMPERIALISTIC EXPANSION IMPERATIVE? But if a

---

terror at any kind of political complication. German commerce and industry are no longer in the foreground of British anxieties." Finally, Metternich was dismissed in 1912, because he continued to report things which Tirpitz and the Kaiser did not like to hear. But Lichnowski vigorously absolved English business interests of any desire for war in 1914.—*Die Grosse Politik,* Vol. 13, pp. 5–7; Vol. 17, pp. 3–14; Vol. 20, Pt. 1, p. 18; Vol. 21, Pt. 2, pp. 470–75; Vol. 28, p. 47.

Brandenburg's conclusion is that "The view so widely held in Germany that Britain engineered the war in order to destroy our economic competition, which was becoming increasingly dangerous to her, has little justification."—*From Bismarck to the World War,* p. 519.

Another German historian's verdict is that "The decisive factor in British hostility towards Germany was not these economic questions but the battleships."—Herman Lutz, *Lord Grey and the World War,* London, 1928, p. 158.

The British historian G. P. Gooch has also expressed his "deep conviction" that "commercial rivalry played no part in the formation of British policy."—"European Diplomacy in the Light of the Archives," *International Affairs,* January-February, 1939, p. 83.

war to defend the economic position of Great Britain was not necessary or desirable, there is still the converse question: Was a war necessary to release into larger fields the expanding economic energies of the Germans? Had the point been reached at which Germany must burst her imperial boundaries or suffer stagnation?

There can be no difference of opinion about the swift economic development of Germany after 1871. No nation had ever risen to wealth and power more rapidly. In January 1914 Dr. Karl Helfferich, a director of the Deutsche Bank, published a book to celebrate the first twenty-five years of the reign of William I, a volume which justly says that "enjoying the protection of peace and working with unresting, unflagging energy of head and hand, the German people have made up for the centuries lost in impotence and self destruction; they have broadened all the conditions of their life from a contracted narrowness to an undreamt-of expansion."[41]

During the twenty-five years before 1914, bank deposits had increased in Germany from 6,500,000,000 marks to 30,000,000,000 marks; the national income had grown from 22 millard marks to 40 millards; the national wealth had risen from 200 millards to 300. The per capita income was larger than in France and the national income equal to that of Great Britain.[42]

So great had been the economic activity of Germany that, though the population had increased from 48,000,000 in 1888 to 60,000,000 in 1914, loss by emigration had entirely ceased. After 1895 there were actually more people coming into Germany than going out. The sinking of emigration to a mere trickle and the continued importation of labor proved to Dr. Helfferich "that economic opportunities have grown more rapidly in Germany during recent decades than the population." Far from suffering from lack of room, the Germans had found that manu-

---

[41] Karl Helfferich, *Germany's Economic Progress and National Wealth, 1888–1913*, New York, 1914, p. 7.

[42] *Ibid.*, pp. 45, 100–1, 123.

facturing and trade "absorbed in a satisfactory way the large increase in population." That the "world is under the sign of trade" was "not more true of any other country than of Germany."[43]

Nevertheless, it was highly improbable that this tremendous expansion could continue at the same pace forever. A generation of industrialists had grown up in Germany that was as grasping and as impatient for greater gains as any country could produce. They bought up old established businesses at high prices, combined and "developed" them at break-neck speed and invested all gains in plant extensions. This process of frenzied industrial expansion could not continue indefinitely, unless Germany's foreign markets expanded with equal rapidity. The swift aggrandizement of the industrialists and merchants had also steadily made more irksome the proud but increasing penury of the Prussian landed gentry. It was they who commanded the army. They had done so in 1870 and another glorious victory of German arms might restore again their impaired position in the state.

Both Junkers and industrialists were still riding the crest of the great tide of self confidence which had been loosed in Germany by the military successes of 1864–1870. When miracles of national achievement had followed these wars, it was easy to suppose that other victories would again enable the gentry to conserve their power and the industrial promoters to expand their empires.[44] In the absence of fresh military victories, German industry would be compelled to stabilize, a drop in the birth rate would have to occur, the overweening self confidence of Germans give place to a more moderate pursuit of wealth, and the effort to consolidate Germany's great place in world trade succeed the dream of world empire.

Such changes in national temper and objectives were doubtless

[43] *Ibid.*, pp. 17, 19, 79.
[44] Wickham Steed, *Through Thirty Years*, Garden City, New York, 1925, Vol. I, pp. 352, 357.

incompatible with the Napoleonic assumption of all great military machines that a defensive position is dangerous and ignoble. German captains of industry were more likely to resent the indications that the Entente powers would not permit them further territorial expansion. Their one great effort at imperialistic expansion, the Baghdad Railway, had been obstructed at every step, and while the last difficulties were finally overcome in agreements initialed early in 1914, no other comparable field seemed available. It was true that another contingent agreement between Germany and England for the division of the Portuguese colonies was made in 1914, but it might produce no greater results than the similar treaty of 1898.[45]

A WAR OF CONQUEST WIDELY ADVOCATED Beginning in 1911 a stream of imperialist pamphlets poured forth from the presses in Germany, explaining that expansion was a veritable law of nature. The Pan-Germans argued for the economic union of all Central Europe down to Constantinople and the outright annexation of most of Asia Minor and Mesopotamia, when Turkey should break up of course. Concerning the power of the Pan-Germans, Delbrück, editor of the *Preussiche Jahrbücher,* was forced to conclude, in December 1913: "It used to be possible to console one's self with the thought that they were a small, semi-comic sect without influence. That is no longer true. The Pan-German press is very widely circulated and has a very zealous following. No wonder that wide circles are alarmed by its success." On April 19, 1914, the executive committee of the Pan-German League predicted an attack upon Germany and Austria "at the first favorable opportunity." To prepare German youth for its destiny, a leading young people's magazine sang that "War is the highest and holiest phase of human activity."[46] The right of Germans to increase their numbers indefinitely was

[45] For an excellent account of German colonialism, including the story of the Baghdad Railway and the projected disposition of the Portuguese colonies in Africa, see Mary E. Townshend, *The Rise and Fall of Germany's Colonial Empire,* New York, 1930.

[46] Carroll, pp. 763–65.

taken for granted, even if that implied the subjection of other peoples.

In 1914 Germany was a mighty and wealthy nation, one of which every German had a right to be proud, and as long as peace continued Germany was assured a great place in the sun of the world's trade. Should war come, and be either unfavorable in outcome or of long duration, her splendid share in the economic and cultural life of the world would be lost. But the only kind of wars which the Germans of 1914 envisaged were short and victorious ones. War was an inevitable and ennobling part in the life of a nation. It was the business of statesmen to choose a favorable time for the coming of its invigorating impact.

THE LAST SPURT While the belief of most German leaders in the vitalizing effects of war was not shared to the same degree in the older nations, every Great Power recognized that its continued existence depended primarily upon armed force, and that with each succeeding crisis the threat to invoke it was increasingly likely to end in war. Accordingly, the arms race grew in intensity each year, on land and sea. The defense expenditures of Great Britain increased from $295,000,000 in 1908 to $375,000,000 in 1913; those of France from $220,000,000 to $410,000,000; of Russia from $300,000,000 to $460,000,000. In this period of five years the big six had expended $36,500,000,000 for arms and armies—a sum which, if expended productively, would have lifted the standard of living everywhere so high that even the poorest of the Powers would have had a great place in the sun.[47]

From the beginning of 1913 to the crime of Sarajevo the preparation for the last test of the alliances was furiously accelerated. Germany increased her standing forces by 170,000 men. For this purpose a capital levy tax of $265,000,000 was laid, a drastic measure which convinced the French that the

[47] Philip Noel-Baker, *The Private Manufacture of Armaments*, New York, 1937, Vol. I, pp. 399–400.

end had come. Surely a capital levy could not soon be repeated. To be ready, France extended her term of military service from two years to three, after a long and bitter internal struggle. It was the only way that the French with their smaller population could have an equal number of men standing in arms.

These final spasms of preparation were taken so simultaneously that both sides can claim that the other made the first move. Fresh loans poured out of France to Russia and in St. Petersburg $250,000,000 was spent from a fund set aside for war. Russia also increased her period of service from three years to three and a half and the number of her effectives by 135,000. The British Mediterranean and Atlantic Fleets (Gibraltar) were largely brought home to the North Sea, while the French Fleet moved from Brest to the Mediterranean, creating another moral bond between France and Britain which was far stronger than any of the reams of paper alliances written down after 1871.

The Balance of Power: A Fatal Semi-internationalism

In this feverish jockeying, the "balance of power" was "forever being unbalanced, re-balanced and unbalanced again." It was a frenzy which could not increase much longer. Unavoidably these measures generated increasing alarm.

GERMAN FEAR OF RUSSIA   In Germany it was fear of Russia, an emotion fanned both by the Austrians and by the German militarists. No German feared the French army alone, but the specter of hordes of barbarous Russians ravaging the land could be brought home to the humblest German peasant. The General Staff knew that the miserable barracks of the Russian soldiers could hardly be extended to cover the new levies, even with all the expenditure envisaged. Moltke wrote to Conrad, March 13, 1914, that "all the news from Russia points away from a deliberately aggressive attitude at this time." France, too, was in a very bad military position, due to the effort to train the extra batch of recruits.[48] But in the same month the Russian Ambassador to Germany reported that "in 1916, it is believed here, our siege artillery will be ready, and then Russia will become the terrible rival. . . . Naturally Germany tries to frighten us and to give no sign that she fears Russia. Yet in my opinion this fear peeps out of every line of recent articles on Russo-German relations."[49]

The idea that Russia would be ready in 1917 grew until everyone accepted it. The Kaiser had gotten it by grapevine from the Tsar. Bethmann had a regular supply of Russian information from his spy Siebert, a German Balt in the Russian Embassy at London. Siebert copied everything, enough to fill a great volume eventually, and kept Bethmann constantly brooding over the Russian peril.

All informed Germans knew that the German army was such a superior weapon, in both technical and human efficiency, that the numbers in the Russian army meant little. Still the conviction deepened that Russia must be dealt with and that no reasonable opportunity prior to 1917 should be neglected, a feeling which found another strong basis in the enormous French loan to Russia in 1913. By its terms France would advance 500,000,000 francs a year for five years, to be used in building railways leading down to the German and Austrian frontiers.[50]

Mansergh believes that by 1914 a great war had become inevitable, because the growth of Slav nationalism in the Balkans and in the Hapsburg Empire could not be halted; because great animosity toward Austria-Hungary in St. Petersburg precluded Russian passivity in the next crisis; and because the Germans, headed by the Kaiser, were "convinced of the inevitability of a war for supremacy between Teuton and Slav." Even Bethmann

[48] Spender, pp. 373–74.
[49] Gooch, p. 259.
[50] Michon, p. 147.

spoke frankly of this possibility in the Reichstag on April 7, 1914. Also there had been so many crises "that statesmen in every country had begun to despair of averting a final crisis." Their preoccupation with preparation for the war was an admission that "because statesmanship was bankrupt, therefore war was inevitable."[51] As a writer in the *Echo de Paris* put it in 1913: "All Europe, uncertain and troubled, prepares for an inevitable war, the immediate cause of which remains still unknown to her."[52]

On February 24, 1914, the Berlin *Post* urged that "at the moment the state of things is favorable for us." France was "not yet ready for war," England had internal difficulties, and Russia recoiled from the conflict "because she fears internal revolution at home. Ought we to wait until our adversaries are ready?" A few days later the *Kölnische Zeitung* published an article from Russia predicting that in 1917 Russia would be ready and would undertake a war against Germany, an article which started another of the bitter press wars which occurred so often during these years.[53]

But for the Russian specter and the deep hostility of Russia and Austria, Germany could have put aside all fear of France. Schöen, the German Ambassador to France, reported August 20, 1913, that "aggressive intentions lie far from the thoughts of the ruling powers and the people." In the autumn he reiterated that the French government was "obviously inspired" by a wish for better relations between the two nations, and on February 5, 1914, reported that "the wound of 1871 burns in every French heart; but nobody is inclined to risk his bones or those of his sons for Alsace-Lorraine—unless a constellation appears to open up a good chance of success. That, however, becomes ever more improbable. The hope of reaching the goal by Russia's aid has vanished long ago. . . . The idea is steadily growing

---

[51] Mansergh, *The Coming of the First World War*, pp. 195, 205–6.
[52] George M. Thomson, *The Twelve Days*, New York, 1964, p. 25.
[53] Schmitt, p. 100.

that France's salvation is to be sought in better relations with Germany."[54]

In February also a Franco-German agreement on the Baghdad Railway cleared the slate of all pending questions between Berlin and Paris, and Poincaré, the Lorrainer, dined at the German Embassy, the first French President to do so since 1870. Nevertheless, the legacies of recent crises and the pressure of the arms race made it certain that if war came France would stand with Russia. The grinding logic of the alliance system decreed that any further change in the *status quo* would imperil the existence of each of the Powers. A worse method of regulating civilized life could hardly be imagined, but it was now enforced by a rivalry in arms that bound both sides to this deadly form of international organization. The idea of European unity had indeed hovered about continually, but it was always to be unity imposed by one group or nation, never a unity of equals. Europe had reached a stage of semi-internationalism in which the nations were organized into two groups, without any bridge between them. "The equilibrium was so delicate that a puff of wind might destroy it, and the immense forces on either side were so evenly balanced that a struggle between them was bound to be stupendous."[55]

An ideally perfect balance of power had been created, too perfect to last. Time could only tip the balance one way or another, and neither side could save itself without bringing world civilization to the brink of dissolution. Was it to be believed that after the catastrophe had occurred the nations would again set out on the same road?

[54] Gooch, pp. 263–64.
[55] Spender, p. 399.

V. The 1914 Crisis

———◆———

"Of Germany's dissatisfaction and restlessness in the Spring of 1914 there can be no question."[1] Her desire for colonies was unappeased. The balance of power in the Balkans favored the Entente. The internal weakness of Austria increased. England and Russia were negotiating for a naval agreement and the armaments of Germany's opponents were rising faster than her own. The European hegemony of Germany was plainly endangered. It would not be possible much longer for even the diplomacy of sudden action to snatch the appearance of diplomatic victory. Four times within ten years the Central Powers had challenged the governments of the Entente: Tangier, 1904; Bosnia, 1908; Agadir, 1911; Serbia, 1913. Each time the Teutonic allies had sought gains which were legitimate according to the standards of power politics, but the main result had invariably been to arouse one or more of the Entente powers to the necessity of tightening their union and preparing for the future. Soon Germany's authority would have to be exerted with finality or it would cease to exist.

CONSERVATIVES ACCEPTED WAR To the conservatives and nationalists in Germany this belief meant that war was inevitable. In March 1914, Colonel Frobenius published Germany's *Hour of Destiny*, a book which soon ran into twelve editions in which he urged Germany to take aggressive action before Russia and

[1] The conclusion reached by the leading student of German public opinion before the war, E. M. Carroll, *Germany and the Great Powers, 1866–1914*, New York, 1938, p. 769.

France completed their preparations.[2] On April 19, 1914, the executive committee of the Pan-German League proclaimed that "France and Russia are preparing for the decisive struggle with Germany and Austria-Hungary and they intend to strike at the first favorable opportunity."[3] On May 12, 1914, Moltke wrote to Conrad that "if we delay any longer the chances of success will be diminished." Moltke added that he hoped to make an end of France in six weeks and on June 1 he said to Baron Echardstein: "We are ready and the sooner the better for us."[4]

In France, the same groups were matched by bellicose strategists and writers, one of whom wrote *La Fin de la Prusse et le Démembrement de L'Allemagne*. Especially after the Agadir crisis in 1911, the number of intellectuals who welcomed the inevitability of war greatly increased. In France, also, it was the conservatives who led the jingoes. "There marched side by side with the nationalist forces an extremely militant clericalism," which saw in war an opportunity to recapture the position of power lost by the secularizing of education and the disestablish-

[2] Camille Bloch, *The Causes of the World War*, London, 1935, p. 35.

[3] Carroll, p. 763.

[4] Conrad von Hötzendorf, *Aus meiner Dienstzeit*, Vienna, 1922–1925, Vol. III, pp. 670, 673; Bloch, p. 33.

In her book on the pre-1914 period, Barbara Tuchman called her chapter on Germany "Neroism in the Air." The musician Richard Strauss produced the depraved opera *Salomé*, which was a huge success, and *Electra*, which the London *Times* thought "unsurpassed for sheer hideousness in the whole of operatic literature." Tragedy was "the staple of the German theater." "Death by murder, suicide or some more esoteric form resolved nearly all German drama," as "an endless succession of heroines illegitimately pregnant were driven . . . to hysteria, insanity, crime, prison, infanticide and suicide." Over all the German scene "the all-pervasive influence of Nietzsche was at work." Already mad in 1890, "living in solitude, disillusionment and chronic drug-blurred battle against insomnia" he produced "a body of work around the central idea of the Superman which was to reverberate down the corridors of his country's life." His countrymen, and some others, found his alluring concept of "rule by the best" seductive.—Barbara Tuchman, *The Proud Tower*, Macmillan, New York, 1966, pp. 291–351, especially pp. 299, 321–23.

ment of the Church a decade earlier. The strongest opponent of these forces was the Socialist leader Jaurès, whose assassination they continually and openly demanded in their press; and accomplished on the day of mobilization.[5]

AUSTRIA RESTRAINED   In neither country was the number who desired to kill the pacifists and accept war more than a section of the élite and a tiny fraction of the nation. In the summer of 1914 the great mass of Frenchmen and Germans desired only to enjoy their vacations, secure in the peaceful protection which their governments and armies had given them for forty years. The German "statesmen," too, had recovered from the pessimism which succeeded the Balkan Wars. On March 23, 1914, the Kaiser said to Francis Joseph, and again two days later to Victor Emmanuel, that he had no belief in a coming war. Count Berchtold was unduly nervous.[6] Though the Kaiser never recalled the *carte blanche* which he had given to Conrad and Berchtold during October and November 1913, he reacted rightly to the continuance of Austria's morbid fears that Serbia might gain a port by union with Montenegro. When, to forestall that horrendous possibility Austria talked of seizing Montenegro's microscopic bit of coast line, William minuted "Idiocy! Incredible!" A war for such a purpose "would leave us entirely cold." On April 21 he tried to have Bethmann go to Vienna to quiet the Austrians and on May 8 the Chancellor instructed Jagow that it was "urgently necessary to speak plainly," for "Vienna is beginning to emancipate herself rather decidedly from us in the whole of her policy and must be checked in time."[7]

[5] Theodor Wolff, *The Eve of 1914*, London, 1935, pp. 279–80, 293–94. On July 7, 1914 Jaurès called the attention of the Chamber to the continued threats of the Nationalist-Clerical *Ligue*, particularly to a prediction of *La Liberté* that he would be "executed" on mobilization day.

[6] Wolff, p. 391.

[7] *Die Grosse Politik*, Vol. 28, pp. 335–38, 348–51.

The Decision for War

THE HAPSBURG HEIR ASSASSINATED But, as always, when the next crisis came the two German chiefs forgot all of their sound resolutions and took exactly the opposite course. When the Archduke Francis Ferdinand, heir to the Hapsburg throne, and his wife were assassinated at Sarajevo, the capital of Bosnia, on June 28, 1914, the war party in Vienna at once concluded that the time to extirpate Serbia had finally come.

The dead Archduke was a strong but somewhat unbalanced character. He inspired admiration in some and terror in others. Like the Kaiser he was a mighty hunter of animals, having slain his many thousands, and when he blazed away at the shepherded animals he terrified everyone around him. Other outbursts led to doubts of his sanity and he was hated by the Court because he had made a morganatic marriage. His children were barred from the throne and his wife was subjected to the most galling indignities. His passing was therefore not mourned. Every effort was made to keep his funeral as small and plain as possible, and only the forcible intervention of the Viennese aristocracy provided any procession to and from the tiny Hofburg chapel.[8]

The Archduke was not mourned by the Magyar nobles, because he was their sworn enemy. He intended to break their dominance in the Monarchy by introducing universal suffrage in Hungary, and by building up the South Slavs of the Monarchy into a third kingdom. Because he was an advocate of trialism and federation he was feared by his dissident South Slav subjects, and this was one of the motives for his assassination. He was a threat to an independent Yugoslavia also because

[8] Luigi Albertini, *The Origins of the War of 1914*, New York, 1953, Vol. II, pp. 1–6; Wolff, pp. 199–201.

he "had a horror of war with Serbia, as sure to cause a breach with Russia," the very eventuality toward which the Pan-Serbs looked.[9]

The protection offered to Francis Ferdinand when he made his visit to Sarajevo was as inadequate as his funeral was disgraceful. The date was an especially dangerous one, the anniversary of the Serbian defeat by the Turks at Kossovo, which had been observed as a day of mourning for 525 years and was to be celebrated as a day of rejoicing in 1914 for the first time, after the Serb victories of 1912–1913. The Austrian minister Bilinski, who was in charge of Bosnia, had warned the reactionary Governor Potiorek, but the latter, an advocate of war with Serbia, provided only 120 police to handle the Sarajevo crowds, instead of the double cordon of troops which lined the streets during the visit of Emperor Francis Joseph in 1910. Some 70,000 troops were near, available for similar duty on June 28, 1914.[10]

SERBIA'S ROLE   In contrast to this flagrant negligence, the Austrian officials could not at first establish any complicity of the Serbian Government in the crime. The investigator, von Wiesner, reported that "complicity on the part of the Serbian government in the crime itself, in its preparation, or in the provision of weapons, is in no way proved, or even to be presumed; and there are, furthermore, reasons which lead me to regard such complicity as impossible."[11] Leo Pfeffer, the Austrian trial judge who made the preliminary inquiry into the crime also put Serbia out of court, saying: "The documents assembled in the course of my investigation proved unquestionably not only that official Serbia had no knowledge of the outrage, but that those who prepared it had concealed themselves from her."[12] These official reports compelled the government to fall back

[9] Albertini, Vol. II, pp. 7–18.
[10] Ibid., pp. 112–15.
[11] Bloch, p. 40.
[12] Ibid., p. 41.

principally on the general charge that Serbia was seeking to detach territories from the Monarchy by propaganda and terrorism.

The crime had been committed by Austrian subjects armed and trained in Serbia by the Serbian secret society of the Black Hand, the moving spirit of which was a remarkable man named Dimitrievic, who was a powerful leader of men and an able conspirator. He was later executed in 1917 by the Serb government after a treason trial at Salonika, on flimsy evidence, because he was considering coming to terms with Austria. He is, nevertheless, still widely revered in Yugoslavia.[13]

In 1914 the power of Dimitrievic and the Black Hand, to which many military officers belonged, was so great that Prime Minister Pashitch and the other Serb Government leaders feared assassination if they opposed its anti-Austrian intrigues. This appears to be the reason for the somewhat round-about warning which the Serbian Government sent to Vienna that the Archduke's life might be in danger. In Vienna, the Serb minister, being *persona non grata* at the Ballplatz, gave the warning in indirect form to Bilinski, who in turn had little authority over Governor Potiorek.[14]

GERMANY FOR ACTION   The lack of proof of any complicity of the Serbian Government in the crime was not a factor in the deliberations in Vienna. So many opportunities for erasing Serbia had been missed lately that this one seemed too perfect to let pass. Only Kálmán Tisza, the Premier of Hungary, objected strongly and repeatedly. He knew that the Empire already contained too many Slavs. To persuade him, it was agreed that Serbia should not be annexed, only dismembered for the benefit of her Balkan neighbors, though several of Tisza's colleagues

[13] Albertini, Vol. II, p. 30.

[14] *Ibid.*, pp. 104–6. Albertini thinks that the Russian military attaché in Belgrade knew of the plot and encouraged it, but that the Russian Minister Hartwig was not aware of it. Giesl, the Austrian Minister to Serbia agrees with this, since Hartwig was opposed to any war between Austria and Serbia because of Serbia's military weakness.—(p. 84).

expected that after the war nobody would quibble about annexations.[15]

Tisza also wished to be certain of German support. So did they all. A "double faced letter for Francis Joseph to sign"[16] and send to William was prepared. It was accompanied by a long memorandum outlining a plan for a general diplomatic offensive in the Balkans which had been prepared before the assassination. Its focal point was now changed from Rumania to Serbia. The Austrian letter to William spoke plainly of eliminating Serbia "as a political factor in the Balkans." Count Hoyos was sent with it to explain verbally how this was to be done. But there was no need to handle William with great care. The Kaiser had been deeply moved by the murder of the Archduke and his wife, whom he had visited at Konopischt in Austria but two weeks before. He was thoroughly opposed to the assassination of princes and felt that the monarchical principle itself was attacked crucially in Austria-Hungary, where it was the chief means of holding the many peoples together. "Now or never!" he commented on the early efforts of his Ambassador in Vienna to calm the Austrians: "matters must be cleared up with the Serbians, and that soon." The quicker the better, he felt, while European opinion was shocked by the tragedy.[17]

Already, on January 1, the German publicist Victor Haumann, who was in close touch with the German Foreign Office, had called on Hoyos to say that it was now "a question of life or death for the Monarchy" and this was the time "to annihilate Serbia." He would guarantee that German public opinion would stand by Austria to a man "and regard war as a liberating

[15] Bernadotte Schmitt, *The Coming of the War, 1914*, New York, 1930, Vol. I, p. 364; Pierre Renouvin, *The Immediate Origins of the War*, New Haven, 1928, p. 57; Count Max Montgelas, *The Case for the Central Powers*, New York, 1925, p. 147; Sidney B. Fay, *The Origins of the World War*, New York, 1928, Vol. I, pp. 421, 423.

[16] Fay, Vol. II, p. 201.

[17] Fay, Vol. II, pp. 209, 221.

action." England would remain neutral, and if a general war came they could see it through.[18]

Similar sentiments were communicated to the Austrian Cabinet on July 4 through the correspondent of the *Frankfurter Zeitung*, who advised the Austrians that "Germany will support Austria through thick and thin, whatever she may decide to do against Serbia. The sooner Austria-Hungary acts, the better it will be. Better yesterday than today, better today than tomorrow. Even if the German press, which is entirely anti-Serb now, cries again for peace, Vienna should not be led astray; the Empire and the Emperor will stand by Austria-Hungary unconditionally. A great power cannot speak more frankly to another."[19]

AUSTRIA GIVEN CARTE BLANCHE, JULY 5–6 This was exhilarating news for Vienna. The next day Hoyos had talks with the Kaiser and Bethmann and soon returned with assurances which removed the last lingering doubts that "the day" for which they had long chafed had come. Telegrams from the Austrian Ambassador in Berlin, Szögyényi, confirmed the reports of Hoyos completely. William, Bethmann, and Zimmerman had offered no objections whatever to the plainly intimated desire to crush Serbia. Quickly, without any sustained conference or careful survey of the international situation, they had told the Austrians to go ahead and do as they thought best. It was "not our function" to advise what was to be done: the Austrians must "themselves judge." It was Germany's business to "stand loyally by Austria-Hungary's side." This she would do by using "every means" to localize the war. The Germans only hoped that Austria would act quickly, a desire which was repeated to Vienna by von Jagow (who had been absent from Berlin on July 5) again and again in the succeeding days.[20]

While the German chiefs were giving Austria their blessing at Potsdam, on July 5, the head of the Austro-Hungarian armies

[18] Albertini, Vol. II, p. 130.
[19] Ö.-U.A., VIII, p. 294; Schmitt, Vol. I, p. 269n; Carroll, p. 776.
[20] Wolff, p. 430.

was in consultation with Emperor Francis Joseph at Schönbrun. Conrad von Hötzendorf was sure that war with Serbia was inevitable. His Majesty replied: "Yes, that is quite right, but how are you going to wage war if they all pounce upon us, especially Russia?" "We are protected in the rear by Germany" was the Field Marshal's reply. It was enough for both of them if they knew that they could depend absolutely upon Germany. The Emperor couldn't feel certain of that, nor could his subordinates, until Hoyos returned from Berlin and official telegrams had been received.[21]

TISZA WON OVER   Even then Tisza held out. He insisted at the Ministerial Council of July 7 that the demands upon Serbia must not be "such as could not be complied with" and that no ultimatum be sent until after acceptable demands had been rejected. If war finally came, he "must still emphasize that we aim at the diminution, but not the complete annihilation of Serbia, both because that would never be permitted by Russia without a life and death struggle, and because he, as Hungarian Premier, could never consent to have the Dual Monarchy annex any part of Serbia."[22] Tisza protested that Berlin had no right to "judge whether it was the moment for us to march against Serbia or not." He would never "give his approval to a sudden attack on Serbia . . . such as, he regretted to say, Count Hoyos had suggested in Berlin without prior diplomatic action." But the other ministers were all for war.

Tisza then wrote to the Emperor, and Berchtold countered

[21] Alfred von Wegerer, *A Refutation of the Versailles War Guilt Thesis,* New York, 1930, pp. 328–29.

[22] Fay, Vol. II, p. 230. The Austrians later gave many assurances that they would not annex Serbian territory or destroy the independence of the kingdom. These declarations, however, at no time convinced the leaders of the Entente that Austria did not mean to reduce Serbia to impotence. It was all too clear that something much beyond a diplomatic humiliation had been determined upon. The fact that Vienna avoided promising to respect the territorial integrity of Serbia suggested partition. For the exchanges on this score, *see* Schmitt, Vol. II, pp. 154, 220–21, 254.

with pleas of Germany's impatience and of her probable deser-
tion of an ally who was so weak, whereupon Tisza went to
the German Ambassador Tschirschky to protest against German
criticism of Austria's lack of resolution and her hesitation. But
on July 9 Szögyény reported that Jagow recommended that
"the projected action against Serbia should begin without delay,"
and after it was decided not to send the ultimatum to Serbia
until after Poincaré had left Russia, William said "a great
pity" and Jagow "infinitely" regretted the delay.

The German role throughout the crisis, up to the last hectic
days when the fear of Britain intervened, was much more than
that of a loyal ally standing behind. There was incitement
throughout the period of the blank check and afterward. The
Germans knew that Berchtold, the Austrian Chancellor, was
weak and irresolute and that Vienna was likely to be paralyzed
by indecision. Zimmerman urged action upon Hoyos "without
too much arguing and changing our minds." It was the German
thesis that Austria not only must strike to preserve the Monarchy
but to prove herself a worthy ally of Germany.[23]

Denying Fay's contention that the Kaiser and his advisers
were only "simpletons putting a noose around their necks" for
"a stupid and clumsy adventurer" like Berchtold to pull, Albertini maintains that Berchtold was not an adventurer, that
throughout the long crisis he had qualms, that the violent and
domineering personality of Tschirschky kept him firmly in line
and that "The evidence here brought together demonstrates
beyond a doubt: (1) that Germany in 1914 wanted Austria
to take advantage of the Sarajevo crime in order to finish with
Serbia once and for all, and restore her own damaged prestige;
(2) that if Germany had not wanted this, neither Francis
Joseph, nor Berchtold, nor even Conrad would have gone
ahead with the venture." He is sure that the Germans never
stopped prodding Austria-Hungary "right up to the moment
when they realized their reckoning on British neutrality was

[23] Albertini, Vol. II, pp. 144, 156.

mistaken," and that Germany drove the Monarchy into war on Serbia, "thus plunging Europe into the most terrible war."[24]

THE DAY FIXED It was not until July 14 that Tisza yielded. July 23 was fixed as the day of action. Five P.M. was to be the hour, but on advice from Berlin it was later delayed until six, to make sure that Poincaré and Viviani would be out on the Baltic Sea. On July 14, also, a stock exchange panic in Vienna gave the world its first inkling that drastic decisions were being made.

Tisza's resistance had merely delayed for a week the formal recording of the decision for war. The die was fully cast on July 5 and 6, when the German chiefs approved of Austria's plan to dispose of Serbia, told her to choose her own ways and means and promised that Germany would hold the ring. Once that fatal blanket assurance was given, events were certain to move surely to the greatest clash between the grand alliances which had yet occurred. What impelled the German leaders suddenly, without any mature consideration, to turn loose the Vienna Cabinet which they had held in leash during 1913 and the spring of 1914?

FACTORS FAVORING SUCCESS The Kaiser's monarchial sensibili-

[24] *Ibid.*, pp. 159, 162.

The Austrian historian Heinrich Kanner has described Berchtold as "agreeable in outward manners, inwardly malicious and deceitful; superficial in his ideas and irresponsible in his acts. . . . Wavering in his decisions and of unfathomable ignorance, he treated his office as a secondary occupation of less importance to him than clothes or the Turf." The Austrian diplomat Szilassy adds that he was weak-willed and timorous, giving the impression of a guileless child in the hands of the Ballplatz officials.

Certainly Berchtold was childish in his audience with the Emperor on July 30 when at that 11:59 hour, after he had brought the crisis to the point of war, he said that Austrian mobilization "will cost millions," and "If the army is stationed in Galicia, it will mean war with Russia."— Albertini, Vol. I, pp. 383–84; Vol. II, pp. 669–70.

By contrast the implacable Tschirschky never relaxed his pressure upon Berchtold from the moment that he received the Kaiser's first reaction to the Sarajevo crime.

ties were deeply injured. Surely those of the Tsar would be. The teetering Hapsburg Monarchy was undoubtedly further weakened by the assassination. But would the Triple Entente allow Serbia to be trampled to death before their eyes? The Kaiser was certain that France and Russia were not yet ready for war.[25] Russia was also contending with very serious strikes, strongly reminiscent of the revolution of 1905. Great Britain, likewise, appeared to be at the point of civil war over Irish Home Rule. Rival armies were drilling illegally in Ulster and in South Ireland, while all England was divided into two strained camps over the proposed coercion of the Ulstermen. The British Cabinet, in fact, hardly took its eyes from Ireland until after the Austrian plan to stamp out Serbianism was published.

There were reasons then for believing that another crisis could be weathered. A vigorous diplomatic initiative had hitherto always given at least the appearance of victory.

WOULD RUSSIA SUBMIT? The specific danger, of course, was Russia. Russia had defended Serbian aspirations in 1908 and again in 1913. Each time Russia had backed down, swallowed her resentment and told the Serbs that the future was theirs. Would Russia now accept a final crushing of her prestige in the Balkans, if not as a European power? This was the towering question which the Germans had to decide on July 5, and they apparently wasted little time on it, though Bethmann had written to one of his ambassadors only two weeks before the Sarajevo crime that while he did not believe that Russia was planning "an early war" she would surely wish "in the event of a new Balkan crisis to make a stronger stand than she did in recent Balkan complications."[26]

Nothing was more probable. But the Germans would make a still stronger stand. As Jagow put it to Prince Karl Marx Lichnowsky, German Ambassador to Great Britain, on July 18, "The more resolute Austria shows herself, the more resolutely we

25 Fay, Vol. II, p. 211.
26 Schmitt, Vol. I, pp. 102–3.

support her, the more likely Russia will be to keep quiet."[27] Von Lerchenfeld, the Bavarian Minister to Berlin reported, on July 18, that Under Secretary Zimmerman "counts on the fact that bluffing is one of the most cherished requisites of Russian policy."[28] Russia and France would be bluffed down; England would not intervene.

THE PROBABILITY OF A GENERAL WAR WEIGHED AND ACCEPTED

But as the days passed and the Teutonic allies meditated on the blow at Europe's peace which they were about to deliver, they decided that if Russia did resist and a world war came it would be just as well.

On July 18, Jagow wrote to Lichnowsky that "We shall not fail to hear some blustering in St. Petersburg, but fundamentally Russia is not ready," whereas in a few years she will "crush us by the number of her soldiers . . . her Baltic fleet and her strategic railways." Russia was accordingly "quite willing to have a few years of peace yet," especially since she knew that the German group would grow steadily weaker. Therefore, if the conflict came now, "we ought not to shirk it."[29]

Four days later, July 22, Count Hoyos sent to the Austro-Hungarian minister in Sweden the view that now was the time

---

[27] Lichnowsky warned that, on the contrary, the Sarajevo murder could not be made a political issue. If military measures were attempted, world public opinion would be unanimously for Serbia. He replied also: "I believe as little in the imminent collapse of Austria as I do in the possibility of mastering internal difficulties by an active foreign policy. The nationalistic feelings of the Southern Slavs and their craving for union cannot be destroyed by war and will perhaps be brought only the more violently to the surface. And it is by just such active proceedings on the part of Austria that the Balkan nations will be driven more and more under the ascendancy of Russia."—Wolff, *The Eve of 1914*, pp. 436–37; Schmitt, *The Coming of the War, 1914*, Vol. I, p. 328. The quotations are taken from Lichnowsky's replies on July 16 and 23.

[28] Alfred von Wegerer, *A Refutation of the Versailles War Guilt Thesis*, p. 69.

[29] Schmitt, Vol. I, p. 321. Six weeks earlier, on June 3, 1914, Bethmann Hollweg had said to Lerchenfeld that a preventive war "was demanded by many soldiers" and that some circles believed a war would improve internal conditions, 'in a conservative sense."—*Ibid.*, p. 324.

for a decision with Russia. If Russia remained neutral, "the entire campaign directed towards the formation of a Balkan combine against us will collapse. . . ." Russia would have to break away from the Pan-Slav movement. Conversely, if she decided to fight, it would be proved beyond a doubt that she was back of "the Pan-Serbian movement and that this movement is actually only part of a plan of aggression, mapped on a big scale, to the realization of which Russia, as soon as her important armaments were complete, would have proceeded anyway."[30]

These statements were made just as the Austrian ultimatum was about to be delivered, while the Germans waited nervously but confidently, fortified by the tremendous prestige of the German army. Its careful training and iron discipline, its elaborate organization and perfect equipment made it an engine of warfare such as had never before existed. To the German people, in the main, it meant only defense, all the more necessary to a people living on a plain. In their minds, as in others, it counterbalanced superior numbers and constituted an instrument that even the same long, intensive effort could not duplicate elsewhere. Its final defeat in 1918 later obscured the memory of what it was.

The Period of Dissimulation

HOLIDAYS AS USUAL While the thunderbolt against Serbia was being fashioned, both Berlin and Vienna took the greatest pains to lull Europe into a feeling of false security. William sailed

[30] Alfred von Wegerer, *A Refutation of the Versailles War Guilt Thesis*, p. 242. Advised that Russia would certainly defend the integrity and independence of Serbia, the Italian Ambassador to Russia urged, on July 16, that Russia announce her firm determination since "it was his impression that Austria was capable of taking an irrevocable step against Serbia." Baron Schilling replied that Austria could be halted by her allies more effectively than by Russia. Schilling's Diary, *How the War Began in 1914*, London, 1925, pp. 25-26.

away on his annual cruise. Von Moltke placidly stalked the
promenade at Karlsbad. The King of Saxony asked whether he
should return from the Tyrol and was told to stay. The King
of Bavaria was advised to go ahead on a proposed visit to remote parts of his realm. Orders were given on July 8 that
recalls from leaves be avoided, lest the packing of trunks in
hotels might disturb Europe's calm.[31]

In Vienna Conrad, most fiery warrior of all, went away into
the country, exulting that his often given advice was at last to
be followed. The Austrian Minister of War also departed on
leave and the significant news of these vacations was duly recorded in the *London Times* of July 15. When the Italian
Minister to Germany read these items his state of "extreme
anxiety" was allayed.[32] Austrian ministers and diplomats became
conciliatory.

Meanwhile, unofficial war flared between Vienna, Budapest,
and Belgrade. On June 30 the Austrian Governor of Bosnia
had permitted the riffraff of Sarajevo to do a million dollars'
worth of damage to the property of Serbs, no matter how
responsible and respected the owners might be, before he intervened.[33] In Belgrade there had been open and unseemly exultation over the death of the Archduke. It was easy for the newspapers to build on these beginnings, and for Vienna to inflame
the Germans and Magyars by doling out bits of alleged evidence
of Serbian complicity in the killing of Francis Ferdinand.[34]

SOOTHING PRESS REPORTS For the benefit of foreign governments, the official press of both Austria and Germany spoke soft
words of reassurance. The German *Norddeutsche Allgemeine
Zeitung* announced on July 9 that no diplomatic action had
been agreed upon at the July 7 meeting of the Austrian Cabinet.
At Belgrade, on July 11, the Austrian Minister, Baron Giesl,

---

[31] Wolff, pp. 438–40.

[32] R. W. Seton-Watson, *Sarajevo,* London, 1925, p. 203.

[33] *Ibid.,* p. 114.

[34] J. F. Scott, *Five Weeks: The Surge of Public Opinion on the Eve of
the Great War,* New York, 1927, pp. 46–47, 49, 58–59.

assured a Hungarian journalist that the steps to be taken at the conclusion of the Sarajevo inquiry would be "in the most conciliatory fashion," and on the same day five leading German papers reprinted the statement of the *Neues Wiener Tageblatt* that the *démarche* at Belgrade would contain nothing "that could be construed as an affront or a humiliation." The *Vossische Zeitung* spoke on July 12 of Austria's "wise and moderate demands." The *Berliner Lokal-Anzeiger* printed a Budapest dispatch, July 14, which purred that Austria's action "would take the politest form, according to the usual practice between states." Two days later the *Norddeutsche* again reproduced a Vienna article affirming Austria's desire for a peaceful settlement. Even after Tisza's declaration to the Hungarian Diet, July 15, that war might be necessary to clarify relations with Serbia, the nationalist *Münchener Neuest Nachrichten* still insisted, on July 18, that Serbia would be "approached in a peaceful spirit and in a calm, friendly manner."

On the same day Bethmann telegraphed to Tschirschky that the *Norddeutsche Allgemeine Zeitung* was deliberately publishing moderate comments so as "not to sound the alarm in advance," but the Ballplatz must not think from this "that Germany proposes to dissociate herself from the determination displayed in Vienna." It was not until July 19 that the official *Norddeutsche* lifted the curtain a little by stating that Austria's right to clear up her relations with Serbia was being more and more generally recognized in the European press. To avoid a grave crisis it was "desirable and imperative" that the reckonings "which may take place between Austria-Hungary and Serbia" should remain localized. Most German newspapers at once began to stress the necessity of "localization."[35]

THE AIM TO RULE MIDDLE EUROPE MASKED The German Government had waited just as long as it could to prepare German public opinion for the localization demand, which might other-

[35] Carroll, *Germany and the Great Powers, 1866–1914*, pp. 780–83; Wolff, *The Eve of 1914*, p. 442; Bloch, *The Causes of the World War*, pp. 66–68.

wise shock a large part of German opinion, as it was bound to astonish Europe. The success of the localization campaign, upon which the fate of Germany and the world hung, depended on the fulfillment of two gigantic and tenuous assumptions, the first of which was that all Europe, including Russia, would stand by while huge Austria-Hungary invaded the small but renascent Serb state and ground it to fragments. The second and even more startling assumption of the German powers was that by enforcing "localization" they would oust Russia from her existing position of predominant influence in the Balkans and destroy for all predictable time both her prestige among all the Slav peoples of Southern Europe and her age-old and newly stirred hopes of gaining control of the Straits.

Nothing less was wrapped up in the localization demand which Germany was now about to thrust upon Europe. If this demand were accepted, all of Russia's political hopes must die or be centered on war. The *Drang nach Osten* would sweep unimpeded down through Constantinople to Mesopotamia. The many millions of South Slavs, whether they be the pawns of the Russian imperialists or the blood brothers of the Russian Pan-Slavists, would hate and despise Russia from the bitterness of their subjection to German and Magyar domination. Technically considered, the German localization demand was only another application of the German cry to England during the Agadir crisis that what Germany demanded of France was none of Britain's business. But actually the 1914 version required the Triple Entente, and all Europe, to confess openly and irrevocably that the will of the German powers was supreme on the European continent, that no small nation which opposed them could exist, and that no opposing coalition dared interfere.

THE HOUR CAREFULLY CHOSEN   It is not to be wondered at that this supremely presumptuous demand was sheltered from the astounded gaze of Europe until the moment when its delivery would cause the greatest amount of paralysis. This time would be the hour when President Poincaré and Premier Viviani had sailed from Kronstadt on their return journey from their state visit to Russia, a visit announced in advance of the Sarajevo crisis. Then for several days the French chiefs of state would be out of effective touch with their Russian ally, with London, and with their own governmental associates. To gain full advantage of this precious interval, the Wilhelmstrasse carefully figured the exact time when the French leaders would be safely out to sea and, to make certain, had the instant for the delivery of the ultimatum delayed an hour, to 6:00 P.M., July 23.

THE ENTENTE DIPLOMATS DECEIVED   In the meantime, the campaign of dissimulation and deceit was, of course, carefully waged in the diplomatic field. To avoid questioning, Berchtold discontinued his weekly reception. In sending Conrad on leave, July 8, his parting words were: "Above all no measures which could betray us; nothing must be done which could attract attention." A friendly but sober warning had been received from Russia as early as July 5, which indicated the need for extreme caution. In reply to an admonition from Sazonov, the Russian Minister of Foreign Affairs, against the irritating effect upon Russian opinion of the constant Austrian press attacks upon Serbia, the Austrian chargé, Count Otto Czernin, had nearly let the cat out of the bag by mentioning the possibility of his government itself instituting a search in Serbia for the Sarajevo criminals. To this Sazonov had replied with the advice: "No country has had to suffer more than Russia from crimes prepared on foreign territory. Have we ever claimed to employ in any country whatsoever the procedure with which your papers threaten Serbia? Do not embark on such a course."[36]

The course having been determined, the Ballplatz became so placid and its assurances to the Russian Ambassador to Vienna so strongly pacific that as late as July 22 he actually left on

[36] The German Ambassador to Rome reported, July 14, that the Italian Foreign Minister, San Guiliano, refused to admit that under international law a Government could be made responsible for the criminal act of an individual, or for political propaganda, unless the offenses amounted to an overt act.—Fay, II, p. 256.

an extended leave. In St. Petersburg the Austrian Ambassador replied, July 21, to an inquiry from Poincaré as to what demands Austria intended to make on Serbia that "the inquiry was still proceeding and he knew nothing of the result." Of course, the Austrians thought it quite rude when Poincaré warned, at the close of this conversation, that "The Russian people are very warm friends of the Serbians, and France is Russia's ally."[37] In Vienna, on July 23, the French Ambassador called at the Ball-platz to warn of the anxiety which was growing in Europe. He was assured by Baron Macchio that the demands contained nothing with which a self-respecting state need hesitate to comply. To an inquiry as to when the demands would be presented, Macchio replied, "probably tomorrow." While he was speaking they were being delivered in Belgrade, at the moment so carefully decided upon. The final text had been approved on July 19 at a very secret rendezvous of the Cabinet and dispatched to Giesl at Belgrade the next day, before the Emperor had approved it.

CONSULTATION WITH ITALY REFUSED Nor were the Vienna leaders any more scrupulous about permitting their own allies to see the exact text of the diplomatic masterpiece which they had fashioned. Throughout the period of dissimulation they were torn between two fears: that if they did not consult with Italy in good time she would denounce her alliance with them; and that if they did advise her she would not only refuse to go along but make their explosive plan public before the chosen time came. Premature exposure might well spoil the plot. That was the greater danger. So Berchtold resisted the pleas of Jagow, on July 15 and 18, that he ought to give Italy something, since her course would have a vital influence on Russia's decision. Actually, Italy was plied with reassurances and evasions to the end. She received the text of the dynamic Note on the morning of July 24, when all the governments in the two great alliances

[37] Fay, Vol. II, p. 248. Fay agrees that the warning was "rude and severe."

knew what was in it. Like the Triple Entente, Italy was presented with a *fait accompli*.[38]

ACTION URGED BY GERMANY AFTER HEARING THE CHIEF DEMANDS

Vienna's deceit of Germany was of a quite different order. The Germans had given their full and unconditional support to the destruction of Serbia. Since they would profit greatly, probably chiefly, from the extinction of Russia's influence in the Balkans, they could be depended upon to hold the ring firmly unless the actual terms of the Note, when read in cold print, should cause a revulsion. Hence Vienna became less and less communicative as the time for the delivery of the ultimatum approached. There was, however, no reason why they should be solicitous about German approval, since they had sent to Berlin the principal demands to be made, and had even invited comment. On July 10, Tschirschky had wired about the proposed Austro-Serbian investigatory organs in Serbia and about the forty-eight hour time limit, saying: "And Count Berchtold says he would be glad to know what Berlin thinks on the subject."[39]

The Bavarian chargé was able to report from Berlin, on July 18, three of the most important Austrian demands, with the comment: "It is evident that Serbia cannot accept such demands, which are incompatible with her dignity as a state. Thus the result would be war." Here, the dispatch continued, "they are thoroughly willing that Austria should use this favorable moment, even at the risk of further complications. But whether they will actually rise to the occasion in Vienna still seems doubtful to Jagow as well as Zimmerman."[40]

---

[38] Seton-Watson, *Sarajevo*, pp. 205, 208, 223, 233, 235. Francesco Nitti, former Premier of Italy, who knew Berchtold well, wrote in 1927: "No one who did not know ministers like Berchtold can really grasp the tragedy. He possessed neither the intelligence, nor the earnestness, nor even the moral dignity to manage properly a factory with ten hands, and he it was who directed and determined the fate of an empire with a population of fifty-four millions."—Nitti, *Bolshevism, Fascism and Democracy*, London, 1927, p. 27.

[39] Bloch, p. 63.

[40] Fay, II, p. 261.

The Ultimatum Delivered

Vienna now made the most of this doubt. From this time on, Berchtold paid little attention to Jagow's repeated requests, on July 17 and 20, for further information about the contents of the Note. He instructed Szögyény not to show the text to the Germans until July 24, after it had been delivered to the Serbs. But Jagow made it so plain that this would not do that Berchtold reluctantly gave his consent, on the afternoon of July 22, for Jagow to see the Note. That official, after reading it the same evening, told Szögyény that it was "too sharp" and went too far. The latter replied that nothing could be done about it, since the Note was already in Belgrade and would be presented the next morning.

WHY DID GERMANY PERMIT DELIVERY? This "inaccuracy" is sometimes cited in extenuation of the failure of Germany to call a halt at this point. But no one knew better than Jagow that the ultimatum would not be presented until 6:00 P.M. the next day. He himself had had the time advanced from 5:00 to 6:00 in order to be certain that the French chiefs of state were out to sea, and since the principal reason for delay had been to achieve the great advantage of their isolation, there was small reason for believing that Vienna was spoiling all the fruits of its patience by rushing matters at the last moment. Nor does the claim of Fay that it would have been "virtually impossible" for Germany to get the terms modified within twenty-four hours seem relevant. The Germans saw, as did everyone who read the Note, that it was a challenge to European opinion which could hardly pass. They had ample justification also for a sharp modification of the "blank check attitude" in the marked reluctance of the Austrians, for days past, to let them know the full extent of the demands. There was plenty of time to countermand the presentation of the demands and to secure a reconsideration. Another day or two would not have mattered when the result would be to eliminate the practical certainty of a final clash of the alliances.

The truth is, as Fay adds, that if the Germans had seen the text "much earlier, it is not to be assumed that they would have modified or stopped it." They would have reasoned that the "internal dissolution of Austria" would be accelerated, that her "evaporating prestige in the Balkans" would completely dry up, that Russia would dominate the Balkans and hasten "the day for controlling Constantinople and the Straits."[41]

Here is the crux of the matter: a shattering thrust of German-Austrian diplomacy was deemed necessary to halt the internal dissolution of the Hapsburg Monarchy and to keep open the German *Drang nach Osten*. Both purposes would be served by letting the ultimatum explode at the agreed hour. Far from wiring frantically and peremptorily to Vienna that there must be consultation before the Note was delivered, the Germans actually urged Vienna ahead on the agreed course. On July 25, Szögyény wired to Berchtold that it was "taken for granted here that a negative reply from Serbia will be immediately followed by our declaration of war, accompanied by military action." It was "felt here that any delay in the opening of hostilities would, on account of the interference of other Powers, be very dangerous." It was "urgently advised" that Austria should "act at once, and present the world with a *fait accompli*."[42]

NO LOOPHOLE LEFT When the ultimatum was published the German press generally agreed "that Serbia could not possibly yield and that Austria knew it." The ultimatum, wrote the Progressive *Freisinnige Zeitung*, on July 25, "left not a loophole through which the Serbs could escape."[43] This was the verdict alike of the average citizen and the diplomat. At least two of

[41] Fay, Vol. II, pp. 267–68.

[42] *Diplomatische Aktenstüche zur Vorgeschichte des Krieges*, Vienna, 1919, Second Part, No. 32; Bloch, p. 92.

[43] Carroll, p. 786.

the ten demands appended to the long and belligerent Note plainly nullified Serbia's independence. When the vacationists in Holland read the ultimatum on the placards at Scheveningen they were "horrified and alarmed." Sir Edward Grey pronounced it "the most formidable document he had ever seen addressed to one State by another that was independent."

The terms of the ultimatum were significant enough, but its most ominous feature was the forty-eight hour time limit. This was the device which was intended to prevent any effective decisions between Serbia and Russia. With France immobilized, Russia was to be rushed off her feet and paralyzed by the swift movement of events. She would be able to do nothing in a time so short, except to fume ineffectually and tell the Serbs for the fourth and last time that she could not fight for them. If there should be a great outburst of determination in Russia the German mailed fist would quell it by a stern demand for "localization."

BERLIN "ENTIRELY IGNORANT" As the fateful hour approached, the Germans joined wholeheartedly in the Austrian campaign of prevarication. Naturally, Jagow knew nothing when the Serbian chargé inquired on the 20th. After he had read the full text of the Note, Jagow wired on the 23rd to the German Ambassadors in London and Stockholm that "we are not acquainted with the Austrian demands." The next day, when the coup had been sprung, he maintained to the French that Berlin "had really been entirely ignorant," and to the British, on the 25th, "no previous knowledge." His circular dispatch to the German Ambassadors, on July 24, stated: "We have had no influence of any kind on the text of the Note, and we have had no more opportunity than the other Powers to take sides in any way before its publication."[44]

[44] Schmitt, I, pp. 383–84; Fay, II, p. 263; Bloch, p. 204. Fay acknowledges that in the above statements Jagow was "virtually" lying, but he excuses the wholesale lying of the Austrians and Germans throughout the crisis by saying: "This kind of diplomatic lying, unfortunately, was not

HANDS OFF! While Berlin was thus strenuously denying all foreknowledge of an ultimatum from its ally which startled Europe as it had not been since 1870, its ambassadors in the three Entente capitals were delivering notice that the war which the Austrian note to Serbia carried on its face was to be strictly an affair of the huge monarchy versus the small kingdom. The Austrian demands became known in Europe on the morning of July 24. With too miraculous speed the German government advanced upon the Triple Entente on the same day. While professing no previous knowledge of the Austrian demands whatever, the ambassadors of the Wilhelmstrasse managed to make, on the day of their publication, an identical *démarche* in St. Petersburg, Paris, and London which was far too serious for

the monopoly of any one country, but was indulged in all too freely by Foreign Secretaries and Ambassadors almost everywhere in July 1914." The only case of possible non-German lying which he cites is the remark of Sir Edward Grey to the German Ambassador, on July 20 that he "had not heard anything recently," whereas the Foreign Office had received a message from the British Ambassador in Vienna, on July 16, which reported that the Austrian Government was "in no mood to parley with Serbia," but would use force if forthcoming demands were not immediately complied with. After alleging that in this case Grey "lied just as deliberately," Fay does add that Grey might have been ignorant of the dispatch in question, though "such ignorance seems hardly likely." (Fay, II, 263–64.) On the contrary, it would seem that if Grey had had the Vienna dispatch in mind it would have been excellent strategy to try it out on the German Ambassador and see what his reaction would be. If Grey had been alarmed by this report from Vienna it would have given him an obvious basis for cautioning Berlin. In any event, Grey was not striving daily to conceal by constant lies the most deadly secret which men ever carried about with them.

On July 25, Jagow maintained to Theodor Wolff that they had deliberately avoided prior acquaintance with the Note, and that Russia would not be ready for two years more. Stumm also declared that in two years war would be inevitable, but it was impossible that Russia should want it now. France, too, could not desire it, after Senator Humbert's revelations in the Senate. Such a good situation would not come again.—Wolff, pp. 451–52.

instant improvisation. The Entente was informed that "We urgently desire the localization of the conflict, as the intervention of any other Power would, as a result of the various alliance obligations, bring about inestimable consequences."[45]

Inestimable consequences indeed! Thus did Germany convict herself of more than she was guilty. She had hoped and expected to be able to avoid a world war, but when a week later she was desperately anxious to do so, no one believed her. Her "Hands off or beware!" demand seemed in Berlin to be justifiable support of an ally that must be preserved, but the Germans could never overcome the shock it caused in St. Petersburg, Paris, and London. Thereafter, she was to bear bitterly for many years the most terrible brand which nations ever laid upon another, before her conquerors could learn that her responsibility for the war was not absolute. Germany had won an empire by the sword and attempted to preserve it by alliance; trying to preserve the alliance she was to lose her empire to the sword.

THE SERBIAN REPLY With the immense power and prestige of Germany holding the ring, the Vienna Cabinet plunged toward their objective, the crushing of Serbian nationalism. Their ultimatum had stunned the Serbian Ministers as completely as they could have wished. After reading it in deathly silence, one of them at length stood up exclaiming "We have no other choice than to fight it out." Moving appeals to Russia and her allies, preparation of the reply to Austria, packing up to move the government into the interior and mobilization of the army, all before their two days of grace expired, taxed the Serb Ministers as all European Cabinets were to be for the next ten days.[46]

Although it did not accept the ten demands of Austria quite as completely as appeared on its face, the Serb reply "won the

[45] Pierre Renouvin, *The Immediate Origins of the War,* New Haven, 1928, p. 73.
[46] Albertini, Vol. II, p. 348.

approval and sympathy of all the Powers"[47] and nonplused
Vienna. It took Berchtold more than forty-eight hours to decide
to send it to Berlin,[48] and when the Kaiser read it he declared
it "a brilliant performance for a time limit of only forty-eight
hours. This is more than one could have expected! A great
moral victory for Vienna; but with it every reason for war
disappears, and Giesl might have remained quietly in Belgrade."[49] Thirty minutes after he had received the reply, Baron
Giesl had been aboard the train for Vienna with his entire
staff, archives, and baggage.[50]

WITHHELD FROM GERMANY The Serb reply was first received
in Berlin from the Serbian chargé, on the afternoon of July 27.
It did not arrive from Austria until 11:30 P.M. on the same
day, swelled out with many Austrian interpolations. This final
Austrian draft on the German blank check killed what was
in all probability the last chance of peace. For three days
Vienna had prevented the publication of the Serb reply in
Germany. During this time all that the German press and public
knew was that diplomatic relations had been broken and that
there was great enthusiasm in Vienna for the expected war.
Wolff believes that "If the German public had been able to
read the Serbian note of reply at once, and if the German
press had been able to express its opinion at the first moment
with a knowledge of the text, it would scarcely have been

[47] Fay, Vol. II, p. 340. The American Minister to Rumania, Serbia and
Bulgaria reported on July 30 that Serbia had yielded everything that her
sovereignty would permit. On August 19 he wrote: "Taking everything
into consideration without prejudice, it seems to me that Austria wanted
to have war with Serbia and that the death of the Archduke Ferdinand
was welcomed as a *casus belli.*" *Foreign Relations of the United States,
1914 Supplement,* Washington, 1928, pp. 103, 106.
After he read the ultimatum, Pashitch was convinced that if he accepted it without the smallest reservation Austria would inundate his
country with police and investigators, arrogate all rights and inevitably
provoke incidents which would bring in Austrian troops.—Bloch, p. 812.
[48] Renouvin, p. 99.
[49] Schmitt, Vol. I, p. 538.
[50] *Ibid.,* p. 535.

possible to leave Germany in the hands of the Viennese war clique." Everyone, Wolff thinks, would have said what William did, and the Emperor's reaction could have saved the situation. There is indeed much force in Wolff's observation that during that week three days was everything. Though Carroll is not so sure that a halt would have been called, he suggests that "a considerable section of the press would have been favorable" to the Serb reply.[51] Even if this had been all, the German government might have been led to use its last chance to call a halt, before Austria declared war on Serbia.

As things did develop, the certainty of war and war feeling increased in Germany during the crucial three days while Vienna withheld the Note. Then Austria declared war on Serbia early on July 28, before the German people had a chance to read a line of the far-reaching Serb reply. Vienna made sure that when it was published, interlarded with rebuttals after almost every sentence, it would merely be noted as one of the scraps of paper which no longer mattered. Consequently, there was an almost unprecedented unanimity of German public opinion in support of Austria's drastic action. Only two Pan-German newspapers and the Socialist press refused to join in the chorus of approval. The Social Democratic *Vorwärts* alone held out until all hope was gone. From the beginning, *Vorwärts* protested against the idea of holding the whole Serbian people responsible in advance for one particular outrage. It denounced the will to war in the ultimatum and emphasized that its most extreme demands were "utterly contrary to the law of nations." It refused to admit that Germany had any right to give her adherence to this "infinitely reckless and criminal" policy and struck at the "localization" idea as "a summons of Austria to war, rather than a warning to her." The Socialists also inaugurated a great campaign of public protest meetings, twenty-seven of which, in the Berlin area, merged into a great demonstration in Unter

[51] Wolff, p. 455; Carroll, p. 791.

den Linden, on July 28. Thereafter the Socialists were rapidly won over by the prospect of seeing "our wives and daughters the victims of Cossack outrage."[52]

War on Serbia Declared

THE CRUCIAL EVENING OF JULY 27 When Bethmann read the Serb reply, late on the evening of July 27, he agreed with the Kaiser that the Austrian demands had been substantially met. On his desk he found also six other very important telegrams. Four of them reported active Russian military preparations along the German frontier. Here was warning of the utmost gravity. A telegram from Lichnowsky also related that Grey was losing patience with Germany. Grey found that "Serbia had agreed to the Austrian demands to an extent he would never have believed possible." If Austria now challenged Russia, by refusing to negotiate or by occupying Belgrade, said Grey, the "result would be the most frightful war Europe had ever seen." Would not Germany therefore use her influence in Vienna?

This was news of extreme seriousness. It indicated strongly that Germany could no longer escape her responsibility as the senior member of the Triple Alliance. The localization idea was wearing dangerously thin. Instead of a localized military victory and a continental diplomatic triumph, a world war between the two grand alliances stared Bethmann in the face.

In his pile of telegrams was another message which should have galvanized the Chancellor into instant and decisive activity. It was a telegram from Tschirschky announcing Austria's decision to declare war on Serbia "tomorrow, or the day after tomorrow at the latest, primarily to cut the ground from every attempt at intervention." The irrevocable plunge was about to be made. War was about to be declared, after everyone agreed that the excuse for it had been removed. William, Bethmann, Grey,

[52] Bloch, pp. 159-70

all who read the Serb reply, knew that Austria had overreached herself and that she would be discredited if she forged ahead in the same manner. Bethmann now knew that a general war was straight ahead. Did he then dispatch a telegram to Vienna which would command instant attention, and make it impossible to issue the proposed declaration of war until the two allies had consulted further? Did Bethmann block instantly the possibility of further evasion on Berchtold's part, such as he had shown in withholding both the final terms of the Note and the Serb reply? Warning could not have been clearer that Berchtold meant to cash the check dated July 6 to the full amount of Germany's wealth and resources.[53]

AUSTRIA PERMITTED TO TAKE THE FINAL PLUNGE Bethmann was now compelled to hold up a restraining hand. He sent a message to Vienna at once which warned that Germany really couldn't "refuse the mediator's role" and must submit a second English proposal, for "by refusing every proposal for mediation we should be held responsible for the conflagration by the whole world, and be set forth as the original instigators of the war. That would also make our position impossible in our own country, where we must appear as having been forced into war." Therefore, said the Chancellor, "I request Count Berchtold's opinion on the English suggestion, and likewise his views on M. Sazonov's desire to negotiate directly with Vienna."[54]

It is not necessary to go into the great controversy over Szögyény's famous telegram, filed at 9:15 P.M. on the same

[53] The role of Bethmann Hollweg as the good man overwhelmed by events has been somewhat blurred by the publication of some of his papers in 1965. They show that he "in fact advocated a policy of aggression which might have come out of *Mein Kampf.*" This led the German authorities to withdraw from publication the memoirs of Bethmann's assistant and the offending author was forbidden permission to go on a lecture tour of the United States.—H. R. Trevor-Roper, "Why Hitler Did Not Invade Britain," *The New York Times Magazine,* June 6, 1965, pp. 29, 85–89.

[54] Fay, Vol. II, pp. 409–17; Renouvin, pp. 122–24; Schmitt, Vol. II, pp. 68–75. The dispatch was sent at 11:50 P.M. on July 27.

evening, wherein he explained, under seven points, that all this mediation business was merely to humor England. We need not make everything depend on whether Jagow did "very decisively inform" Szögyény to this effect, whether he "repeated his attitude and begged me . . . to assure Your Excellency. . . ." His Excellency Count Berchtold was too busy on the morning of July 28 to give his "opinion" to Bethmann on anything. He was intent upon getting the signature of the old Emperor Francis Joseph to his declaration of war. The aged monarch dreaded the results, but when he saw in the proposed draft a statement that Serbian troops had already attacked his army he could hardly refuse. Berchtold then scratched out from the declaration of war the untrue reference to Serbian aggression and dispatched it on the morning of July 28.[55]

In the afternoon the German Ambassador to Austria found time to drop in to deliver Bethmann Hollweg's explanation of why he must offer to meditate, accompanied by its English enclosures, all of which had been in his office since 5:30 A.M.[56] He need not have been so careful, since Bethmann's message did not even contain a suggestion that the declaration of war against Serbia be postponed. It is difficult to believe that during this most critical period Bethmann's telegram would not have been presented much sooner had the German Embassy officials attached any importance to it. How could they, when Berlin had urged, only three days earlier, a quick declaration of war and immediate attack on Serbia?[57]

Berlin had failed to grasp the last opportunity to stop the

[55] Schmitt, Vol. II, pp. 82–3; Albertini examines the Austrian denials that the Emperor was deceived, concluding that there had been a false report which Berchtold exploited for a couple of days, if he did not invent it. Earlier Francis Joseph had firmly made up his mind about the crushing of Serbia, but on July 25 and 27 he had said that the sending of the ultimatum did not mean war, seemingly hoping to avoid it.—Vol. II, pp. 460–65.

[56] Schmitt, Vol. II, p. 82.

[57] Fay, Vol. II, p. 417; Schmitt, Vol. II, pp. 3–4.

onrush of a European conflict. After Austria had confirmed the fears of all Europe and the world that she was determined to run amok, it was useless for Germany to protest that she had had no determining hand in starting the avalanche.

DÉMARCHES IN PARIS AND ST. PETERSBURG   In reality German effort was still centered on bluffing the Entente powers. In Paris, four attempts had already been made to induce France to join in a public statement which would cause a split between her and Russia, and a fifth trial was made on the morning of the 28th, as Austria declared war. On the evening of July 28, after the Austrian declaration of war, "Willy" was mobilized to use his strong personal influence over the Tsar in a telegram pointing out to the Russian monarch that there were regicides to be punished and "In this case politics play no part at all." This message and one following it made a deep impression on "Nicky." They induced him to cancel general mobilization for a time, but they could not overcome the effects of the Austrian declaration of war. That step supplied swift and unavoidable evidence that Austrian vengeance upon resurgent Serbia would not be denied. The declaration convinced all literate Russians that the small Slav nation which Austria had sought since 1905 to strangle by economic war and by exclusion from the sea was now to be throttled by armed force.

RUSSIAN MOBILIZATION   It is useless for German historians to argue endlessly that all would have been well, if only Russia had not mobilized. The decisive steps had already been taken, long before Russia's decision was made. On three separate occasions Germany had it in her power to hold the crisis down to a severe humiliation of Serbia, with every demand exacted that Serbia's independence would permit. On July 5 and 6 the decision was put squarely up to Germany. She advised full steam ahead. On July 22 her leaders read an ultimatum which they knew would make a terrific crisis certain and they lifted not a finger to stop its delivery. On July 27, with full evidence that the clash of the grand alliances was upon them, the Germans

permitted Austria to launch her little war, now looming as a
world struggle. In all three of these crucial decisions the Germans
chose the road to war. When Russia mobilized in reply to the
declaration of war which Austria hurtled swiftly after her revealing ultimatum to Serbia, that was one of the consequences of
the heedless German-Austrian decision to grasp control of *Mittel
Europa* while the bloody crime at Sarajevo gave them a favorable
opportunity, not the cause of the World War.[58]

[58] Though he cites factors on all sides throughout his study, in his conclusions Fay lets the blunders and omissions of Germany, her incitements
and catastrophic failures to halt the headlong course of Austria's brazen
challenge to the Entente all slip into the background. He thinks that the
whole Austrian plan to smash Serbia was unsound and that it would only
have made a final reckoning certain two or three years later. The Monarchy
would only have been made more explosive and Russia "quite certain" to
aim shortly at wiping out this "second" humiliation "which was so much
more damaging to her prestige than that of 1908–09."

But after Germany had deliberately backed and promoted a foolish and
provocative policy by every means in her power for twenty-four days, a
policy which at the best deliberately gambled with world war, Fay excuses
her from the chief responsibility by arguing that Russia's reaction to the
headlong Austro-German plunge "precipitated the final catastrophe." Thus,
"It was the hasty Russian general mobilization, assented to on July 29
and ordered on July 30, while Germany was still trying to bring Austria
to accept mediation proposals, which finally rendered the European war
inevitable." And again, "But it was primarily Russia's general mobilization,
made when Germany was trying to bring Austria to a settlement, which
precipitated the final catastrophe, causing Germany to mobilize and declare war."—Fay, II, pp. 551–52, 554, 555.

Against this verdict are these considerations: (1) that Germany opened
the clash of the alliances with statements which no one could believe;
(2) that everyone believed her to be the controlling member of the Austro-
German alliance and there was no convincing evidence of any change of
heart on her part; (3) that Austria's course upset completely the new
balance of power in the Balkans, where Russia had deeply cherished interests which were valid by balance of power standards; (4) that the
Austro-German combination appealed to force but forbade a counter appeal by Russia; (5) that speed in mobilization was just as vital to Russian
victory as to German; (6) that if the Russians rushed to arms too quickly
under the lightning hammer blows of (a) the Austrian ultimatum; (b)
her declaration of war, (c) her bombardment of Belgrade, this error was
far less culpable than the carefully planned and deliberate springing of these

The individual responsibility for the final decision on Russian general mobilization fell on Russian Foreign Minister Sergei Sazonov, a man "sickly by nature, finely sensitive and a little sentimental, nervy to the point of neurasthenia . . . open handed and generous, but refractory to all sustained effort of thought, incapable of pursuing a train of reasoning to its logical conclusion."[59]

All accounts agree that Sazonov was horrified at the thought of a general war and sought to avoid it from the first. He was at the same time the official who had to express Russia's firm determination not to permit the crushing of Serbia, without at least a very strong stand. It was to exert effective pressure upon Austria that the idea of partial mobilization, against Austria alone, was invented, a proposal which Grey thought natural and Jagow permissible. It was an impracticable idea militarily, but it was not rejected out of hand either by his allies or opponents. Indeed, Maurice Paleologue, the French Ambassador,

---

successive coups upon Europe by Austria and Germany. It was the Austro-Germans who cold-bloodedly planned the crisis and brought it to the boiling point.

In Fay's own words: "The news of the bombardment of Belgrade, followed by Pourtalès' warning that the further continuation of Russian mobilization measures would lead to German mobilization and war, removed any last doubt which Sazonov may have had as to the need of immediate general mobilization."—(II, 461.)

Luigi Albertini, the author of the definitive history of *The Origins of the War of 1914* (Oxford Press, 1953) quotes many dispatches expressing belief that Russia—and even France—would stand aside and says: "it is not permissible for a historian like Fay to be oblivious of the admissions made immediately by the German Government in the *White Book*." He holds that the evidence demonstrates beyond a doubt that in July 1914 Germany wanted Austria to restore her prestige by finishing with Serbia and that otherwise no one in Vienna, even Conrad, would have gone ahead with the venture. (Vol. II, pp. 160–63).

For the strongest presentation of the view that Russia was responsible for the war because of her mobilization, see, H. E. Barnes, *The Genesis of the World War*, New York, 1926.

[59] The estimate of Baron Taube, a permanent official in the Russian Foreign Ministry.—Albertini, Vol. I, p. 367.

was ever at his elbow urging him to be unyielding and stiffening the pacific instructions which he received from his superiors in that critical interregnum while President Poincaré and Prime Minister Viviani were almost isolated on the cruiser *France*, returning from their visit to Russia.

From 5:00 P.M. on July 23 to 8:00 A.M. on the 29th, when the *France* reached Dunkirk, France was almost without a government, so far as the crisis was concerned. The Foreign Office was in charge of Bienvenu-Martin, the Minister of Justice, who knew little of foreign affairs. He did the best he could, but was able to attempt little in the critical days when a firm hand in Paris might have cautioned both Germany and Russia. In St. Petersburg, Paleologue was free to speak for France, and his influence was on the side of belligerency, whereas Viviani was consistently for moderation and against mobilization. The result of the late return of the French leaders was that they were imperfectly aware of what was going on in St. Petersburg on July 30 and 31, where partial mobilization had first been approved by the Tsar, then cancelled by him, after which he was forced to sign orders for both partial and general mobilization when Sazonov came to the aid of the generals, the order for general mobilization being finally issued, at 5:00 P.M. on July 30.[60]

Albertini believes that Sazonov made a terrible mistake when he proceeded on to general mobilization, instead of canceling all mobilization. However, he emphasizes that too much stress cannot be laid on the ignorance as to what mobilization implied among all of the political leaders of the Great Powers. Sazonov did not know that in Germany mobilization would be practically simultaneous with crossing the Belgian and Luxemburg frontiers. Even Tirpitz did not know that, and probably neither did the

[60] Albertini, *The Origins of the War of 1914*, Vol. II, pp. 528–650. *See* especially pp. 619–26 for his evidence that Paleologue deliberately deceived his government about the imminence of Russia's general mobilization.

Kaiser. Thus Sazonov could believe that there would still be some days in which to negotiate, while the mobilizations were being carried out.[61]

For Russia to have abandoned all mobilization would also have convinced Berlin and Vienna that the game was won. Such a decision would have had to be taken in a general European atmosphere of belief that the German powers meant to demolish Serbia at any cost, and that a European war was now finally inevitable, in a matter of days.

A GAMBLE WHICH FAILED   The whole attempt to upset the existing balance of power by staging a "localized" war in the heart of Europe, while Russia wrung her hands in impotent humiliation and France and England stood by, consenting to the reconsolidation of German power over Europe, was a gigantic gamble, one in which all the surface considerations favored success and all the basic factors were against it. The latter were at once brought into play by the extreme terms of the Austrian ultimatum, as all who read it with any discernment saw. "We must make no mistake about it—this means general war," said Francis Joseph.[62] Moltke was of the same opinion. As soon as he could reach Berlin, he drafted the ultimatum to Belgium, July 26, in which he assured the Belgians that the French forces were about to be moved to "the Meuse-Givet-Namur sector," with the object of "crossing Belgian territory in order to attack Germany."[63]

Down the Steep Incline

LAST MINUTE "REVERSAL"   On the night of July 29–30, British Ambassador Goschen divined from a conversation with Bethmann Hollweg that Germany meant to march through Belgium, with

[61] Albertini, Vol. II, pp. 479–83, 579–81.
[62] Kanner, *Kaiserliche Katastrophenpolitik*, p. 251; Bloch, p. 74.
[63] Bloch, p. 75.

all the inherent probabilities of permanent control, and to take French colonies. On the same night, a telegram came from Lichnowsky in London which shattered Bethmann's expectation of British neutrality, and the shock led to the famous series of telegrams to Vienna urging the necessity of respectful attention to British mediation and ending in one on the evening of the 30th warning that "If Vienna declines to give in any direction, it will hardly be possible to place the guilt of the outbreak of a European conflagration upon Russia's shoulders."[64]

This last appeal was countermanded and never delivered. By that time Bethmann Hollweg had recovered his nerve. Obviously, tortured nerves, strained by terrific responsibility and protracted lack of sleep, were not conducive to the best judgment in any of the capitals during the final days of the crisis.[65]

By this time Austro-German diplomacy had created a situation in a balance of power era from which it could not extricate itself, except by the use of the military power in which it placed such great reliance. This was true for three reasons: (1) public opinion, especially in Austria and Russia, would not now permit a retreat; (2) the plans of the military chiefs took control; and (3) there existed no means, either within the alliances or without them, of securing a little delay and a meeting of minds that would allow the alternatives to war to be considered.

INFLAMED PUBLIC OPINION In the month which had elapsed since the murder at Sarajevo, public opinion had reached such a pitch of resolution in Vienna that it would have been dangerous for the government to abate its purpose to crush Serbia. The anger of the ruling elements against Serbia was cumulative

[64] Fritz Fischer, *Germany's Aims in the First World War,* New York, 1967, pp. 78–82. Fischer holds that these telegrams had only tactical importance and represented no reversal in policy.

[65] See also, Renouvin, *The Immediate Origins of the War,* pp. 176–82, 186–89 and Monteglas, *The Case for the Central Powers,* pp. 146–48, 153–54.

from previous crises, as was their disgust with the turmoil and losses which these periods of tension involved.[66]

Similarly in Russia, the wrath of the controlling classes against what appeared to be the final suppression of Serbia by Austria mounted rapidly upon the fires which still smoldered from 1913 and from 1908. As soon as he had read the Austrian ultimatum Sazonov declared *"C'est la guerre Européenne!"* Then a veritable cascade of plans to prevent the catastrophe poured forth from him. He made six proposals in rapid succession, all designed to forestall an Austrian declaration of war, gain time and get negotiations among the Powers started.[67] Even after Austria had rejected the Serb reply, the German military attaché in St. Petersburg wrote, July 26, "There is still a desire to avoid it"—war.[68]

The Russian Cabinet had decided at once to ask the Tsar's consent to mobilize against Austria, if it should be necessary,

[66] J. F. Scott, *Five Weeks: The Surge of Public Opinion on the Eve of the Great War*, pp. 49, 67, 72. Up to the end of the crisis the German press testified to the pacific conduct of France. "The French press," said the *Rheinische-Westfälische Zeitung* on July 27, "is peaceful." On the same day the nationalist *Berliner Neueste Nachrichten* spoke of "friendly Paris" and the Paris correspondent of the *Kölnische Zeitung* reported on July 30 that there was "not a trace" of a desire for war, an evaluation in which the Catholic *Germania* entirely concurred.—Carroll, *Germany and the Great Powers, 1866–1914*, pp. 808–9.

The widely quoted report of Colonel House to President Wilson, from Berlin in May 1914, that "whenever England consents France and Russia will close in on Germany" was followed by another from Paris, on June 17, 1914, saying that he did not find the war spirit dominant in France nor a desire to recover Alsace-Lorraine.—Charles Seymour, *The Intimate Papers of Colonel House*, New York, 1926, Vol. I, pp. 249, 262.

Count Julius Andrassy, the son of the man who with Bismarck framed the first of the alliances between Germany and Austro-Hungary in 1879 and who was himself the last Foreign Minister of the Dual Monarchy, was of the opinion in 1914 that "in view of Germany's superior strength, it did not appear probable that France, which was visibly growing more peace loving, would go to war for the sake of Alsace-Lorraine."—*Diplomacy and the War*, London, 1921, p. 63.

[67] His moves are listed in Fay, II, p. 355.

[68] Kanner, II, pp. 20–34; Bloch, p. 100.

and to urge an extension of the time limit to Serbia.[69] When none was given, and a declaration of war swiftly followed, the "psychotic explosion" in Russia was terrific. "Into the kindling fire of Russian resentment was thrown this fresh inflammable fuel. Anger blazed high."[70]

UNCONTROLLABLE MILITARY MACHINES Then it was that the plans of the generals became decisive. Sazonov moved quickly to put into effect his plan for partial mobilization against Austria alone, instructing his ambassadors abroad to announce that measure on July 28. But the generals, understandably enough, had planned a war only against the Triple Alliance. They had no plans for mobilizing against Austria singly. To attempt to do so would unmistakably have thrown into wild confusion the general mobilization which the continued support of Austria by Germany would soon compel. The launching of millions of men cannot be improvised; it takes miracles of detailed planning, long in advance, to enable it to be done with any efficiency. To attempt to change the plans at the last crucial moment promised paralysis of the blow by which, in the grand strategy of the alliances, France was to be saved from the shattering power of the first German thrust.

Frantically then must the army leaders strive to persuade

[69] Fay, Vol. II, p. 297. The American chargé in St. Petersburg telegraphed to the State Department at noon on July 26 that diplomatic and political circles there considered "Russian intervention inevitable in case of Austro-Serbian conflict."—*Foreign Relations of the United States, 1914 Supplement*, Washington, 1928, p. 15.

[70] Scott, p. 172. Also pp. 167–72. The feeling in Russia was never adequately reported by the German and Austrian diplomats during the crisis and it is equally ignored by post war German scholars in justifying their "localization" policy. See Montgelas, *The Case for the Central Powers*, p. 130; Scott, pp. 175–76; Fay, Vol. II, pp. 441, 446–48; Schmitt, Vol. II, pp. 104–5.

The American chargé wired home an account of the rising excitement in Russia on July 28, 11:00 P.M., and another on July 31, 4:00 P.M., in which he said: "Whole country, all classes, unanimous for war. Last week's serious political strikes ended." The next day he telegraphed that "reports from all parts of the country show determination to support Serbia fully." *Foreign Relations, 1914 Supplement*, pp. 17, 26, 27, 36.

the Tsar and his Foreign Minister that any mobilization must be aimed at the main antagonist, according to the plan, and it was inevitable that they should succeed. The agonized Tzar locked himself in from them in vain. He could resist them for a while, but the conversion of Sazonov left him no recourse. In desperation he revoked his first signature only to have to yield another.[71]

Meanwhile Bethmann Hollweg in Berlin struggled to hold off his own General Staff, in the vain hope that Vienna would agree to "Halt in Belgrade," as the Kaiser and Grey had proposed. Would not that satisfy the honor of the Austrian army, which had mobilized twice in recent years without conquering anyone? Perhaps, but apart from the resolve of the Ballplatz to dispose of Serbia, Conrad von Hötzendorf's arrangements did not call for the achievement of so limited an objective as the seizure of the Serb capital alone.[72] Furthermore, the Austrian chief of staff was too intent upon securing general mobilization against Russia to improvise an attack at Belgrade. His victory came on July 31, a few hours after the Russian staff had achieved its objective. It was made certain by advice, in the strongest terms, from General von Moltke to order full steam ahead.

On July 30 Moltke told Conrad that if Austria-Hungary did not mobilize against Russia at once the situation would be "highly critical." They should reject any proposal by Great Britain and "mobilize at once. Germany will mobilize."[73] Lutz says that Moltke's pressure "would have led to a European war even without the Russian order for mobilization on the afternoon of July 30." He regards this as "irrefutable."[74]

Austria accepted Moltke's advice on the same day it was

[71] S. D. Sazonov, *Fateful Years 1909–1916*, New York, 1928, pp. 199–206; Schilling's Dairy, *How the War Began in 1914*, pp. 62–64.

[72] References to the strategy of the Austrian General Staff are cited in Schmitt, Vol. II, p. 181.

[73] Conrad von Hötzendorf, Vol. IV, p. 152.

[74] Herman N. Lutz, *Die Europaische Politik in der Julikrise 1914*, Berlin, 1930, pp. 232–33.

given and issued the order for general mobilization early the next morning, July 31. Austria mobilized without knowledge of the decision to mobilize made by Russia on the afternoon of July 30. This news did not arrive in Berlin until 11:40 A.M. on July 31.[75]

Thus undermined in Vienna by his own high command, Bethmann could scarcely hold out longer in Berlin. But could not Germany have mobilized while bringing Austria and Russia to terms? Repeated mobilizations in Austria had not meant war and the Russians would have been glad to postpone hostilities.

Not so the Germans. Their plan of campaign called for a conquest of France through neutral Belgium, so swift that it would be completed before the Russians arrived in full force. Everything depended upon speed in executing this plan and all others had been thrown away. Accordingly Moltke's horror was genuine when for a few hours it seemed that England would stand aside, if France were not attacked. The Kaiser's "We march, then, with all our forces, only toward the East!" was unbelievable. Moltke "stood trembling and mottled" as he tried to convince William that the thing could not be done. For the moment the best he could get was an agreement that the armies should concentrate toward France and then face about toward Russia.

Brief respite, until the Chancellor discovered that "the plan" called for the occupation of Luxemburg the next morning, August 2, and the Emperor ordered that detail of the great movement held up! "It was a great shock to me" said Moltke, "as though something had struck at my heart," and when protest was this time unavailing, "I was overwhelmed."[76]

[75] Camille Bloch, *The Causes of the World War*, pp. 155–57; Renouvin, pp. 212–13; Albertini, Vol. I, pp. 673–79.

[76] Renouvin, pp. 252–53; George M. Thomson, *The Twelve Days: 24 July to 4 August, 1914*, (Putnams) New York, 1964, p. 153. Like his Imperial colleagues in Austria and Russia, the German Emperor signed the order for general mobilization with the future heavy upon him, warning the circle of officers around him that they would live to regret it. Schmitt, Vol. II, pp. 323–24, quotes various accounts of the occasion.

Von Moltke was soon revived by the arrival of news from London that there had been a misunderstanding of England's attitude. She would not guarantee to hold France neutral. Moltke's great military machine could now begin its advance with the unbounded confidence that all Germans had every right to feel in it. It was free to roll on until it reached Paris—almost.

However, Moltke never quite recovered from the Kaiser's proposal to change the plan. He wrote afterward that "I never recovered from the shock of this incident. Something in me broke and I was never the same thereafter."[77]

SCRAPS OF PAPER Germany was the victim of the military maxim that the best defense is a swift offense. In the crucible of a four years' war the theory proved to be disastrously false.[78] Had Germany been content to stand on her own frontiers, her ally might indeed have been forced to compromise her demands on Serbia. The general war, too, might still have come at a later time, but the heavy onus of the first invasions would have fallen on Germany's enemies. Few will doubt that the Central Powers could have defended their main frontiers almost indefinitely, or that they could have won battlegrounds in France and Russia large enough to spare themselves serious devastation.

How "in reality" did the swift conquest dreams of the German

---

[77] Barbara W. Tuchman, *The Guns of August,* New York, 1962, pp. 81–82. She feels that his less than dynamic handling of the rush to the Marne was related to the impairment he suffered, though it is to be remembered that he was a personal appointee of the Kaiser's and had few qualifications to be a great commander.

[78] The general staffs of Europe in the years before 1914, says a noted British military critic, "blinded by the after-glow of Napoleon and deceived by the superficial quickness of the German victory of 1870, dreamed of new battlefields where the issue would be decided by neo-Napoleonic coups."

A minority school had "analyzed the improved range and deadliness of modern weapons, and predicted that future war would develop into a deadlock, with the opposing armies passively entrenched."—Captain B. H. Liddell Hart, "New Armies for Old," *Current History,* March, 1933, p. 641.

general staff work out? That group of stern realists had left nothing out of account except the reaction of mankind. So little had they thought of that that they could not understand why their Chancellor proceeded in haste to declare war on every-body. Admiral von Tirpitz complained again and again that he couldn't see why it was necessary. His complaint was especially pertinent in the case of Russia, since it was intended to place the burden of war guilt on her.[79] Poor civilian that he was, Beth-mann foresaw enough of what was ahead to feel that he could not demand the surrender of Belgium without the gravest reason, the state of extreme necessity arising from being at war on both fronts. Therefore hasty ultimatums and garbled declarations of war were sent to Russia and France so that Belgium's sacri-fice might seem to be justified. Declarations of war hurled right and left gave both enemies and neutrals alike the impression that here was aggressive intent of the most hardened variety.[80] But would not Germany's case have been still worse if she had attacked neutral Belgium without being at war?

THE CRUCIAL ROLE OF THE GERMAN PLAN TO INVADE BELGIUM

As one studies the fine account of August 1914 and its anteced-

[79] Admiral Alfred von Tirpitz, *My Memoirs*, New York, 1919, Vol. I, p. 364. Tirpitz gives a vivid glimpse of the distressed Chancellor, caught in front of his own war machine. "Through all these days Bethmann was so agitated and overstrained that it was impossible to speak with him. I can still hear him as he repeatedly stressed the absolute necessity of the dec-laration of war, with his arms uplifted, and consequently cut short all further discussion."

[80] Lichnowsky, the German Ambassador in London, says: "The im-pression grew stronger and stronger that we wanted war under all cir-cumstances. It was impossible to interpret our attitude on a question that did not concern us in any other way." Lichnowsky, *Heading for the Abyss*, New York, 1928, p. 75.

His reference to the Serbian quarrel as one that "did not concern us," considered apart would be too harsh an appraisal of his own government's position. More justified is Wolff's criticism of another urgency in Beth-mann's mind, that he must declare war on Russia to enlist the aid of the German Socialists. A Russian declaration, or a Russian invasion without it, would have served this purpose better.

ents by Barbara Tuchman, the central role of the German attack on Belgium in determining responsibility for World War I stands out very clearly.[81]

In an era of rival alliances the Balkans were likely to be the cause of a great explosion. Bismarck had predicted that "some damned foolish thing in the Balkans will ignite the next war." But Belgium was the lynch pin on which peace rested in West Europe. Its neutrality was guaranteed by a treaty signed in 1839 by Britain, France, Russia, Prussia, and Austria. Before the treaty there had been a dangerous squabble among the powers over Belgian independence for a dozen years, during which Lord Palmerston had maneuvered incessantly and finally successfully for her neutralization. Thus he preserved Wellington's victory at Waterloo and kept Britain's front door partly free from hostile menace. It was a precious achievement and it had stood for seventy-five years, surviving even the Franco-Prussian War in 1870, and giving Belgium her first real peace in centuries.

If nations have "vital interests," Britain had one, long sanctioned in law and custom, in Belgian neutrality.

Nevertheless, Germany had planned for fifteen years to violate Belgium's neutrality, deliberately and in wholesale fashion. As early as 1899 Alfred von Schlieffen, Chief of the German General Staff, began to plan to attack France through Belgium, in case of war, to avoid the fortified Franco-German frontier. At first he was only going to violate a small corner of Belgium, but year by year he expanded the plan into a tremendous enveloping movement over all the Belgian plain, to roll up the French armies in a giant *Cannae* on the model of his hero Hannibal. But he and all the ruling Germans had imbibed heavily from the famous German writers—Clausewitz, Fichte, Hegel, Nietzsche, Treitsche, and Bernhardi—who had taught the Germans that only their superiority and power mattered. Later the Nazis found ample foundations for asserting the *Lebensraum* rights of the Master Race.

[81] Barbara W. Tuchman, *The Guns of August.*

After the Franco-Russian Alliance it was all very simple. When war came France must be crushed before the slow-mobilizing Russians could reach Germany. This meant trampling Belgium ruthlessly. It was military necessity, the highest of all laws.

In November 1913 a major effort was made to intimidate the young Belgian King Albert, who was visiting in Berlin. The Kaiser pointed out General Alexander von Kluck as the man designated to lead the march on Paris. Pouring forth a tirade against France, he told Albert that war with France was not only inevitable but near at hand, and when Albert vouched for France's pacific mood he kept insisting that war was inevitable. Then Moltke stressed to Albert that war with France was coming and terrible destruction would mark the path of his invincible army. To the Belgian military attaché he insisted that war with France was "inevitable" and "much nearer than you think." Citing several minor evidences of French unfriendliness, he asked what Belgium would do if invaded and received a firm reply.[82]

The Belgians went home and tried to push their defenses, but too late, especially since they ordered (or had ordered) heavy guns from Krupps, who delayed delivery.

But wouldn't the invasion of Belgium bring Britain in? Moltke's common sense told him that it would. In a 1913 memorandum he wrote: "then England will and *must* join our enemies." He did not think anyone in England would believe German promises to evacuate, but concluded that England would fight anyway "because she fears German hegemony."

This was sound thinking, but no Frenchman could be sure of England's entry, against the powerful pacific sentiment in the country and in the ruling Liberal Party. France therefore pulled her troops back ten kilometers from the German frontier on July

---

[82] *Ibid.*, pp. 17–24, 17, 106–7. She cites half a dozen accounts of Albert's visit to Berlin. Before the war the Kaiser also told a British officer at maneuvers: "I will go through Belgium like *that!*" cutting the air with his hand. (P. 164.)

30, under rigorous orders to avoid any clashes, to prevent any precipitation of conflict before Belgium had been invaded.

Since 1905 the British armed forces had been making plans to fight jointly in France, with an Expeditionary Force of at least six divisions, and the protection of French Atlantic coasts had been left to the British Navy while the French fleet concentrated in the Mediterranean. These arrangements, both morally and practically binding on Britain, had been covered by exchanges of notes saying that Britain was still free to decide in the event of war. So Parliament had to honor the obligation to defend the coasts of France, but the Cabinet was badly split on going to war with Germany, a clear majority being against the German hegemony argument. Two leading members of the Cabinet resigned when the naval pledge was honored and two more quit on August 3. But Churchill, at the Admiralty, kept the fleet mobilized at the end of the maneuvers and managed to get its reserves called up. At the War Office Haldane mobilized the army reserves.

It was only after Belgium had decided to resist that Grey won the strong support of Parliament on August 3, and the next day dispatched an ultimatum to Germany to stop the invasion of Belgium.[83] The country, deeply split over current events in Ireland, was at last united for resistance by the actual invasion of Belgium. G. P. Gooch, who knew all the members of the Cabinet, wrote that they were split into three groups—the interventionists, abstainers and uncommitted—before the invasion of Belgium swept them all into one, except those who resigned.[84]

United States Ambassador Walter Hines Page also recorded the vital importance of the Belgian invasion in Grey's statement to him on August 4 that it meant the end of Belgian independence and that it would be followed by the German annexation of Holland, Denmark, and the other Scandinavian states.

[83] Tuchman, *The Guns of August*, pp. 112–18, 121.
[84] G. P. Gooch, "European Diplomacy Before the War in the Light of the Archives," *International Affairs*, January 1939, Vol. 18, pp. 83–84.

"England would be forever contemptible if it should sit by and see this treaty violated," Grey said, "and its position would be gone if Germany were permitted to dominate Europe."[85]

In his August 4 address to the Reichstag, Bethmann Hollweg ignored Jagow's assurance to one of its committees a year earlier that Germany would never violate Belgium and the promise of the War Minister that the Supreme Command would respect Belgium's neutrality as long as Germany's enemies did. Now he confessed the invasion, because "We knew that France was standing ready to invade Belgium and we could not wait." It was a case of military necessity and "necessity knows no law." But he did go on to say, to the great relief of the Liberal and Socialist deputies, that "Our invasion of Belgium is contrary to international law but the wrong—I speak openly—that we are committing we will make good as soon as our military goal is reached."[86]

To the British Ambassador, Bethmann Hollweg harangued about the "unthinkable" thing England was doing, "all for just a word—'neutrality'—just for a scrap of paper."[87]

Germany's Responsibility

Before 1914 the militarist-imperialist-nationalist groups in Germany had conceived a plan for the swift crushing of all op-

[85] H. H. Asquith, *The Genesis of the War*, New York, 1923, p. 317.

[86] Tuchman, p. 128. This promise is sadly similar to that of President Johnson in 1965 to rebuild North Vietnam, through the Mekong Delta plan and otherwise, while for many months he supervised the bombing of that little country as "an aggressor" against our client regime in Saigon.

[87] In 1965 the United States' government calmly violated plain provisions of the UN Charter and the most vital rules of international law in North Vietnam and Santo Domingo, plus the central provisions of the OAS Charter in the latter case, without any confession of guilt. It was not even alleged that national existence was at stake, merely that a relatively minor expansion of Communism, in one case hypothetical, could not be tolerated.

position in Europe in case of war, which they then convinced themselves was inevitable. Then the Plan made it essential to have a European war in 1914, before the completion of Russia's strategic railway system "in 1917" nullified it by greatly speeding Russia's mobilization. This factor was bound to loom ever larger as the allegedly fatal date approached.

Superior power, they thought, and its ruthless use, was all that mattered. Little neighbors would simply have to be overridden. The Plan for swift mastery then brought Britain into war against them, in time to help defeat it, and outraged the vast neutral world deeply, helping to combine it ultimately against Germany.

Of course in Germany the fatal war plan was dressed up as "defense," but it made a defensive war impossible in her ruling minds. The Plan made it seem to them safe to pursue aggressive diplomacy and in a period of recurrent crises it made a saving pause for sober thought unattainable.

Germany's power was so great that she could have fought off any combination against her, had an offensive one existed, which was not the case, but she chose a plan that would make a mighty victory and great imperial expansion swift, "certain" and immensely profitable. Then her leaders awaited "Der Tag" with confidence. But after the disaster the German Crown Prince remembered the invasion of Belgium as a time "when we Germans lost the first great battle in the eyes of the world," and Austrian Foreign Minister Count Czernin recalled it as "our greatest disaster." In the end the outraged feelings of mankind became more powerful than German "necessity."[88]

Six months after the great Plan had failed, with such catastrophic results for Germany and the world, Moltke admitted to Matthias Erzberger, Centrist Party leader, that it was a mistake

---

[88] Tuchman, p. 123. Similarly, in 1965, the leaders of the Johnson Administration showed little awareness that their acts in Vietnam and Santo Domingo had launched great waves of disapprobation, ranging from disapproval in West Europe to fear in Latin America and hatred in Asia. They thought that their raw power was so great that they could determine the affairs of small states everywhere with impunity.

to attack France first. The larger part of the armies should have been sent East to smash the Russians first. Tuchman discovered also that until 1913 there had been an annually revised alternate plan to send the army trains mainly to the East. After the war the Chief of the Railway Division wrote a book to prove that the Plan could have been reversed. It had not really been sacrosanct after all. Shelving it would have been a relatively minor matter, when compared to the measureless damage it did.[89]

GERMANY WILLED THE WAR Moreover, evidence for the conclusion that Germany precipitated the war in 1914 for her own aggrandizement continues to accumulate. In 1967 a great book by Fritz Fischer, *Germany's Aims in the First World War*, was published in the United States. Fischer is Professor of History at the University of Hamburg.[90] Based mainly on a long search of many German archives, his monumental study documents unassailably the intense thrust of German arms and business interests throughout the war to carve out a great empire in the East, extending from the Baltic Sea to the Persian Gulf, one to be expanded in the West at the expense of France and Belgium and buttressed by a rich colonial domain covering all Central Africa, from coast to coast.

Fischer finds that in Germany the whole crisis of July–August 1914 was "viewed in the light of a general war." Germany "willed and coveted the Austro-Serbian war." He quotes an Austrian politician, who was pro-German, as saying in his diary in December 1914: "Germany seized her opportunity and made an Austrian grievance her signal for action. That is the history of the war." The Director of the Deutsche Bank wrote in late August 1914 that in the Wilhemstrasse "they were determined to force a conflict. . . . The whole campaign against Serbia was arranged in advance to make a conflict inevitable." Fischer is certain that

[89] Tuchman, pp. 79–80.
[90] Published by W. W. Norton & Co., New York. 652 pages. No serious student of World War I can fail to consult it.

Bethmann Hollweg himself expected a general war, one lasting as he predicted "at the most four months, a short but violent storm." He observes also that "The July crisis must not be regarded in isolation. It appears in its true light only when seen as a link between Germany's world policy, as followed since the mid-1890s, and her war aims policy after August 1914."[91]

GERMANY'S WAR AIMS   As early as September 9, 1914, Bethmann Hollweg set down a program of annexations from France, vassalage for Belgium, friendly dependence for Holland, absorption for Luxemburg, and *Mittel Africa* for Germany—all designed to so weaken France as "to make her revival as a great power impossible for all time," while Russia "must be thrust back as far as possible . . . and her domination over the non-Russian vassal peoples broken." The Chancellor conceived this as a moderate program to check "the wave of annexationist feeling" that was sweeping over all Germany. Indeed four outstanding unofficial leaders, including August Thyssen, laid down annexation programs much more extensive, and Centrist leader Matthias Erzberger demanded a war indemnity high enough to cover all war costs "and in addition pay off the Reich's entire internal debt." Both the Emperor and a former German official in Warsaw argued for deporting the natives out of annexed zones in France and Poland. Bethmann Hollweg proposed an indemnity for France high enough to keep her from rearming for twenty years.[92]

Naturally these early aims had to be held in abeyance after the failure of the first rush into France, but they were never abandoned until the very end. On the contrary, a firm majority for the world power war aims was formed in the Reichstag, containing all of the bourgeois parties, which were vehemently annexationist, and unofficially "a considerable proportion of the Social Democrats." This Parliamentary War Aims Majority was always stimulated by the powerful urgings of the great organiza-

[91] Fischer, pp. 84, 89–92.
[92] Fischer, pp. 103–4, 106–9, 111, 115, 117.

tions of industrialists and merchants, who developed "the famous Memorandum of the Six Economic Associations" in the spring of 1915. Their demands invariably included acquisition of the Longwy-Briey iron basin in France. Fischer's book contains literally scores of urgings toward this prime prize, but everything of economic value was reached for, including Rumanian and Russian oil and Ukrainian wheat, iron and manganese. After German annexations in the Baltic states, Poland and Western Russia, suitably disguised in the Wilsonian garments of self determination, all other powers were to be excluded from Rump Russia. Trade agreements, control of railways and customs unions would make German exploitation certain in the vast areas of the East. These details were the subject of "innumerable representations from heavy and light industry and from commerce." All national groups were to be isolated from each other, "and the whole *Ostraum,* its political and economic unity smashed beyond repair, was to be made into a 'Hinterland' for Germany." Russia was to be thrust back from the Black Sea and the Straits and separated from the Balkan states to "secure Germany's road from Berlin to Baghdad."[93]

A VAST EMPIRE ACHIEVED IN THE EAST When the new Soviet Government balked at these draconian terms in February 1918, after Germany had helped to bring it to power by sending Lenin and many of its other leaders across Germany from Switzerland, a new German advance occupied additional territories and enforced the separation of the Ukraine from Russia.[94]

Then the independence of Finland was forced and she was bound to Germany by three treaties on March 7, cutting Russia

[93] *Ibid.,* pp. 173–78, 108, 485–86.

[94] Fischer, p. 504. A leading German Protestant church magazine scoffed at "Peace without annexations and indemnities" and celebrated the "uncountable booty" brought by the Brest-Litovsk Treaty. A long paragraph enumerated the things taken, all adding up to "a true peace of God." Fischer adds that it cannot be denied that the article "reflects what was in the spring of 1918 the feeling of the great majority of the dominant classes of Germany."—pp. 507–8.

off from the North Sea and obligating Finland to admit all German goods duty free, a privilege that was not reciprocated. In the South, Rumania was made a German vassal, at the expense of Austro-Hungary, in the Treaty of Bucharest, May 7, 1918. Firm control of Rumanian oil was taken and a similar hold fastened on agriculture. Simultaneously, Bulgaria was taken in hand and the usual German economic dominance established.

Yet German private interests were deeply dissatisfied. "The Deutsche Bank was grumbling, Stinnes raging, Ballin up in arms." Led by Ludendorff, others criticized the diplomats sharply, "saying that the power position attained in Bucharest was far too modest." The aim of the generals was to secure the centers of raw materials and industry near Germany's frontiers, thus making not only Poland and Austria-Hungary but France and Belgium into weak dependents of Germany.[95]

FINAL AIMS IN THE WEST   With a vast empire carved out in the East, the generals began on March 21, 1918, the last grand offensive in the West which would bring German predominance there and gain the riches of middle Africa, especially the copper of Katanga. All the expansionist forces now converged on the West and renewed their demands in a big Chancellor's conference on May 30. A "new tide of annexationism" rose throughout the spring and summer. Even at the end of July, after the great military offensive had been turned back, Foreign Minister Kühlmann was fired for suggesting that the war could no longer be won by *purely* military decisions. A great official conference at Spa, July 2–3, still sure of victory, "reflected exactly the ambitions and political philosophy of the overwhelming majority of the German people." When the last great German lunge on July 15 failed, and the initiative passed to the Allies on the 18th, and after the Black Day of August 8, another Spa conference on August 14 could give great weight to the war aims. Even on September 29, the day when Ludendorff and Hindenburg told

[95] Fischer, pp. 512–13, 521–22, 524.

the Emperor that he must request peace from Wilson at once, "Hindenburg still hoped for the annexation of Longwy-Briey."[96]

FAILURE DUE TO STABS IN THE BACK   Then when the vast new empire in the East also collapsed the rage of the military machine turned inward. As early as 1917 the generals had been talking of "a stab in the back" at home. This charge was propagated in the press, especially after November 1918, when it was turned against the government which had to make peace, against the Socialist parties and finally against the Weimar democracy. Later it became the foundation of Germany's second swift thrust for world power under Hitler.

This false interpretation of Germany's defeat in 1918, says Fischer in closing, "was accompanied by another popular illusion: that Germany had been the victim of an organized assault and that her war had been exclusively one of justifiable self-defense."[97]

Such illusions can destroy nations, and these two almost did destroy Germany from 1940 to 1945.[98]

Believing, as all belligerent peoples did, that they had fought purely in self-defense, it was easy for the average German to rebel against the verdict of Article 231 of the Treaty of Versailles, which said:

"The Allied and Associated Governments affirm, and Germany accepts, the responsibility of Germany and her allies for causing all the loss and damage to which the Allied and Asso-

[96] *Ibid.*, pp. 620, 623, 628, 634–35.

[97] *Ibid.*, pp. 635–36, 637.

[98] There is also sober food for thought in contemplating the illusions which led the American government to the brink of national disaster in Vietnam from 1950 to 1968—the illusions that South Vietnam was a prize strategic spot, that it could be held against the decisions of the 1954 Geneva Conference, that international communism was the issue, that we were containing an aggressive Chinese dragon, that our bombers could enforce our will and that the failure of all guerrilla wars would be demonstrated.

ciated Governments and their nations have been subjected as a consequence of the war imposed upon them by the aggression of Germany and her allies."

Germany's responsibility for the war was predominant, but it was not total. Though her sins of commission were decisive, the failure of the British Government to become deeply aroused to the onrush of disaster at an earlier date was a lesser factor in the final crash. The system of rival alliances had organized Europe for war and all were virtually certain to be involved when a final confrontation occurred, and there had already been several grave ones.

Britain's Role in 1914

Most students of the period have agreed with Prince Lichnowsky, German Ambassador to Britain, that Sir Edward Grey "left no stone unturned in his efforts to insure peace."[99]

There can be no doubt that British opinion was deeply opposed to becoming involved in a war over a Balkan squabble. A member of the British Cabinet has recorded Lloyd George's report of his consultations with the banking, cotton and steel and coal interests. "They were all *aghast* at the bare idea of our plunging into the European conflict; it would break down the whole sys-

[99] Lichnowsky, *Heading for the Abyss*, New York, 1928, p. 41. Lichnowsky did not believe that Russia had any thought of precipitating war, for "If Russia had wanted the war, in order to attack us, a hint to Belgrade would have been enough and the unprecedented Note would not have been answered." (P. 74.)

As the crisis developed he was convinced that even if Grey had declared in St. Petersburg that England would not join in, "Russia would nevertheless have moved." (P. 41.) This judgment is supported by the third telegram predicting Russian intervention which the U. S. Chargé Wilson sent to Washington at 11:00 P.M. on July 28, saying: "It is believed here that England and Italy will try not to be drawn in unless forced by later complications."—*Foreign Relations of the United States, 1914 Supplement,* p. 17.

tem of credit with London as its center," cut up commerce and manufacture, "hit labor, wages and prices, and, when winter came, would inevitably produce violence and tumult."[100]

The danger to British existence was so appalling that at least three-quarters of the British Cabinet were determined not to be drawn in unless Britain herself was attacked, which was not likely, "and a powerful section of the press clutched at the German thesis of a localized war between Austria and Serbia."[101] Preoccupation with the Irish crisis was also nearly complete in the early stages of the crisis.

These considerations, plus a widespread veneration for Sir Edward Grey's character, have led most students of this period to conclude that he could not have done more than he did to avert the war of 1914. Yet Albertini's evidence that Grey was very slow in exerting the power he did possess to avert a European war is impressive.

Grey quickly assessed the Austrian ultimatum to Serbia as "the most formidable document I had ever seen addressed by one State to another that was independent," but in his first talk with French Ambassador Paul Cambon on July 24, he assumed the Austro-Serb dispute to be of no concern to Britain and talked of stopping the Austrian and Russian armies for conference after they had been mobilized. This in effect supported the German localization thesis, and instead of intervening in Vienna he sought

[100] Lord Morley, *On the Eve of the Catastrophe.* Quoted in C. Hartley Grattan, *Why We Fought,* New York, 1929, p. 128. This estimate is fully confirmed by Lichnowsky, who after calling attention to the fact that Anglo-German trade in 1913 amounted to $681,000,000, adds that "aside from this huge commerce, British prosperity was based on international commercial values and not on agrarian or home products." In short, "the outbreak of the war was an unspeakable catastrophe for Great Britain, even could she have been sure of crippling us." *Op. cit.,* pp. 40–41.

Herbert Feis records also that by investing about one-fourth of her national wealth abroad Britain had "created a preponderating interest that the world should be orderly and peaceful."—*Europe, The World's Banker, 1870–1914,* New Haven, 1930, p. X.

[101] J. F. Scott, *Five Weeks, The Surge of Public Opinion on the Eve of the Great War,* p. 222.

only to persuade Berlin to do so. Telegraphing to Buchanan in St. Petersburg on the 25th he also assumed Russian mobilization to be inevitable.[102]

On the 26th, Grey urged Germany more solemnly to mediate in Vienna, but his statement in the House of Commons on the 27th reiterated the distinction between the Austro-Serbian and the Austro-Russian war. Berlin kept its conviction that Britain would remain neutral and Russia was left with Grey's advance approval of her mobilization, but Lichnowsky's talks with Grey on the 27th caused the German Government to send its first to-be-disregarded admonition to Vienna.[103]

It was not until July 29th, after the Austrian declaration of war on Serbia, that Grey made the "Halt in Belgrade" suggestion to Lichnowsky, intimating strongly that Russia could not be expected to stand aside. This was the warning which Buchanan in St. Petersburg had advised on the 24th and which finally made, five days later, galvanized the Germans into their last minute effort to slow up Austria and to make their request for British neutrality, which reached London on the morning of July 30.[104] In return Germany would not take any French territory in Europe, though no "assurance as regards colonies" could be given and Bethmann-Hollweg could not tell to what operations Germany might be "forced" in Belgium.

That such a proposal could be made revealed how ineffective Grey had been in Berlin, where the strongest pressure had to be exerted if the peace was to be saved. When Grey read this German bid for the victory the Germans had been counting on all along, he saw at last the abyss which had faced Europe ever since the publication of the Austrian ultimatum on July 24. In the evening he telegraphed to St. Petersburg linking the "Halt in Belgrade" idea with the "suspension of further military preparations"

---

[102]Albertini, Vol. II, pp. 329–38.

[103] *Ibid.*, pp. 410, 415–16. Probably in the Cabinet meeting on the 27th Grey said that "If the Cabinet was for neutrality, he did not think he was the man to carry out such a policy."—p. 417.

[104] *Ibid.*, pp. 512–14, 521.

on Russia's part, hitherto taken for granted. But when this telegram left London, Russian general mobilization had already been decreed. His restraining hand came much too late.[105]

On the 31st Grey had a talk with Lichnowsky in which he at last insisted strongly that Austria make real concessions, implying that otherwise Britain would be drawn in if France was. This pressure was also much too late. The usual defense of Grey is that the division in the Cabinet and Parliament was so great that he could not take decisive action. Albertini's reply is that if he could go as far as he did on July 31, on his own authority, he could have done so much sooner. All along he correctly foresaw that if France was attacked Britain could not stand aside, and in spite of his constant assertion that no treaties bound Britain to action he knew that she was morally bound by the 1912 naval dispositions. Therefore, reasons Albertini, it was his duty to take timely and energetic action to save the peace or resign. Grey's defense in his *Twenty Five Years*,[106] implies "abstention from all endeavor to influence the course of events." Up to August 1, when events compelled a decision in Britain, Grey was so indecisive that on the afternoon of July 31 he almost drove Paul Cambon to despair.[107]

There is no suggestion in Grey's conduct of the positive culpability for the 1914 catastrophe which clearly falls on some of the

[105] Albertini, Vol. II, pp. 632–35.

[106] Volume I, pp. 312–13.

[107] Albertini, Vol. II, pp. 637–40. An eminent British journalist, George M. Thomson, who studied the action of these days, agrees that Grey did not act in Paris and St. Petersburg as promptly and strongly as he should, or in Berlin. But his position was "one of extreme delicacy." By operating so much on his own authority he had laid himself open to challenge. His policy had really been bi-partisan, winning more support in the Tory party than in his own. In the crisis "almost the whole influence and moral weight of the Liberal press was eloquently against him," as Thomson demonstrates in detail. If Grey had spoken earlier, as the moral arbiter of Europe, it might have made the difference, but withal he was "by a perceptible margin the noblest of the cast."—George M. Thomson, *The Twelve Days: 24 July to 4 August, 1914,* (Putnams) New York, 1964, pp. 146, 157, 206–8.

other actors. Theirs were acts which originated and propelled the crisis forward. His responsibility is solely in the failure to take earlier action.

The Breakdown of the Alliance System

DISCUSSION IMPOSSIBLE   The system of rival alliances had come to its logical end. The opposing forces had been lined up once too often. All were now engaged in a general war which the people of no nation wanted and which even the stubbornly blind men of Vienna had hoped to be able to avoid.

In the last hectic days all initiatives for peace were lost in a maze of telegraph wires. When time was more precious than it had ever been in human history, the distracted rulers of Europe sat in their capitals writing telegrams that it would take hours to encode, transmit, and decode. Six hours appears to have been a reasonable time, very often it was longer. Delivered, they were hastily read or suspiciously analyzed; often misinterpreted, the proper answer was pondered as disturbing messages from other quarters arrived.

Was it not possible to secure a meeting of representatives of the two alliances that could sit down and examine the situation, face to face? It was not. All of Grey's proposals to that end failed. Yet he never ceased to believe that if conferees could have been assembled, the war would have been averted.

A conference might well have failed. Nevertheless it was assuredly the supreme tragedy of the post-Napoleonic century that one could not be held in July 1914, the month in which European civilization collapsed. This catastrophe should have clinched the case for a permanently organized guardian of the peace, the assembly of which no nation could prevent. It should never have been possible for any other empire to again assert sovereign rights which destroy the right of many nations to live in peace, or even to exist.

THE FRUITS OF BISMARCKIAN REALISM The high priests of *realpolitik* greatly prided themselves on their realism. They did not need to bother about justice or the rights of peoples. But in the end "it was found that the excluded sentiments and moralities had a realism of their own which was ruinous to the schemes of those who disregarded them."[108] The realistic politicians of Germany had no timely presentiment of the great surge of feeling over the invasion of Belgium, no suspicion that it would become a world tide and finally overwhelm them. Those of Russia persisted in playing the game of power-politics when only the greatest concentration on internal reform could save them from a far greater upheaval than that of 1905. The warriors of Vienna and Budapest thought that they could repress the many rising nationalisms, both inside their borders and without, by a bold display of force. They failed completely to see that the appeal to force would make all the subject peoples far greater liabilities than they were.

It was Bismarck's habit to deride Gladstone when the great English Liberal thundered periodically against the oppressions practiced by the Turks upon the Balkan peoples. Who but the sentimental Gladstone did not know that the Balkans were "not worth the bones of a single Pomeranian Grenadier"? So Gladstone's wise realism was pushed aside and Bismarck's spirit of blood and iron and of tricky bargaining, sometimes working through Disraeli, ruled the Balkans and Europe from 1870 to 1912. Then the unsolved grievances and problems of the Balkan peoples burst through the bonds long laid upon them and overwhelmed all the successors and disciples of Bismarck.

When at last the hard realists in Vienna burned their bridges and anounced that they would solve everything by resolute use of the sword, the organ of the Pan-Germans sang with delight of the fresh wind blowing through the country, "purifying and clarifying the air." It "heard the tread of world events" and

[108] Spender, *Fifty Years of Europe, A Study of Pre-War Documents*, New York, 1933, pp. 418–20.

found it "a joy to live." But the liberal Berlin *Morgenpost* predicted, on July 30, that Italy would remain neutral, that England would not, and that she would eventually bring in Japan and the United States on the side of the Entente. The war would last from three to five years and so exhaust the world that Germany would gain nothing.[109]

Even Moltke, the successor of Schlieffen, could see that back in 1906. Then he had said to the Kaiser: "It will be a national war which will not be settled by a decisive battle but by a long wearisome struggle with a country that will not be overcome until its whole national force is broken, and a war which will utterly exhaust our own people, even if we are victorious."[110]

This was genuine realism, in 1906 and 1914, but by 1914 Moltke believed that Germany was in a condition of hopeless isolation which was growing ever more hopeless. Unlike Germany's civilian leaders he did not believe in Britain remaining neutral, but he still thought that the Schlieffen plan would crush France before her allies could move.[111]

[109] Carroll, pp. 815–16.
[110] Barbara W. Tuchman, *The Guns of August*, p. 22.
[111] Fritz Fischer, *Germany's Aims in the First World War*, p. 50.

VI. The Entry of the United States

———————⟡———————

How did it happen that the United States, with its long tradition of neutrality during European wars, was drawn into the First World War in 1917?

THE INITIAL IMPACT Nothing seemed more unlikely when the conflict began. Only a few people had followed the recurrent crises in Europe enough to know that a constant danger of war existed. The crime of Sarajevo, on June 28, 1914, was a sensation in the American press for three days only. Then a heat wave and other matters occupied attention until the Austrian ultimatum to Serbia was published on July 24.

The next day alarm became keen and big black headlines marched across the front pages until all the great powers of Europe were at war. By that time public opinion had set strongly in favor of the Allies. The Austrian ultimatum seemed to carry war on its face. Our sympathy for the little underdog, Serbia, was quick, and Germany's hasty declarations of war hastened the process of decision. Then the invasion of Belgium completed it.

At this distant time, after the manifold trampling of little states under foot during World War II, it seems strange that so much feeling could be aroused by the violation of Belgium's neutrality. Yet all contemporary accounts agree that this was the step which cost Germany heaviest. The able German Ambassador to the United States, Count Johann-Heinrich von Bernstorff, testified before a German parliamentary inquiry, on October 22, 1919, that throughout the entire war "the Belgian question was the one which interested Americans most and which was most effective in working up American public opinion against us."[1]

Here again it was partly a matter of sympathy for the small nation, so ruthlessly overwhelmed, but there was also a powerful revulsion against treating treaties as scraps of paper. For a century treaties had had an increasing degree of observance and there was great resentment against the brutal scrapping of a long standing treaty, a resentment which the many and sometimes exaggerated stories of German atrocities in Belgium kept alive.

Behind the general belief that the Central Powers had convicted themselves during the outbreak of the war was, of course, a large backlog of predisposition toward the Anglo-French side. The counter feelings of the Irish-American and German-American citizens were strong, but they were far outweighed by the common heritage of Anglo-Saxon culture in most of our citizens and by the personal ties of leading Americans with their counterparts in Britain and France.

Yet the national desire to see the Allies win did not mean that we expected to take part in the war. Far from it. Almost nobody had the slightest idea that we could be involved. Nearly everybody congratulated himself that we were safely apart and had nothing to do with the old world madness.

The Defense of Neutrality

NEUTRALITY AXIOMATIC The proclamation of neutrality, promptly issued by President Woodrow Wilson on August 4, 1914, was accepted as axiomatic by all. Two weeks later, on August 19, the President sought to lessen the strong taking of sides which was already evident. In a speech to the Senate

[1] Carnegie Endowment for International Peace, *Official German Documents Relating to the World War*, New York, 1923, Vol. I, pp. 253–54.

he reminded us that we had many different national origins. He urged that we be "impartial in thought as well as in action." Deep divisions among us would be fatal to our peace of mind and also impair our ability to mediate between the warring powers as a friend.[2]

Wilson's hope that we might be neutral in thought may have been a vain one, but it was not bellicose advice. His wish to mediate the conflict was as steadfastly held, and in 1920 Bernstorff testified that the policy laid down in August 1914 was "unwaveringly adhered to until the rupture."[3]

This did not mean that Wilson forgot his deep admiration for English institutions and literature or that he was wholly impartial in dealing with the belligerents. A protest against the growing rigors of the British blockade of Germany in September 1914 was toned down and understood to be for the record. Secretary of State William Jennings Bryan was much less inclined to sympathy with Britain, and was a staunch opponent of war, but Counsellor Robert Lansing, who wrote most of the diplomatic notes to Britain, was firmly resolved that none of them should cause a breach. Lansing's conviction that Germany must not be allowed to win was strong, but his *Memoirs* show that Wilson consistently resisted that argument.[4]

British control of the seas led at once to Allied orders for munitions and supplies. Such trade was clearly legal under international law and the administration had no disposition to change the rules for Germany's benefit in the middle of the war, especially since the trade ended a minor depression in progress and compensated for the abrupt loss of German markets. Our trade with the Allies in munitions alone during the first half of our period of neutrality was $508,269,245, and in the second half, $1,679,679,544. Wheat exports also jumped

[2] Newton D. Baker, *Why We Went to War*, New York, 1936, p. 30.

[3] *Ibid.*, p. 38.

[4] Charles Seymour, *American Neutrality, 1914–1917*, New Haven, 1935, pp. 139–40; Robert Lansing, *War Memoirs of Robert Lansing*, New York, 1935.

from $89,036,428 in 1913 to $333,552,226 in 1915, and the loss of German orders for cotton was made up after a period of stagnation by larger Allied buying.[5]

NEUTRAL TRADE PLACED UNDER BRITISH CONTROLS From the beginning it was essential to Allied success that new ways of blockading Germany be devised. The British were unable to maintain the traditional offshore blockade, whereby a cordon of ships physically prevented neutral commerce with the enemy by visiting and searching them for contraband.

To begin with, the old definitions of contraband were much too narrow. London therefore resisted successfully a long effort of the State Department to persuade Downing Street to accept the international Declaration of London of 1909, which regulated such matters. Instead, the British carefully refrained from mentioning any free list and gradually extended the contraband lists to include anything that might be useful to the enemy.

At the same time new techniques were evolved to throttle all trade with the enemy, without doing so in any open proclamation. Innumerable cases piled up in the British prize courts, which found ways of condemning all kinds of formerly legitimate trade with the enemy. An avalanche of protests by American commercial interests to the State Department led to so many protests to Britain that the Department got lost in the complexity and futility of the resulting correspondence.

So did the American shippers, until they discovered that they could go to the British Consuls here and get full approval for any shipment to the Allies, provided that they submitted their cargoes and manifests to rigorous scrutiny for any goods going to the Germans. Then London embargoed the export from the

---

[5] C. C. Tansill, *America Goes to War*, Boston, 1938, pp. 53, 116, 222. Tansill's book is the most thorough and exhaustive study of our entry into the First World War. Though written from the standpoint of one who believed in the feasibility of neutrality, and who opposed our entry into the Second World War, the volume records the whole story with fairness and restraint. For his attitude toward World War II, *see* the *New York Times*, April 23, 1939.

Empire of a long list of raw materials essential to American manufacturers, and released them only when individual agreements were signed by our people guaranteeing no re-export to the Central Powers.

These two effective controls of American commerce being established, there remained the problem of neutral shipments to Germany through the neutral Dutch and Scandinavian states. This great hole in the new, long range blockade of Germany was filled by two new measures on the European side of the Atlantic. First the Dutch and others were compelled to set up corporations for the receipt of goods, under contract to see that they were not re-exported to the enemy. These measures were enforced by the ability to cut off all of the oceanic trade of the small European neutrals. Then the British insisted that all neutral ships going into the North Sea should call first at British ports, because of the danger of mines. There they would be advised about lanes through the mine fields—and thoroughly searched for any goods which might be destined for Germany.

In October, a German auxiliary cruiser laid mines out in the Atlantic, beyond Iceland, and London avowed that only some merchant vessel flying a neutral flag could have done it. Therefore, on November 2, 1914, Britain declared the whole of the North Sea a military area and increased the pressure on American ships to stop in the Straits of Dover. The few which did not were picked up by British patrol vessels. By November 11 a German submarine could and did swim under a hundred merchantmen anchored in the Downs awaiting inspection and torpedoed a British gunboat.[6]

From the early months of the war the British caused great and vexatious losses to our shippers by detaining vessels bound for neutral ports for long periods without apparent cause and by replacing the international law of the sea with British municipal law in all their judgments on neutral ships.[7] On their

[6] Walter Millis, *The Road to War*, Boston, 1935, pp. 109–19.
[7] Lansing, *War Memoirs*, p. 123.

side it was obviously most difficult to search the cargo of a large merchant ship on the high seas with a submarine likely to sight a sitting target in the British warship concerned.

THE GERMAN WAR ZONE RESISTED   The failure of the United States to join in the protest of the Scandinavian countries about the British North Sea proclamation increased the deep resentment in Germany against the United States for providing ammunitions base to the Allies and for acquiescing in their effort to starve out the Central Powers. An intense debate as to methods of retaliation led to a decision in December and January over the advisability of declaring a war zone all around the British Isles, to be enforced by submarine warfare. Admiral Tirpitz opposed the move partly because he believed that too few U-boats were ready, but the submarine school won on February 4, 1915, and Secretary Bryan was notified three days later that after February 18 all *enemy* merchant vessels found in British waters would be destroyed.

In the meantime, on January 25, Germany had placed certain cereals and flours under government control to prevent hoarding and speculation. Two days later Sir Edward Grey notified our Ambassador, Walter Hines Page, that since the German Government had taken control of all food in the Empire all food cargoes to Germany would hereafter be subject to seizure.[8] This led to a strenuous effort by Secretary Bryan to work out a compromise whereby food would be allowed to go to Germany for civilian use alone, to be distributed by American agencies, if the Germans would use their submarines only under visit and search rules. Grey at first expressed approval, over the protests of Page, who sometimes helped Grey to compose replies to our notes of protest, but Grey effectively declined on March 15. Germany had accepted the proposal on March 1, subject to the addition of certain raw materials.[9]

The German war zone notice led our Government to dispatch

[8] *Foreign Relations, 1914, Supplement,* p. 317.
[9] Tansill, pp. 237–40.

notes on February 10 to both Britain and Germany warning Britain against the use of the American flag as a ruse, and Germany against the assumption that such use of our flag justified sinkings. Germany was to be held to "strict accountability" (Lansing's phrase) for any loss of American life and property due to a failure to visit, search and provide for safety of passengers and crew.[10]

German Submarine Sinkings

WHAT WAS THE STATUS OF ARMED SHIPS AND THEIR PASSENGERS? This warning led to much vacillation in Germany and delayed the opening of the submarine campaign. Simultaneously, after some wavering, the United States Neutrality Board on March 3, 1915, legalized the entry into American ports of the growing number of armed British merchantmen. In Tansill's opinion, a contrary decision would have compelled the disarmament of British ships and enabled German submarines to avoid sinking on sight. He feels that this decision was "the supreme crisis in the story of American neutrality."[11]

As matters developed it was only a question of time until Americans traveling on British ships would be killed, even if an American ship was not mistakenly torpedoed. The inevitable happened on March 28 when the U-28 pursued the British liner Falaba in the Irish Sea and torpedoed the ship after allegedly allowing two short extensions of an original ten minutes for evacuation, in the presence of approaching trawlers.

[10] Foreign Relations, 1915, pp. 98–99. The flag note to Britain was "a mere gesture," vaguely phrased, which had been devised by Lansing to give an impression of impartiality.—Ray Stannard Baker, Life and Letters of Woodrow Wilson, New York, 1935, Vol. V, p. 252. Baker adds that the note to Germany made a most favorable impression on the dominant, pro-Allied opinion in the United States.

[11] Tansill, p. 250.

The ship sank at once, with a loss of 104 lives, including an American, Leon C. Thrasher.

This event precipitated an intense struggle between Secretary Bryan and Lansing for the President's decision. Lansing's memorandums argued for the strict application of the accepted rules of sea warfare and contended militantly that the German government wanted war with the United States anyway. Bryan suggested that the arming of some British merchantmen justified the submarine commander in assuming that the *Falaba* was armed. He questioned the right of one man (Thrasher), acting without consulting his government, to involve the whole nation in war, noted that we had not protested Britain's blockade of food for the German civilians and asked: "Why be shocked at the drowning of a few people if there is no objection to the starving of a nation?" Bryan proposed the alternative of warning Americans not to travel on British ships.

Wilson inclined to accept Lansing's legalistic view, but Bryan's homespun contentions caused him to pause for a month, uncertain as to the best course. On April 28, the American ship *Cushing* was attacked by a German seaplane. Apologies were promptly offered. On May 1, the American tanker *Gulflight* was torpedoed, though not sunk, and towed into a nearby British port. Two American sailors were drowned and the captain died of shock. The Germans offered extenuating circumstances for the attack, but Lansing contended still more strongly that they wanted war.

THE LUSITANIA DISASTER   While Wilson continued to hesitate, the great British liner *Lusitania* was torpedoed without warning on May 7, 1915, with a loss of 1195 lives out of 1959 on board. Of 159 Americans, 124 perished, including several famous persons. The huge ship went down in eighteen minutes, due to a second explosion, probably coal dust in her bunkers. No disaster at sea had ever been so immense, so well reported by the survivors or so heart-rending.

It is difficult to recall any incident in American history which set off a comparable explosion of wrath. When the *Falaba* sinking had killed a hundred people, including one American, the great newspapers of the East greeted it as "a crime against humanity," "murder," "piracy," "a triumph of horror," "Barbarism run mad," "an atrocity which the civilized world should protest with one voice."[12]

When the much greater tragedy of the *Lusitania* burst upon the nation, Henry Watterson thundered from Louisville that "the nation of the black hand and bloody heart has got in its work." The editors of the *Literary Digest* concluded that "condemnation of the act seems to be limited only by the restrictions of the English language." The cartoonists contributed "every kind of stirring and terrible visual appeal." Preachers added to the passion which stirred many millions in the Eastern half of the country so deeply.[13]

After the illimitable horrors of World War II it is not easy to realize how much emotion the *Lusitania* disaster stirred. People then were still not accustomed to wholesale death in every form. Death at sea, too, stirs the imagination and sympathy as no other kind does. People prefer almost any other end to life. Pictures in the newspapers of the woman passenger with her six children—all lost—or the death photograph of the woman with a tiny baby clutched to each breast, struck home. If this kind of thing could happen no one could be safe at sea. The right to travel safely at sea, even during wartime, also seemed to the majority something which could not be given up, especially after it had been so "savagely" attacked. Immense numbers of people were conditioned for war by the

[12] Tansill, p. 251n.

[13] Millis, pp. 172–74. The West was much less disturbed. Newton D. Baker, Secretary of War during the war, wrote later that the shock of the disaster "literally overwhelmed America and public opinion never recovered from it. Then in truth began a process of 'tramping out the vintage, where the grapes of wrath are stored,' which never let up." N. D. Baker, *Why We Went to War*, p. 59. Ray Stannard Baker described the tragedy as "a horror which shook the nation to its depths."—Baker, *The Life and Letters of Woodrow Wilson*, Vol. V, p. 330.

Lusitania's end, but not many wanted it then. The newspapers overwhelmingly demanded that the President "should instantly compel Germany to disavow, to make reparation and to abandon her submarine war, though taking care not to get the United States into trouble while doing so." Those who did cry for war then did so in belief that Germany "had no fleet we can sweep off the briny deep, nor army near enough to be exterminated."[14]

OLD RULES VS. NEW WEAPONS   People were not then accustomed, either, to the idea that all modern war is wholesale murder, and murder of all ages and sexes. We still thought of war as something between the fighting men. We refused, also, to have the traditional rules changed abruptly and dramatically by new fighting weapons. The British had gradually changed the rules of war to fit their new necessities, but it was done slowly, silently and relatively painlessly. Even the long detained cargo of an American ship would be paid for by the British in the end, and not one American was killed. The result might condemn great numbers of German babies to slow death, but this was not seen or felt in the mind's eye. Besides the Germans could always save their babies by confessing defeat.

The sole alternative before the Germans was to develop a new weapon which could bring economic paralysis and starvation to Britain. The submarine was the weapon, but it could not be used according to the old rules if merchant ships were armed. Even if the ship was warned, also, it was poor safety to put hundreds of people out on the sea, perhaps stormy, far from shore. Only ruthless use of the new arm could really make it a winning weapon. In time the German public and leaders were sure to demand its unrestricted use.

Wilson understood the basic difficulty. He said to a press conference on March 2, 1915, "that the conditions of war had radically changed but the rules had not." The President's chief advisers did not grasp this principle, or were unwilling to do

[14] Millis, p. 175.

so. Wilson's official biographer describes Lansing as "spinning empty logic based upon the traditions of a world that had utterly vanished—a world that had not known aeroplanes, or the transmission of information by radio, or submarines, or leviathan ships—trying to strait-jacket a war bursting with new devices into the legalisms of 1864 or 1870 or 1898." Page, the President's most important diplomatic agent, was, says Baker, "actually taking the part of our chief diplomatic opponent, playing the game of the British." Colonel Edward M. House was "wandering anxiously about Europe seeking peace, being used as a pawn in their deliberate and most effective policy of delay."[15] Only Bryan urged the realities of the situation, and he was often uncertain in a very confused series of situations.

THE LUSITANIA NOTES When President Wilson heard about the *Lusitania* he at once left the White House for a long walk, noticing no one. The next day he deliberately played his usual Saturday round of golf, to the horror of great newspaper publishers. Hearing that he was on the links one of them shouted to a subordinate "My God! Send out and get him right away. Tell him to declare war on Germany at once."[16]

Wilson insisted to Tumulty, his private secretary, that he would "see red in everything" and "probably not be just to anyone" if he let his mind dwell on the tragic details in the newspapers."[17] Striving to keep his balance he secluded himself until Monday evening, May 10, when he told a great audience in Philadelphia that "peace is a healing and elevating influence and strife is not. There is such a thing as a man being too proud to fight. There is such a thing as a nation being so right that it does not need to convince others by force that it is right."

The crowd burst into tumultuous applause, but the newspaper

[15] Baker, *The Life and Letters of Woodrow Wilson*, Vol. V, pp. 260–61.
[16] George Britt, *Forty Years–Forty Millions, The Career of Frank A. Munsey*, New York, 1935, pp. 281–82. Cited in Tansill, p. 276.
[17] Joseph P. Tumulty, *Woodrow Wilson as I Know Him*, Garden City, 1921, p. 232.

editors took a view so different that Wilson soon retreated and denied that he had been talking about the *Lusitania* crisis.

In the forging of the first *Lusitania* note, House and Page in London of course thought that war was required. In Washington Lansing pressed for stern action, in close consultation with the bellicose Secretary of War, Lindley M. Garrison. Only Bryan, supported somewhat by Postmaster General Burleson, struggled against stern action. He pleaded that "ships carrying contraband should be prohibited from carrying passengers." The *Lusitania* had carried 4200 cases of small arms ammunition. He fought vainly for a statement to the press that would soften the impact of the proposed note, but on May 13 he signed it.

The first *Lusitania* note was couched in relatively friendly diplomatic language, but it maintained stoutly all of our existing rights upon the sea, denied that submarines could be used without disregarding those rights and protested against the irregularity of the notice published in our newspapers by the German Embassy on the day the *Lusitania* sailed, warning all passengers off British ships. The note demanded disavowal of the sinking, reparation and the prevention of similar sinkings. It closed with a stern warning.[18]

The German reply of May 28, 1915 to our note answered it point by point and precipitated another intense contest between Bryan and Lansing. Bryan opposed an immediate answer, argued for arbitration and a strong note to Britain. He sought the exclusion of munitions from passenger ships and argued that "if a submarine is bound by the rules applicable to merchantmen, then the merchantmen ought also to be bound by the rules applicable when the merchantmen are attacked by a cruiser." Fearing acutely that the second *Lusitania* note would

---

[18] The release of the famous Bryce report on Belgian atrocities, on May 11, signed by the most respected Ambassador the British had sent to this country in many years, had a strong impact on the white hot sentiment in the country.

bring war, Bryan resigned on June 8, 1915, and the firm note of June 9 was signed by Lansing, the new Secretary of State.[19]

THE ARABIC CRISIS Two additional *Lusitania* notes were exchanged, both holding firmly to the established positions, before the sinking of the *Arabic* on August 19, 1915, with the loss of two American lives precipitated another acute crisis.

The *Lusitania* case had led to a fresh debate in German officialdom about submarine warfare. Bethmann Hollweg and the Army secured an order from the Emperor, on June 6, directing submarine commanders to spare *large* enemy passenger vessels. The resignations of Admirals Tirpitz and Bachman were rejected, but out of deference to them the order was kept secret. It was violated by the U-boat commander who sank the *Arabic* without warning. This face was discovered by Ambassador James W. Gerard in Berlin, but the German Government refused to disavow the act.

Instead it came to a decision on August 27, after further heated debates, that thereafter no passenger ships, large or small, could be sunk without warning and providing for the safety of lives.[20] On the same day Secretary Lansing told Ambassador von Bernstorff that unless this action were taken "the United States would certainly declare war on Germany."[21] This led Bernstorff to exceed his instructions and give the desired pledge in writing on September 1.

President Wilson proceeded on the assumption that "the people of this country count on me to keep them out of the war."[22] At the same time he tenaciously insisted on a disavowal of the *Arabic* sinking, and after many passages back and forth Bernstorff, on October 5, incurred another reprimand from his government by explicitly disavowing the act of the U-boat

[19] Tansill, pp. 322–37.

[20] Admiral Arno Spindler, *La Guerre Sous Marine*, Paris, 1933–35, Vol. II, p. 335, cited in Tansill, p. 366.

[21] Lansing, *War Memoirs*, p. 47.

[22] Wilson to House, August 21, 1915. Tansill, p. 360.

commander and offering indemnity. Thus another crisis was bridged. In May 1915, also, the U-boats were equipped with cannon and in the next three months managed to sink ninety-four ships according to the rules of cruiser warfare. Some 22 were sunk without warning, indemnity being paid for the neutral ships destroyed.[23] On the other hand, doubt was cast on the feasibility of submarine warfare according to the rules by the *Baralong* case of August 19 in which a British "mystery ship" used the American flag as a means of exterminating the last man of a U-boat crew, in a most brutal manner.

THE ANCONA CONTROVERSY The long continued negotiations over the *Lusitania* were exacerbated by the sinking of the Italian liner *Ancona* in the Mediterranean on November 7, with a loss of twenty Americans. The reaction of the American press was intense. The Germans eventually agreed to pay indemnity, but would not admit liability and disavow the submarine commander. Secretary Lansing's threat on January 25 to break relations, without express authority from Wilson, drew a quick surrender from Bernstorff, but not from Berlin. On February 1, 1916, however, Germany admitted "liability," though she still refused to agree that the sinking was "illegal."

THE ARMED SHIP CRISIS A compromise finally seemed to be in sight when on February 11, 1916, a German note announced that armed merchant ships would be sunk without warning.[24] Another struggle in German councils over the renewal of unfettered submarine warfare had been won by a combination of the Army with the Navy, to the alarm of the Chancellor who thought the entire world would be affronted, with grave danger of Germany's destruction.

Before the armed merchant ship warning came, Lansing had already notified Britain, on January 18, 1916, that if the submarines observed the rules merchant ships "should be prohibited

[23] Admiral Spindler, *op. cit.*, Vol. II, pp. 146–48, 238–40.

[24] "The President's pacific attitude towards Germany is revealed in his evident disappointment at this failure to find a solution for the *Lusitania* difficulty."—Tansill, p. 406.

and prevented from carrying any armament whatever."[25] There did not appear to be any rule that protected armed merchant ships from being sunk at sight by a submarine. Lansing held to this view until deterred by stern advice from Colonel House, coupled with a strong anticipation of renewed all-out submarine war.

Charges by Bryan that the preparedness campaign pointed toward intervention in the war led to a White House conference between the President and the majority leaders of Congress, on February 21, 1916, in which the President's defense of the right of our citizens to travel on armed ships deeply aroused Senator Stone. Something like panic swept through the Congress and the most strenuous efforts by the President were required to defeat the McLemore and Gore resolutions, forbidding Americans to travel on the armed ships of the belligerents. The battle was concluded on March 7, by a vote of 276 to 142 in the House of Representatives. "It was a result for which the two (political) parties were about equally responsible, and one applauded by nearly the whole press."[26]

THE SUSSEX CASE   On March 24 a new crisis was precipitated by the torpedoing of the passenger steamer *Sussex* in the English Channel, with the loss of eighty lives, including several Americans. Lansing, Page, and House were for an immediate break with Germany. Lansing wrote the note and House worked mightily for its acceptance, but Wilson demurred. A second Lansing draft, on April 10, 1916, was still "too severe and uncompromising" for the President.

On the same day a note arrived from Germany based on the submarine commander's report, denying that the *Sussex* was torpedoed by the U-29 and suggesting that it struck a mine. This note was, in Bernstorff's later opinion, "probably the most

[25] *Foreign Relations, 1916, Supplement,* pp. 146–48.

[26] Millis, *The Road to War,* p. 279. A simple, clear resolution banning travel on armed ships would apparently have commanded a larger vote than the 142 mustered by the opposition.

unfortunate document that ever passed from Berlin to Washington." Wilson thought he detected a direct untruth and he approved a note to Germany, on April 18, which while stopping short of breaking relations, declared that "unless the Imperial Government should now immediately declare and effect an abandonment of its present methods of submarine warfare against passenger and freight-carrying vessels, the Government of the United States can have no choice but to sever diplomatic relations."

After a sharp struggle, the German government decided to accept the American demand. Admiral von Tirpitz, who had resigned on March 12 because of restrictions on the submarine campaign, opposed surrender but Admiral von Holtzendorf, his successor, took the opposite view. The German note of May 4, 1916, promised that "In accordance with the general principles of visit and search and destruction of merchant vessels recognized by international law, such vessels, both within and without the area declared as a naval zone, shall not be sunk without warning and without saving human lives, unless these ships attempt to escape or offer resistance."

The Final Crises

EFFORTS TO STOP THE WAR Wilson had won another diplomatic victory, the last that he could hope to win. If the Germans again resorted to sinkings without warning he would have no choice but to sever relations. This near-certainty made it essential to stop the war, if it could be done. But unfortunately for such an endeavor the American presidential election was due.

Bethmann-Hollweg asked Bernstorff on August 18, 1916, to encourage mediation by Wilson. On August 31 a new drive of the German naval leaders for unrestricted submarine war was turned back. Holtzendorf now favored it but the new army chiefs, Hindenburg and Ludendorff, were hesitant. On September 2 Bethmann-Hollweg inquired of Bernstorff if American good offices would be offered if Germany guaranteed the restoration of Belgium. Colonel House replied, "not until after the election." The Chancellor then turned to Ambassador Gerard, who cabled that Germany was "anxious to make peace."

Time was running out for Bethmann. On October 7, the Reichstag adopted a resolution advising the Chancellor to base his attitude on the U-boat question on the conclusion reached by the Army High Command. Meanwhile, the American electoral campaign was being fought, largely on war issues. The President was being championed because "he kept us out of war," and by no one more effectively than W. J. Bryan. He campaigned throughout the West and was a powerful factor in swinging many close states to Wilson. The President's victory was the closest and most dramatic in history.

There can be no question about Wilson's desire that the United States should mediate the war. It was one of his first reactions to the conflict. He often spoke of it, publicly and privately. After May 4, 1916, also, American relations with the Allies were much worse than with the Central Powers.[27] In addition to the earlier British practices the British blacklists of American firms and citizens caused much indignation and led to two acts of Congress in September 1916. The British also used a considerable part of their Navy to bring American ships into port for the censorship of their mails, a practice which caused the loss and nondelivery of much mail, both ordinary and important. British warships also hovered closely off our ports, intercepting neutral ships, and there were irritating seizures of nationals of the Central Powers from our ships. All of these practices, and the British refusal to make any important concessions about them, aroused Wilson's indignation. Bernstorff testified later that in the latter half of 1916 "Wilson was for the first time during the war really neutral."[28]

[27] Newton D. Baker, *Why We Went to War*, p. 83.
[28] Seymour, *American Neutrality, 1914–1917*, p. 47.

Wilson therefore had every reason to push peace proposals after the 1916 election, but he was so pressed and distraught with cares and duties that it was six days before he could begin to draft his peace note, without any encouragement from Colonel House. Meanwhile, the German civilian officials were hard pressed. Secretary von Jagow cabled Bernstorff on November 16 and 20 about American peace moves. But at this time the deportation of large numbers of Belgians to work in Germany stirred a great deal of American indignation, which Wilson shared, and made it difficult for him to initiate his peace move. It was not until November 27 that Wilson was able to discuss the first draft of his peace proposal with House. It was one of the most moving and eloquent documents he ever wrote, though House objected strongly to the phrase "the causes and object of the war are obscure."[29]

At this juncture the Germans gave up hope of American action and on December 2 published their own peace proposal suggesting immediate peace negotiations. In London this idea received short shrift from the new Lloyd George Cabinet which came into office on December 5, ending the long tenure of Sir Edward Grey in the Foreign Office. Bryan intervened on December 14 with a personal plea to Lloyd George to consider peace, but did not even receive a reply.

Though the German peace move had virtually torpedoed his own chances of success, Wilson at last shook off all his advisers, ignored House, and on December 18 sent the fifth draft of his peace proposal to each of the warring powers. It was a simple inquiry for the terms on which they would conclude peace. His statement that "the objects which the statesmen of the belligerents on both sides have in mind in this war are virtually the same, as stated to their own people and to the world" testified to a high degree of objectivity, but infuriated both the Allies and the President's American opponents. The joint reply of the

[29] The text is in Baker, *Woodrow Wilson, Life and Letters*, Vol. VI, pp. 380–86.

Allies, on January 10, 1917, stated terms which meant the loss of all German war gains, and the Germans refused to state their terms. Their Supreme High Command had decided for unrestricted submarine war. On their side, the Allied leaders were confident, even after the interminable slaughter on the Somme, that they could smash the Western front in the spring.

UNRESTRICTED SUBMARINE WAR The shadow of the submarine, always in the background to say the least, became startlingly real on October 7, 1916 when the giant U-53 put into the harbor of Newport, Rhode Island, got newspapers, with their sailing lists, and sank nine ships close off our coasts within twenty-four hours. There was a sudden slump on Wall Street, a 500 percent rise in marine insurance rates, general uneasiness and fear among our people, and an explosion of wrath against us in Britain.[30]

It was on January 9, 1917, at Pless, that the German Army and Navy leaders secured the Chancellor's acquiescence to unrestricted submarine warfare, to begin on February 1. In the meantime, they insisted that *armed* merchant ships should be destroyed at sight, and on January 10 Bernstorff notified Lansing of this decision.

The German decision was made in full knowledge that war with the United States would probably result. Some thought that it might not happen, but if so the German leaders felt sure that they could starve Britain out of the war before the United States could arm and act. No such feat as the sending of 2,000,000 men overseas in little more than a year had ever been performed. Besides, American armament would likely diminish the flow of supplies to Europe for a time. The number of submarines had been greatly increased from the meager twenty-one of 1915. World crop harvests had been short and British supplies were not high. It was confidently expected that ruthless submarine war on *all* vessels approaching Britain would soon "bring her to her knees," not only by destroying cargoes but even more by destroying ships.

[30] R. S. Baker, *Woodrow Wilson, Life and Letters,* Vol. VI, p. 330.

Admiral von Holtzendorf argued on December 22, 1916, that Germany must bring the war to an end before August 1917. If world opinion should object it could be told that it was better for a few thousand seamen to die than for hundreds of thousands of Germans.[31]

Balked by the unwillingness of the warring governments to consider peace, Wilson reverted to his lifelong faith in the rank and file of mankind and appealed to the peoples in his famous address of January 22, 1917. Believing that there was no hope for the world in either side trying to crush the other he pleaded for a peace between equals, "a peace without victory." An imposed, victor's peace would leave "a sting, a resentment, a bitter memory."

Looking beyond any such momentary pause between wars, the President poured out his heart in support of the central idea of a league of nations, not a balance of power, but "a community of power." He urged that "all nations henceforth avoid entangling alliances which would draw them into competitions of power." There was "no entangling alliance in a concert of power" —one which would promote self government, moderation in armaments and freedom of the seas.

The address won wide acclaim in the American press and among the peoples of the world, but it had no effect at the time on the warring governments. On January 24 Wilson wrote to House that if "Germany really wants peace she can get it, and get it soon, if she will but confide in me and let me have a chance. . . . I genuinely want to help and have now put myself in a position to help without favor to either side." Wilson did not know that Bernstorff had received notice of the unrestricted submarine war on January 19 and had wired back promptly that war with the United States would be "unavoidable."

Bernstorff twice sought vainly to secure a postponement of the date of the ruthless U-boat war, which was to apply to

[31] *Ibid.*, p. 436.

neutral ships as well as belligerent. In Washington, Lansing was recording, on January 28, his convictions that Germany meant to dominate the world, that "the Allies must *not* be beaten" and that "war cannot come any too soon to suit me."[32] Far from being in this frame of mind Wilson wrote to Lansing on January 31 complaining about the offensive use of guns on British armed merchantmen.

Bernstorff presented the notification of all-out submarine warfare on January 31, 1917. One American steamer a week, not carrying contraband, might sail to and from Falmouth under the strictest requirements about flags, huge red and white markings one meter wide, and full lighting at night. All other ships met in the war zone would be sunk. The *Sussex* pledge had been broken and there was no alternative left but to break relations with Germany.

DIPLOMATIC RELATIONS BROKEN   Yet Wilson was slow to decide. He could hardly believe the news at first. He resisted the strong counsel of Lansing and House. He argued that it would be a crime to become involved in the war if it was humanly possible to avoid it. He conferred with the Swiss minister about a joint effort of all neutrals to promote peace. He went to the Senate building for a long conference with Senator William J. Stone of Missouri, Chairman of the Foreign Relations Committee, and other senators. He consulted the Cabinet and found them almost unanimous for breaking relations. The press and public opinion reflected the same view.

On the afternoon of February 3, the President announced the break to a joint session of Congress, which applauded the step as warmly as did the country. The Senate passed a formal resolution of approval, 78 to 5. Even Bernstorff, when handed his passport said: "I am not surprised. . . . There was nothing else for the United States to do."[33]

[32] Robert Lansing, *War Memoirs,* pp. 208–9.
[33] *The New York Times,* February 4, 1917.

Wilson made it clear in his message to Congress that he would await overt acts by Germany before going to war, and on February 15 he wrote: "I am doing everything that I honorably can to keep the country out of war." In his agony he hammered out a draft of "Bases of Peace," which contained the central idea of the League of Nations—mutual guarantee of territorial integrity and political independence. As war sentiment mounted he thought the nation's clergymen were "going crazy." An abortive effort to promote a separate peace by Austria-Hungary was pushed and he tried vainly to organize the terrified smaller neutrals into a common front.[34]

Fear had also blockaded our own East coast. Ports were clogged with cargoes and with ships refusing to put to sea without guns aboard or other protection. Wilson thought he needed authority from Congress to put Navy guns and men aboard the ships and he resisted this step through five Cabinet meetings covering three weeks, until the Cabinet was aroused and angry over the issue. Then, at precisely the right moment, the British played a trump card. On February 25 they turned over to him a remarkable document which had been in their hands since January 16, the Zimmerman note.

The German Foreign Secretary, Gottlieb von Jagow, a strong opponent of submarine war, was replaced on November 23, 1916, by the Under Secretary Arthur Zimmermann, who was more pliable and also more indiscreet. He conceived the natural but not too brilliant idea of offering an alliance with Mexico, inviting her to reconquer "the lost territory in Texas, New Mexico, and Arizona," and to enlist Japan's help. To add insult to injury this highly unrealistic but provocative proposal was sent through our own secret code, a privilege granted to Bernstorff to facilitate communication with his beleaguered government.

Wilson read the Zimmerman note on February 25, 1917 and went before Congress the next day to ask for authority to arm

[34] Baker, *Woodrow Wilson, Life and Letters,* Vol. VI, pp. 461–70.

the ships. The House voted the authority 403 to 14, but a bipartisan filibuster killed the bill in the Senate. A dozen opponents of war talked it to death at the end of the short session. They were instantly and angrily condemned by the President and by the country. On March 12 the ships were armed anyway.

In his second inaugural address, on March 5, the President reiterated once more his hard won belief that all nations were equally interested in the peace of the world, in self-government by all peoples, in free seas and in avoiding armed balances of power. Then he secluded himself in his room for about ten days, seeing only a few officials. On the 19th, Lansing brought him news of the sinking of three American ships, but got no commitment for a declaration of war. On March 20 the President held a three-hour Cabinet meeting, finding them all agreed that war was inevitable. The meeting closed without the President announcing his decision, but the next day he called the Congress to meet in special session for April 2. In the intervening days while he was writing his war message, Lansing could not find out what he was going to propose. When he had finished the message, on April 1, he sent for editor Frank Cobb of the *New York World*. All through the night the haggard Wilson forecast the illiberalism and the "spirit of ruthless brutality" that would be unleashed in the country by war. As day dawned he was still saying: "If there is any alternative, for God's sake let's take it." There was no alternative.

WAR DECLARED   In the evening he faced the élite of the nation in the hall of the House of Representatives. He recounted how international law had been born in attempts to devise some law and order on the sea. Then he called for war, not "for revenge" but "to vindicate the principles of peace and justice in the life of the world as against selfish and autocratic power." He called upon the nation to fight "for democracy, for the right of those who submit to authority to have a voice in their own governments, for the rights and liberties of small nations, for a universal dominion of right by such a concert of free peoples as shall bring peace and safety to all nations and make the world itself at last free."

The vote for war in the House of Representatives was 373 to 50 and in the Senate 82 to 6.

Why Neutrality Failed

After the war was over, a large revisionist literature grew up which sought to prove that the United States had entered the war because of: (a) loans and sales to belligerents; (b) the travel of Americans on belligerent ships; (c) subtle foreign propaganda; and (d) Wilson's many mistakes.[35]

As world order again rapidly broke down, after the Japanese invasion of Manchuria in 1931, Senator Gerald P. Nye of North Dakota, sponsored and headed an inquiry into the munitions business which focussed the dominant isolationist sentiment on the munitions makers, the "merchants of death," and "the international bankers" as the culprits who had dragged us into the World War and would do so again. A revolt of the older Democratic Senators against his effort to make Wilson personally responsible for the war eventually ended the inquiry, but not before the history of our entry into the war had been successfully rewritten. A succession of public opinion polls showed that the American people believed our part in the war had been a mistake and that they favored "neutrality" legislation to prevent a repetition of the errors of the past. A series of stringent laws

---

[35] See: John K. Turner, *Shall It Be Again?*, New York, 1922; Frederick Bausman, *Facing Europe*, New York, 1926; C. Hartley Grattan, *Why We Fought*, New York, 1929; Walter Millis, *Road to War*, Boston, 1935; Charles A. Beard, *The Devil Theory of War*, New York, 1936; Edwin Borchard and W. P. Lage, *Neutrality for the United States*, New Haven, 1937; Hubert Herring, *And So to War*, New Haven, 1938; H. C. Peterson, *Propaganda for War*, University of Oklahoma Press, 1939.

was duly passed, all of which broke down under the force of the Axis onslaught on the pacific powers.

It is important, accordingly, to examine some of the alleged reasons for our entry into the First World War which during a critical period dominated public thought and action.

1. *Allied Propaganda.* In 1939, H. C. Peterson wrote a scholarly book, *Propaganda for War,* which came to the conclusion that the United States entered the war because of the effect of British propaganda upon the American people and upon President Wilson.

British propaganda was very effective. It was well organized and financed. It controlled most of the channels to the American press at the start of the war and afterward. It worked largely through American spokesmen and through promoting personal contact between influential British and American citizens. It was not crude, hot and obvious, as German propaganda was. It unquestionably influenced many Americans to the Allied side.

It was, however, not what Englishmen said which made the Americans pro-Ally. Their common Anglo-Saxon speech, institutions and heritage were a basis of sympathy which no amount of words could greatly affect.

Yet, above all, it was what the Central Powers *did,* during the outbreak of the war, which determined our attitudes. The Austrian ultimatum to Serbia, the hasty German declarations of war and the invasion of Belgium left impressions which could never be removed. Then the long succession of submarine sinkings, culminating in the *Lusitania* disaster, deepened our anti-German feelings. After the greater German offenses and horrors of the Second World War, such things as the deportation of great numbers of Belgians to Germany may not seem greatly shocking, but in the years 1914 to 1917 we were still accustomed to the greater humanity which had prevailed during a century of relative peace.

The atrocity stories, some totally false and others having a basis of fact, influenced many people, but the greatest of all

atrocities was the war itself, for which most Americans believed
the Central Powers to be responsible.[36]

2. *The International Bankers.* During the isolationist reaction
the idea spread that the international bankers had spun a devious
web of inter-allied finance from which we finally could not
escape.

Early in the war the State Department discouraged the making of loans to the belligerents, but after a few months this
policy was relaxed to permit the granting of credits. A year
later foreign government loans were allowed and by the end of
our neutrality loans totalling $2,262,827,544 had been made to
the Allies, excluding Canada.[37]

J. P. Morgan & Company acted as fiscal agents for the Allies
in this country and other international bankers were active in
their behalf. The bulk of the banking community was pro-Ally
and did what it could to help the cause of the Allies. On the
other hand, the bankers had fought Wilson throughout the creation of the Federal Reserve system and many of them never
ceased to hate him for his victory in securing a more decentral-
ized system. No President was ever less susceptible to the society or pressure of bankers. When offers from the great corporations and bankers to place all their resources at the disposal
of the government began to flood into the White House in
February 1917, after relations were broken with Germany, Wilson was appalled. "It is Junkerthum trying to creep in under

[36] Peterson himself shows conclusively that British prestige among Americans declined progressively during 1916 and that Wilson swung even more
strongly against British attitudes and practices.—H. C. Peterson, *Propaganda for War*, pp. 285–88.

Peterson accepted "the appalling political crudities of the Germans" as
"merely the outward manifestation of a deep historical force"—Germany's
rise to power. War was perpetually inevitable in Europe because some nation would always be rising to power. The history of the 1914–1917 period
had demonstrated not that "the United States cannot keep out of war," but
"that it is impossible to be unneutral and keep out of war." (Pp. 327 and
330.)

[37] *Munitions Inquiry*, Part 39, 8981. Cited in Peterson, *Propaganda for
War*, p. 259.

cover of the patriotic feeling of the moment. They will not get in," he declared.[38] His reply to J. P. Morgan was as brief and as cool as it could have been.

There is "not the slightest evidence" that any bankers or big business interests influenced Wilson in any degree during his weeks of decision—after the German decision of January 9, 1917, had virtually removed the power of choice from him.[39]

3. *The Munitions Makers.* The corporations which sold munitions to the Allies made great profits during the war. The profits of Bethlehem Steel jumped from $24,821,408 in 1915 to $61,717,309 in 1916. U. S. Steel cleared $348,000,000 in 1916. One small firm "earned" 1605 percent. "Unbelievable" profits were reported in all branches of industry and commerce. Meat packers' profits doubled in 1916. The West was "immensely enriched by the enormous export of its food products." Even cotton finally came into the big money. Incomes increased in all brackets. There was plenty of money for land speculation and for the purchase of the Allies' war bonds.[40]

(Perhaps some munitions makers saw a chance for still larger profits if we entered the war.) Others could have foreseen the strict control of profits which ensued. That any of them brought influence to bear on the Wilson Administration—anti-big business as it was—is highly unlikely, and still to be proved. During 1916 Secretary of War Newton D. Baker "never saw a munition maker except as I sent for him and urged him to try to help us in the emergency of our border troubles." To equip the Pershing expedition into Mexico, Baker found no airplanes fit to fly and only one industrial plant equipped to build heavy machine guns.

When we entered the war the museums of city police departments were ransacked for confiscated "concealed weapons"

[38] R. S. Baker, *Woodrow Wilson, Life and Letters,* Vol. VI, pp. 461–62. During his tenure as Secretary of War, from 1916 to 1921, Newton D. Baker could not recall any conversation with a banker on any subject.— N. D. Baker, *Why We Went to War,* p. 123.

[39] Tansill, p. 657.

[40] Peterson, *Propaganda for War,* pp. 257–58.

and at the end of the war pistols were still lacking. "For months American manufacturers were unable to make heavy ammunition" and much of our armament had to be obtained from the Allies in Europe. Baker's keenest memory was that in 1917 "a munitions industry large enough to be interested, much less influential, in our going to war simply did not exist."[41]

4. *Impending Allied Bankruptcy*. During the two years and eight months of our neutrality American exports to the Allies totalled seven billion dollars, about two billions for munitions and the balance for foodstuffs, raw materials, etc. Enormous balances of trade in our favor were suddenly created. Paying for this tremendous stream of goods forced the Allies to ship us great quantities of gold and a large part of their stocks and bonds, in addition to the loans they were able to obtain, most of them backed by collateral.[42]

By the Spring of 1917 their financial position was desperate. It does not follow, however, that the much discussed telegram from Ambassador Page, dated March 5, 1917, determined our entry into the war. Wilson had paid little attention to Page's letters since he had proved himself early in the war to be more pro-British than the British. Other evidence did convince him that if we entered the war large credits would have to be given the Allies at once. This, however, could have been done without entering the war, and far more cheaply.

There doubtless were many American investors who had become doubtful about their Allied war bonds during the stalemated war winter of 1916–1917. Some of them may have welcomed our entry into the war on this account, but they did not make the decision for war.

By early 1917 our economic prosperity was tied up with the fate of the Allies. That is patent. Yet no American President was less susceptible to materialistic pressures. Wilson did assist Allied financing, though sometimes putting a check on it. The

[41] N. D. Baker, *Why We Went to War*, pp. 119–22.
[42] Peterson, pp. 256, 259–66.

war trade was as legitimate as the freedom of the seas for which we had fought Great Britain a century earlier. Nor was it wholly immoral for a nation which had suddenly had its whole economic life disrupted by a war to recover, if it could, by trading with the belligerents it could reach. The war trade may have conditioned many people for joining the Allies, but the decision was made in Berlin.

Had the Germans not reversed their *Sussex* pledge it is impossible to believe that Wilson would have yielded to any amount of pressure to save American investments or war business.

5. *Fear of a German Europe.* It has frequently been said that Wilson's great mistake was in his choice of objectives for which we should fight. Instead of summoning us to fight "a war to end war," "to make the world safe for democracy" and to establish a league "of democratic nations," Wilson should have told us that we were fighting for national survival against a German domination of Europe, it is said.

This factor could properly have received more stress. Nevertheless, our stark fear of a Nazi world in 1939–1941 was not duplicated in 1914–1917. Most Americans wanted the Allies to win, but in early 1917 they would have been very reluctant to fight just to prevent a German victory, especially since stalemate was then the prospect. Many thoughtful and influential people felt more strongly about it, and when the crisis came the conviction that a German Europe would be bad for us made many ready to accept war. Wilson himself would have feared a German victory keenly had it been imminent. If we had not been in the war during the great German sweep through France in the spring of 1918 fear would have impelled us toward intervention, perhaps too late, but in March 1917 the defense of national interest involved in the submarine controversy was the decisive consideration. Behind it, to be sure, was a strong feeling that it was time to take a hand.

OUR ONE-SIDED NEUTRALITY Viewed from this distance, our neutrality was one-sided and illogical. We permitted the British to change the rules, gradually and without obvious loss to us, but refused to permit the Germans to change them in the middle of the war. The Administration's legalistic attitude toward the German submarine was influenced by Lansing's legalism and his aversion to Germany's acts and policies, but the German attack on merchant ships, ending in the proposal to destroy *all* of them, "awakened nothing less than horror."[43]

The German object was to destroy cargo space to such an extent that Britain would be starved out of the war. Each sailor killed might save a thousand Germans, but this was not obvious to Americans, nor would it have been appealing to them. They were not impartial automatons, but people who could not avoid making up their minds about the tremendous and stirring events of 1914–1917. "To expect the people of the United States to view the greatest of European events without emotion, without moral judgment, without bias, is to expect from them more than they are capable of."[44]

Throughout the period, too, public opinion approved the President's attitude toward the belligerents. When he tried to lead it he usually went in the direction of being "neutral in thought as well as in action," of being so proud in the right that we did not need to fight, of "peace without victory" for either side. Public opinion eventually pushed him the other way, and when at last he recommended war he was only recording a national decision.

It is arguable that had Woodrow Wilson made one or two different decisions American participation in the war might have been averted, or at least delayed. It is not possible to charge Wilson with any desire to lead the United States into war. Tansill's conclusion is that "in the long list of American Chief Executives there is no one who was a more sincere pacifist than the President who led us into war in April 1917."[45] A

[43] Dexter Perkins, *America and Two Wars,* Boston, 1944, pp. 40–43.
[44] Perkins, p. 38.
[45] Tansill, *America Goes to War,* p. 606.

different turn of the wheels of politics would have put a fire-eater such as Theodore Roosevelt in the White House.

Wilson's long struggle against going to war showed not so much that the most sincere pacifist could make mistakes, but that when the center of western civilization was torn by war the defense of American neutral rights led to war. It was equally demonstrated that when Europe is at war both the interests and the sympathies of the American people are sucked into the vortex. Above all, it was indicated with shattering clarity that a great effort of statesmanship was required to prevent such measureless tragedies from engulfing nations around the world, whose peoples desired only to live normal lives.

VII. World War I

————◆————

The actual onset of the war aroused a strong patriotic response in every participating nation. The often considered general strikes of socialist workers did not develop. The German socialists bowed to the German fear of the barbarian Slav and supported the war. In spite of the murder of their leader, Jean Léon Jaurès, which had been called for publicly by the French reactionaries, the French socialists flocked to the colors. The strikes and riots which had gripped Petrograd for weeks evaporated as the Russian people responded to the Austro-German challenge. In Great Britain the tense postures of civil war over the Irish question were abandoned to the point that the Irish Nationalist leader Redmond told the government it could safely leave Ireland without troops. The German invasion of Belgium had created a moral unity in Britain which no one would have thought possible before the event.

Everywhere mobilization proceeded quietly, or with cheers as well as tears. Each people accepted the version of the war which its leaders gave to it. Each believed it was being attacked and that the national existence was at stake. While the war came as a shock to most plain people it was also accepted as a relief from the mounting tensions, crises, alarms, and taxes of the past ten years. At the end of the age when war was a relatively limited affair it brought an exultation of spirit, a sinking of lesser things in a great cause. Besides, victory would soon be won and the war ended. In German circles especially, but elsewhere as well, thinking was still dominated by the swift, remunerative victories of Bismarck's wars. Economists in both England and

Germany did not believe that the economic structures could support long wars and everywhere people had forgotten how bad a great war can be. It was a full century since there had been a prolonged general war.

The Failure of the 1914 Offensives in the West

Certainly the German General Staff had no idea of fighting a long war. It proceeded to put into operation the plan by Schlieffen, whose dying words in 1913 had been: "It must come to a fight. Only make the right wing strong." As explained above, his plan called for a great wheeling movement through Belgium (but after pausing in force on the Belgian border without a declaration of war, until the French came in to occupy the Belgian heights along the Meuse) which would circle around behind Paris and roll up the French armies on the Jura Mountains and the Swiss frontier. To make certain of success he planned to put seven-tenths of the German troops into the right wing steam roller.[1]

The opening of the war found the French committed to the same doctrine that it is the fierce offensive that wins. The enforced fortress mentality of the years after 1870 had been succeeded by the rise of an *élan vital* which would translate the *mystique d'Alsace* into victory when the Day came. Everything was to depend on dash, fire and *le cran*, guts.

PLAN 17   General Ferdinand Foch, chief military theoretician, was the fountainhead of this doctrine in the Army and a Colonel Grandmaison was the one who set the Army and rightist circles ablaze with his brilliant lectures on "the idea with a sword," offensive to the limit. Supported fiercely by a rightist War Minister, Adolphe Messimy, this idea carried all before it. It was allied with another, that Army reservists were too soft and

[1] H. A. DeWeerd, *Great Soldiers of the World Wars*, New York, 1941, pp. 19–46.

family encumbered to be fit soldiers, except the very youngest, and would therefore not be used in line fighting either in France or in Germany.

These two ideas worked together to defeat the common sense views of General Michel, top French commander in 1911. Reflecting Schlieffen's thinking precisely, he submitted a report calling for holding the France-German border, which was very difficult to attack through, and for concentrating the defense on the Belgian frontier, matching a regiment of reserves with every active regiment.

This "insane" proposal led Messimy to resolve instantly to remove Michel, and to choose General Joseph Joffre to head the Army, which proceeded to adopt Plan 17, in April 1913. It provided for offensives through Alsace, going to Berlin through Mainz. It was not a detailed plan, only a project for two French offensives, one on each side of the German fortified area Metz-Thionville, but its existence almost led to the complete defeat of France in August 1914. The Germans did invade through Belgium, as the evidence indicated, and they did use their reserves in the line to provide the necessary bulk, and they almost won. Jaurès, the martyred French Socialist leader, had argued that reservists from twenty-five to thirty-three were at the peak of their stamina and that without them France would be terribly submerged, but the authors of Plan 17 persuaded themselves that the reserves were fit only for secondary duty, that the Germans would not use them and that a German right wing assault would leave the center so thinned that the French could "cut them in half," according to General Noël de Castelnau's prediction.[2]

In the event, the French Army did manage to liberate Mulhouse in Alsace briefly, while the German thunderbolt hit it in the West, where it could only retreat. The big armies that should have been ready to answer King Albert's pleas for help

[2] See the excellent account of the evolution of Plan 17 in Barbara W. Tuchman, *The Guns of August*, New York, 1962, pp. 28–43.

in Belgium were not there. Moreover, Joffre would not vary from Plan 17 by detaching troops to help the Belgians. Under Albert's heroic leadership they fought stubbornly, as the Germans marched wave after wave of men up to the guns of the Liège fort until they were heaped high in "an awful barricade of dead and wounded."

While all Belgians asked where the British and the French were, Joffre steadily refused to change his plan of deployment for their aid "by so much as a single brigade." His armies and thoughts were still concentrated on the Rhine in accord with Plan 17, about which the French Government had never been consulted and which he failed to explain to an assembly of generals who had hoped to hear it expounded as the war opened.[3]

General Charles Lanrezac, whose Fifth Army was menaced by the German flood through Belgium but still poised for the assault on the Rhine, repeatedly warned Joffre of the peril, and on August 14 both he and General Joseph Simon Gallieni, from Paris, went to Joffre and told him what was happening, but he refused to believe them until mounting evidence compelled him, late on August 15, to order Lanrezac to change direction, though stretching his forces thin by retaining some of them pointed toward the cherished offensive. At the same time Joffre took two divisions that Lanrezac had trained and sent him two new ones, aggravating his despair. Joffre sent some Territorials into the big gap, but would still not "substract a single division" from his planned offensive.[4]

Meanwhile the British Expeditionary Force had landed in France and from that moment its commander, the pugnacious Sir John French, experienced "a draining away of the will to fight." Tuchman gives half a dozen possible reasons for this change, none of which prevented his French allies from being "variously disappointed, startled or outraged" by his attitudes.

[3] Tuchman, *The Guns of August,* pp. 177–83.
[4] Tuchman, pp. 206–12.

On August 18 while Albert was deciding to move his government and his five divisions into the Antwerp fortress, Joffre was issuing his Order 13, the signal for the great offensive in the center. In it he issued an "impossible instruction" to Lanrezac to face both ways. The latter was no longer a "lion," but von Kluck still was, and to tame him he was put under Bülow's orders, which he disputed daily until Moltke relented ten days later.

GERMAN ATROCITIES   Meanwhile a remarkable group of American newsmen reported daily the savagery of the Germans in Belgium. The invaders had come armed with printed proclamations decreeing death for various offenses and mass executions began promptly, villages being destroyed in exasperation and executions ordered on the principle of collective responsibility, expressly outlawed by the Hague Convention. In France also the Germans engaged in "a frenzy of looting, shooting and burning."[5] They began at once to shoot priests, on the theory that they would organize resistance. They were infuriated by the "futile and senseless" resistance of the Belgian Army and their advance was "sullied by orgiastic frightfulness, a pagan saturnalia of burning and killing," which even Moltke thought "certainly brutal."[6]

PLAN 17 EXECUTED   Finally, on August 20, after two German armies had attacked with great force in the center, Joffre released the order to attack there and at Morhange. French *élan* and *cran* hurled waves of red trousered men into the mouths of German cannon until the earth was deeply covered with corpses. Foch, the spiritual father of Plan 17, was there to see how it worked out. Nevertheless, the attack in the difficult

[5] Tuchman, pp. 226–27, 232.

[6] This is the verdict of *The American Heritage History of World War I*, New York, 1964, p. 44. This excellent history of the war by the Editors of *American Heritage* is narrated by Brig. Gen. S. L. A. Marshall, USAR (Ret.).

The Allies soon came to call the Germans "the Huns," but it was the Kaiser who had invented the appellation.—Mansergh, *The Coming of the First World War*, New York, 1949, p. 55.

Ardennes Forest went on under the delusion that the huge German right wing could be lopped off there. When bad news came from the West Joffre simply refused to believe it and the attack continued until all French armies were defeated.[7]

On August 23, Lanrezac decided to retreat instead of counter-attacking and, according to one British source, prevented a decisive Allied defeat, but by this time he was not notifying Sir John French of his movements. French was intent on taking the BEF, thousands of whom had died nobly, out of the war, but was stopped by Kitchener at a meeting in Paris.[8] The great sweep of the German right wing "that Kitchener had eternally talked of," and that Joffre had refused to believe in, was developing, with thirty-eight German divisions enjoying a preponderance of nearly 2 to 1 over the various forces in front of them.[9]

Plan 17 had been put to a full test and it had failed, but Joffre never admitted the failure. Instead, he made a scapegoat of Lanrezac, though he had ratified his retreat by his silence, and lectured the Army on the technical deficiencies which had contributed to its collapse. The authors and executors of the great offensive crusade which had nearly caused the destruction of France could not admit that they had been wrong both in theory and practice.

SCHLIEFFEN PLAN ALTERED On the German side, where the Plan now promised to succeed, Moltke decided on August 25, at the urging of the Kaiser, to send two corps from his armies in France against the Russian invaders of Prussia, and on August 31 he made his crucial error. At the urging of Bülow, concurred in by von Kluck for his own reasons, he assented to their armies wheeling *inside* of Paris, instead of around it, in hot pursuit of the French armies, still intent on enveloping them.[10]

[7] Tuchman, pp. 229–45.
[8] *American Heritage History*, p. 51; Tuchman, pp. 360, 391–94.
[9] Tuchman, p 245.
[10] *American Heritage History*, p. 51.

The change of direction put Paris on the flank of von Kluck's army, but this was disregarded, Kluck expecting to return to pick up the city after the victory. However, the Military Governor of Paris, General Gallieni, a man who had recently outranked Joffre, urged a flank attack, using the Sixth Army in Paris plus the arriving 7th Division, and after many hours he received permission. Using several hundred wheezing Paris taxis to carry the Seventh to the front during the night of September 5, he unhinged Kluck's army and started the great German retreat from the Marne.

During their own retreat the French had been preparing well to make a stand, probably behind the Seine, but they seized the opportunity and made it on the Marne. Their artillery was cleverly placed and fully supplied. Telephone lines were everywhere, tools and weapons properly distributed, machine gunners and infantry in place—all creating a storm of fire, dust and smoke which made a real no-man's land.[11] Behind it all Joffre remained imperturbable. He weighed the main decisions for many hours, even days, sometimes sitting in silence but often traveling long distances by automobile, in spite of his bulk, to see for himself and talk with his commanders.

He was ruthless in replacing them. "He conceived the whole duty of generals to be lions in action and dogs in obedience."[12] In some parts of the Army he removed more than half of the officers for failure in battle, installing younger more militant men. By contrast the British government could not bring itself to remove Sir John French until December 1915.

On the German side Moltke stayed throughout in his headquarters, finally advanced into Luxemburg, the victim at times of "indescribable pain," and nearly always of faulty communications. This was partly because his armies were advancing through hostile people who cut the wires and jammed his radio, but also from lack of communications planning. At the

[11] Bircher and Clam, *War without Mercy*, Zurich, 1940, pp. 88–95.
[12] Tuchman, p. 209.

top of the Marne battle Moltke hardly knew where some of his armies were and he sent an officer with plenary verbal powers to straighten things out, a move which resulted in the order to retreat.

After his armies had fallen back to the general line of the Aisne, both sides began the famous "race to the sea," trying to outflank each other until they reached the North Sea near Ypres in Belgium, while both sides entrenched from Switzerland to the ocean, in that "gangrenous wound," that "brutal, mud-filled, murderous insanity known as the Western Front."[13]

BREAKDOWN OF CIVILIZATION The period of open warfare had been an indescribable ordeal for many millions. On both sides men marched for many days, overtaxing all human endurance, living on uncooked food, falling totally exhausted into the ditches, and the horses suffered no less, but always the march or the battle had to be renewed. The white dust of the roads covered them deeply, as it did the interminable lines of fleeing refugees, carrying babies and pitiful possessions in the grueling August heat, dumbly seeking to get to some kind of safety. Streets and roads were littered with abandoned packs and bloodstained bandages and, wrote a leading American observer in Belgium, "over all lay a smell which I have never heard mentioned in any book of war—the smell of half a million unbathed men. . . . It lay for days on every town through which the Germans passed."[14] Tuchman adds that "mingled with it was the smell of blood and medicine and horse manure and dead bodies."

Thinking over all these things, what is to be said of the sanity, the maturity, or the barbarism of the leaders of civilization in the early twentieth century? But can it truly be called civilization, this welter of incompetence at the top of governments, this military anarchy, this obscene squandering of life and wealth?

[13] Tuchman, p. 438.
[14] Ibid., p. 259.

Was it not likely a ghastly prelude to man's destruction of the human race on this planet?

On both sides a great gamble on a swift knockout had failed in the summer of 1914, but the German failure was the more serious.

THE RUSSIAN THRUST AGAINST EAST PRUSSIA DEFLECTED How- ever, German spirits were soon revived by the victories of another agèd and massive soldier. Moltke was succeeded by General Erich von Falkenhayn as commander in chief of the German armies on September 14. A week later Prittwitz, German commander in East Prussia, revealed his panic on hearing that the Russians under Samsonov had crossed the frontier in his rear while he was heavily engaged with Rennenkampf's army in front, and was displaced by a retired General Paul von Hindenburg, who ate and slept with great regularity during the succeeding campaign while his brilliant chief of staff, Gen- eral Erich Ludendorff, defeated the Russian armies in turn. Just as the "miracle of the Marne" had made Papa Joffre a legendary hero, now Hindenburg, the victor of Tannenberg, became the idol of the German people.

Tremendous battles ensued in Poland culminating in the battle of Lodz during November 1914, a struggle in which the Grand Duke Nicholas showed bold strategic initiative, but which was weakened by the Russian habit of broadcasting orders and plans to each other by radio, first entirely clear and finally in an easily decipherable code. The Russians expended their last reserves of ammunition also, using more shells in a day than were being produced in a month. Thereafter, Russian troops fought increasingly without ammunition and soon without enough rifles, while tales of their disasters spread dejection throughout Russia.[15]

AUSTRIAN REVERSES Yet in the South the Russians had mo- mentarily satiated Conrad von Hötzendorf's perennial desire

[15] C. R. M. F. Cruttwell, A History of the Great War, 1914–1918, Oxford, 1936, pp. 48–54.

for war. He had sent his armies promptly into Russian Poland, instead of standing on the San River and abandoning Eastern Galicia, partly for political reasons, to impress Rumania and Turkey. His strategic concepts were good, but his resources inadequate. His Poles were mostly loyal, but the Czechs and Slovaks deserted in large numbers, along with many South Slavs. His armies were psychologically beaten before the battles started and soon found themselves well behind the San. Lemberg, a great communications center, was surrendered on September 3. Some 350,000 men had been lost and appeals had to be made to Germany for help. A bitter winter campaign by the Austro-German forces failed to relieve the 150,000 men left in the fortress of Przemysl, which fell on March 22, 1915.

In the South Conrad's punitive expedition against Serbia fared no better. This invasion which the Archduke Francis Ferdinand had been rehearsing when he was shot at Sarajevo was carried out, but the Serbs won the first battle of the Great War in the third week of August 1914. The Austro-Hungarians had to retire with a loss of 40,000 men and much stores. A second invasion did take Belgrade on December 2, but since the Russians were pushing through the Carpathians, troops had to be detached and the Serbs again freed their soil of invaders, though not for long.[16]

TURKEY IN THE CENTRAL POWERS CAMP   In the Balkans the Allies were outmaneuvered both diplomatically and militarily. For several weeks they played a comic game with the Germanophile Turkish dictators, Enver Bey and Talaat Pasha. After having signed a treaty of alliance with Germany on August 2, 1914, they toyed with the Allied diplomats for ten weeks, pretending to purchase the German warships *Goeben* and *Breslau* which dominated Constantinople, while they pushed mobilization and their defenses. Late in September they closed and mined the Dardanelles, thus cutting off the munitions-starved

[16] William L. McPherson, *A Short History of the Great War*, New York, 1920, pp. 60–62. The cost in dead was 100,000 on each side.

Russians from their industrialized allies. At last, on October 28, the two German warships shelled Odessa, sinking Russian, British and French ships, with Turkish apologies, but the Allies at last lost confidence in Turkish protestations and declared war.

1915—Year of Teutonic Successes

The Holy War which the Sheik-ul-Islam proclaimed had no effect outside of Turkey proper, but Turkey's participation threatened the Suez Canal and Britain's South Persian oil fields. It necessitated a Russian campaign to drive the Turks back from the Kars-Batum region, which they did January 2, 1915, inflicting heavy losses on the Turks. Most important of all was the closure of the Straits. This one blow could decide the entire war, since Russia was woefully unable to supply her vast armies. To keep them in the field supplies would have to come in from her allies and from the neutrals, yet the Baltic was closed by the German Navy, icebound Archangel on the Arctic Ocean was far away and Vladivostok was 5000 miles from the fronts. Only the Black Sea could serve as an artery to keep Russia's war effort alive.

THE GALLIPOLI CAMPAIGN Seizure of the Straits by the Allies would, moreover, most probably bring in all the Balkan states on the Allied side, make Turkey's part in the war harmless and enable the Central Powers to be attacked from the rear. Since it offered an escape from the trench war impasse on the Western Front the British Cabinet assented on January 2, 1915, to a Russian request for the opening of the Straits, but could not decide whether troops were available for a joint land-sea assault. The attack was accordingly begun by a great Allied fleet led by eighteen pre-dreadnought battleships which were too slow for use elsewhere. Bombardments from February 19 to March 7 reduced the outer forts while some land forces under General Ian Hamilton assembled nearby. The transports, however, were not loaded for quick unloading and Hamilton sent them to Alexandria for reloading, probably a fatal decision. Admiral de Robeck then decided to go it alone and attacked in force on March 18, losing four battleships late in the day. At first he was ready to proceed again, but desisted after a conference with Hamilton, when the Turkish artillery ammunition was nearly exhausted.[17]

On April 25 landings were made on the tip of the Gallipoli peninsula, but trench warfare soon ensued. A landing further north at Suvla Bay by the British, on August 6, was handicapped by antiquated generals and the accident of Allied shells which fell short and drove back the invaders after they had passed the crest of the hills.[18] Thereafter stalemate again ensued and the expedition was withdrawn at the end of 1915. The British casualties had been 112,000, not counting 100,000 men who had been out of action because of sickness. A total of 750,000 Allied fighting men had been engaged.

The Straits remained closed, the Russian giant fought increasingly with bare hands and Allied diplomacy in the Balkans collapsed.

ITALY JOINS THE ALLIES   Earlier in 1915 Italy had entered the war against the Central Powers, after bargaining long with both sides. Under prodding from Germany, Austria gradually increased her offers until they were quite substantial. At different

[17] Admiral Lord Fisher had first conceived the idea of a naval thrust through the Dardanelles, but he went cold on it and Churchill, the Navy Minister, became its advocate. Admiral Carden, on the spot, at first approved the assault but before it began he "fell apart, physically whipped, nervously exhausted by the strain of the undertaking." When it was decided to send land forces, General Sir Ian Hamilton, an introspective man, was sent to command them without instructions. His own planning revealed "throughout an amazing ignorance of, or indifference to, major factors that should regulate operations." He attempted what an earlier General Staff study had declared to be impossible and dissuaded Admiral de Robeck from renewing his attack at the critical moment.—*American Heritage History*, pp. 83–86.

[18] Cruttwell, p. 223.

times both sides agreed to make Trieste a free city, but Italy wanted the whole of the Trentino, Istria and much of Dalmatia, besides a share of Turkey. The Dardanelles campaign led her to believe that the partition of Turkey was imminent.

Finally the offers of the Entente were accepted, including a part of Turkey, a share of the German colonies and of the expected war indemnity. By the Treaty of London, signed April 26, 1915, Italy was also to receive a loan of $250,000,000 from Britain and the Vatican was to be excluded from the peace making. Trieste was to be Italian, but not Fiume. The grant of parts of Dalmatia greatly angered the Serbs. Six days later the big German-Austrian breakthrough at Gorlice, partly staged for Italy's benefit, inaugurated the great Russian retreats of 1915. In mid-May Austria made her maximum offer to Italy, guaranteed by Germany and the territories to be handed over within one month.

This double turn of affairs led Giovanni Giolitti, long the leading Italian politician, to declare for neutrality, backed by a majority of the Chamber of Deputies. Popular demonstrations by interventionists all over Italy broke the deadlock and the Chamber voted confidence in the ministry on May 20, 407 to 72. War was declared against Austria on May 25, but not against Germany until August 27, 1916, a state of affairs which helped to confuse and lower Italian morale.

Italian hopes of a short war with heavy gains were doomed within a few weeks. Italian troops fought splendidly throughout 1915, but everywhere they faced the enemy sitting high up in a great mountain rim around their plains. Even the Slavic parts of the Hapsburg Empire were willing to fight against the Italians, but geography was a much worse obstacle than the Austrian armies. Hard fighting only served to pile up 250,000 Italian casualties during 1915.

BULGARIA ON THE GERMAN SIDE   In the Balkans, Entente diplomacy lost all of its objectives. Greece was pro-Ally, but was restrained by her Hohenzollern King Constantine, and the sympathetic Premier Eleutherios Venizelos was rebuffed by Russia's refusal to consent when he offered three divisions to aid in the Gallipoli campaign. Rumania was on the brink of joining the Allies when their military reverses began. Bulgaria was offered parts of Serbian Macedonia and Venizelos was willing to concede her an Aegean littoral. Like the Turks the wily King Ferdinand of Bulgaria played with both sides until the end. Turkish concessions to Bulgaria on the Aegean were published on September 21, 1915, and Bulgarian mobilization was ordered. To soothe the Allied diplomats it was announced on the 24th that the mobilization was simply intended to maintain Bulgaria's neutrality. When it became imminent the Serbs begged for permission to strike at once, a move which would at least have enabled them to evacuate their armies down the valley of the Vardar to Salonika, but the Allied diplomats, still deluded by the Bulgars, forbade it.

SERBIA CRUSHED   Eventually they discovered the true situation and broke relations with Bulgaria on October 4, 1915, war being declared on the 13th, several days after hostilities had begun. The crucifixion of Serbia which followed was ruthless enough. German and Austrian forces nearly 400,000 strong attacked from the North and an equal number of Bulgarians from the East. The Serbs, numbering no more than 250,000 fought furiously, but were driven across the Albanian mountains to the sea, the Albanian tribesmen taking their toll along with mud, snow and exhaustion. Hardly a hundred thousand Serbs reached the Albanian coast, to be removed eventually to the Island of Corfu where they were revived and later played a part in the last stages of the war from Salonika. One sixth of the Serbian people lost their lives during this catastrophe.

Belatedly recognizing its imminence the Allies had decided on September 25 to send an army to Salonika, but too few troops arrived to matter and Salonika remained a fortified camp until near the end of the war, when its army of 750,000 men issued forth and compelled Bulgaria to be the first of the Central Powers to surrender.

In 1915 Bulgaria received at once the ample spoils promised her and proclaimed the abolition of the Kingdom of Serbia. The Teutonic Powers profited even more, now having firm land communication with their Turkish ally and high hopes of one day using the Baghdad Railway to extend their great self sufficient Middle-European empire to the Persian Gulf. Rumania retired into neutrality.

AUSTRIA RELIEVED   Political considerations dictated an Austro-German offensive against Russia in the spring of 1915. The "twin Generals," Hindenburg and Ludendorff, were strongly demanding it. Bitter winter fighting in the north had not availed the Germans much, while in the south the Russian conquest of most of Galicia enabled them to take a few of the passes in the Carpathians and threaten to erupt into Hungary. Should they do so Italy would surely strike and Bulgaria might not join the German side, while Rumania probably would help the Entente. The effect of such developments on both Turkey and Austria-Hungary might well be decisive.

For these reasons Falkenhayn reluctantly gave up his desire for a smashing blow on the Western front and turned to the East. However, he resolutely opposed the Hindenburg-Ludendorff team's desire, which Conrad shared, for a great *Cannae* in which two giant pincers would start 600 miles apart and encircle all the Russian armies. Falkenhayn resisted any such stupendous commitment of his forces in space and time and was supported by the Kaiser. Instead, a limited breakthrough in Galicia was planned and brilliantly carried out on the Dunejac at Gorlice. Eight German divisions were moved from the Western front through Germany in April, without the Russians knowing it. Some 700 guns were concentrated on a narrow front, though only one to fifty-seven yards, and on May 2 the shell shocked Russians surrendered in droves. They had only one shallow line of trenches, with two unfortified river lines in their rear, while August von Mackensen, the able, tactical German general who opposed them, had worked out an elastic but deep scheme of attack which carried all before it. By this time the Russians were pitiably armed. A third of their 6,000,000 troops had no arms. Battery commanders were threatened with court-martial if they used more than three shells a day and they had no guns larger than six inch caliber. Boys were sent to the front with only four weeks of training, usually without having handled a rifle, and the Germans captured them armed with oak clubs.[19]

After the breakthrough at Gorlice, Galicia was rapidly cleared, the Russians scurrying down out of the Carpathians and retreating also in the north, where Warsaw was taken on August 4 and Brest Litovsk soon afterward. Falkenhayn then resolutely called a halt, ordered his troops to dig in and prepare winter quarters, though Hindenburg insisted on a further thrust in the north which gained no strategic objective. Falkenhayn had a feeling for the vast spaces of Russia which would have served Hitler well at a later time. In September 1915, after their great retreat, the Russians still held a continuous line 800 miles long. They had lost nearly 2,000,000 men, three-fourths of them sturdy prisoners who would do much needed labor for the enemy.

These sacrifices led the deluded Tsar to listen to the Tsarina, who was jealous of the Grand Duke Nicholas, and to proceed to take over the supreme command of the Russian armies himself. Thus a weak man devoid of military ability replaced a commander who had demonstrated both real strategical ability and iron determination. The Grand Duke's hatred of the evil monk Rasputin who dominated the Tsarina had undone him, but after this stroke even the Russian nobility detested the court.

The Russian threat to Austria removed, Falkenhayn sent a division of German troops to the extreme tip of Hungary, just before the entry of Bulgaria, and shipped heavy forces south under Mackensen for the destruction of Serbia.

[19] Cruttwell, pp. 171, 179.

"NIBBLING" IN THE WEST   While these events transpired in the East the war in the West was deadlocked in the trenches. From Switzerland to the North Sea continuous lines of trenches faced each other, often only thirty yards apart. In them crouched great armies of men, often standing in water, through cold and rain, snow and heat. Many dugouts sheltered some of them. These became deeper and larger as the war lengthened, the better to accommodate, it sometimes seemed, the rats and vermin which loved to live with the troops.

This kind of fighting bore no relation to the sweeping victories the armies of all nations had rushed to win in August 1914. The glamour and the glory had all departed, except for the generals who still hoped to execute the great breakthrough. Gloom and misery settled upon the peoples, months of interminable waiting for the fateful telegram at the door, months of dwindling rations and comforts which were also filled with a constantly increasing necessity to produce more and more ammunition.

The fire power of the machine guns, especially on the German side, had driven the troops underground. There they had to remain until the artillery could really destroy the enemy lines. This meant heavy artillery, of which the Allies had little, and ever higher mountains of shells to feed them. And when the guns could thunder for hours it was discovered that the enemy had constructed second and third lines and made his defenses so deep that the elusive breakthrough did not occur even after the awesome bombardments. Elastic zones featured by concrete "pill boxes" still held, until the tank was finally developed to break the stalemate—late in the war.

The war in the West during 1915 is a melancholy tale of a dozen battles, almost all waged by the Allies. Acknowledging the deadlock, Joffre said "but I nibble at them" and the word stuck as descriptive of the year's fighting. Five of these expensive and fruitless French nibbles took place before the British effort at Neuve Chappelle, near Lille, in early March bogged down with a loss of 13,000 men. Like the good cavalry-man that he was General Sir Douglas Haig had his horse brigades assembled to operate in the open country when the lines should be breached, as he often did afterward.

In mid-April the Germans prepared the way for a poison gas attack near Ypres in Belgium. Their first experiment against the Russians in January had not been reported, perhaps not recognized as such. On April 14, 1915, a captured German told about the big cylinders being assembled and he actually had a gas mask on him. On the 17th a false German accusation that the British had been using asphyxiating gas in shells was an equally plain warning. Yet the attack on April 22 was a complete surprise. Men fled in panic from the greenish cloud which deprived them of all chance to live and breathe. Nevertheless, the breach was closed. The Germans had no plans for exploiting it and the chemical resources of the world were now mobilized against them, but not before the Second Battle of Ypres had cost the Allies 70,000 casualties to 35,000 for the Germans.

A combined British-French attack in Artois on May 9 was similarly punishing to the British, whose artillery barrage was so inadequate that their waves of advancing men were mowed down. The French had been able to throw 700,000 high explosive shells, mainly from heavy guns, and their infantry really walked through in the center, but the breach was too narrow and the hole was corked. Piecemeal struggles continued until the end of March before the French desisted, with nearly 400,000 casualties.

These wounds, coupled with the fall of the Asquith Cabinet in Britain on account of the shortage of shells, might have led the Allies to adopt the German policy of standing on the defensive, or at least one of constant feints with artillery and gas, but the woes of the Russians coinciding with Italy's entry argued for further attacks. Nearly all the generals also succumbed ultimately to the fascination of the wall of mud and

men, of concrete, gas and fire, and to the determination to win
world fame by smashing through it. A plan for a grand battle
in Champagne was matured for September 25. Again the barrage
was unprecedented, 2500 guns, including 900 heavies. Joffre
was so confident that he had ten divisions of cavalry ready to
exploit the rout which never came. The news of 25,000 prisoners
and 150 guns captured was trumpeted, but the French losses
of 145,000 men were rigorously kept secret. On the British end
the battle was so mismanaged by General French that he was
removed after its close and Haig succeeded him as British
Commander-in-Chief. Like other generals on both sides, French
lacked the will to stop the battle once his attack had failed.
Haig, in his turn, "gradually acquired an almost Cromwellian
conviction that God had marked him out as an instrument for
the triumph of the Allies."[20]

1916—Attrition War

The year 1915 was one long disaster for the Allies. Even local
successes had been denied them. Yet no Allied government
showed any signs of making peace. Germany, on the other hand,
after being magnificently organized to resist the blockade by
Walther Rathenau, a Jew who proved himself to be one of the
great men of the war,[21] was still constricted economically while
her adversaries drew upon the great resources of the world,
especially those of the United States. The growing strength of the
Allies would surely mean a great offensive in the West in 1916.
Should the Germans remain on the defensive and wait for
disintegration and revolution to complete its work in Russia?
Falkenhayn devised a compromise.

VERDUN Falkenhayn had a plan. Believing that Germany

[20] Cruttwell, p. 169.
[21] Chambers, Grand and Bailey, *This Age of Conflict,* New York, 1943,
p. 49.

would lose a long war for lack of manpower reserves, he planned to bleed France to death at Verdun, a place she would be sure to defend for sentimental reasons. Not wishing to take the divided and almost undefended salient quickly, he deceived the Crown Prince, whose armies were to be used, and his commanders, rejecting attack on a 30-mile front that would have given early victory and confining his assault to a narrow 6-mile front. He deliberately denied the attackers the reserves they needed to take Verdun, and doled them into the battle to keep it going, depending on a tremendous mass and variety of artillery to keep German losses down.

Thus, says General Marshall, he staged "the greatest battle in world history" in the dead of winter, ignoring the great lessons he had learned in the two Ypres battles, in the hope of waging a battle so terrible in its dimensions that it would put the French out of the war and force the Allies to make a tolerable peace with Germany.[22]

Falkenhayn was right in believing that France would defend Verdun to the death. They built an automobile road in the salient and poured men and supplies in by truck to the front where Falkenhayn's big guns always left more men alive than he had thought possible. The assault began on February 21, 1916, and the German mincing machine drew in the legions of France for five months, but the fighting degenerated into the rawest man to man struggles in the steep hills and ravines of the region. At one time the Germans captured two of the great concrete forts, Douaumont and Vaux, only to lose them again. When the ordeal was over France had suffered 535,000 casualties, but the German list was 427,000. Afterward the French gathered up the bones of 80,000 men and built a great ossuary over them. Verdun had been held and Germany had suffered the moral defeat. Falkenhayn's removal as German generalissimo soon followed. Ludendorff succeeded him.

On the French side the great slaughter produced a galaxy of

new heroes led by General Henri Pétain, who in his prime was a tower of strength, and including General Robert Nivelle, the star of the tragedy. It was high tragedy for France because the Verdun salient could have been evacuated and its base defended readily, without any serious military consequences.

AUSTRIAN DEFEATS　Falkenhayn had been cool to Conrad's desire to demolish his most hated enemy, the Italians, and the latter had attempted the feat alone, refusing to content himself with holding the newly won fronts against Russia. The result was defeat for Austria in her Italian campaign of May 1916. Then on June 4 the Russian General Aleksei Brusilov made a feint toward Galicia, intended to relieve his French and Italian allies, and the Austrian front "broke like a pie crust" along a front of 200 miles. The Austrian troops of Slavic blood surrendered in large bodies until by mid-August Austria-Hungary had lost 1,500,000 men, at least 500,000 more than the Russians.

RUMANIA CONQUERED　This disaster at last brought in the Rumanians on the side of the Allies, August 17, 1916. They grasped for the coveted Transylvania, in Western Hungary, leaving their rear open to Bulgarian attack which came speedily while Austro-German forces under Mackensen crossed the Carpathians and completed the conquest of Southern Rumania by December.

BATTLE OF THE SOMME　Before Verdun absorbed most of the French Army a great Anglo-French offensive had been planned for July 1, with forty French and twenty-five British divisions participating. Like Falkenhayn, Joffre conceived of it as a grinding operation. Verdun greatly reduced the French participation, but the Battle of the Somme began nevertheless, in a region of chalk soil which had been indefatigably honeycombed by an immense labyrinth of German dugouts too deep to be disturbed by the heaviest bombardment from the 850 heavy guns disposed by the French and the 460 British heavies.

The preliminary bombardment alone used up 1,738,000 shells, lasting eight days. Then the new British citizen army advanced confidently, each man carrying 220 rounds of ammunition, two bombs and two sandbags, not to mention picks, shovels, telephone apparatus and carrier pigeons, a basic weight of 66 pounds per man. The columns lumbered ahead until by nightfall 60,000 men, or 40 percent of those engaged, had been mowed down by the German machine guns, probably the highest proportionate losses in any recorded battle. The Delville Wood devoured six divisions. The cavalry, once again assembled in the rear, did get one brief moment of activity when a night attack got through and the cavalry cut down fugitive Germans for a few hours, but counterattacks soon closed the breach.

So the battle went until September 15, when a strange new weapon was first used. Adapted from the American caterpillar tractor it had first been developed illegally by the British Admiralty under Churchill, after the Army had scorned the idea. It was called a "tank," to disguise it from enemy spies and because it was hoped it looked that way from the air. The first fifty tanks used in the battle of the Somme did not achieve the terror that the regimented Allied correspondents portrayed. Indeed, most of them broke down or failed to negotiate the great shell holes, but some had a field day and the way to end trench warfare was indicated.

Ten days later another broad attack by seven infantry divisions almost bit through the German fortified zone. German troops had had to be sent to the East and only five divisions remained in reserve, the lowest point of the war until its close. This was the situation which confronted Hindenburg and Ludendorff when Falkenhayn was dismissed. Despondency was general, but Ludendorff's supreme gifts as an organizer were put to good use and in August "General Mud" came to his aid. First the rains and then winter closed down the second great battle of attrition in 1916, one which wore down the German Army as Verdun had the French. The British casualties totalled 400,000 men, the French 200,000 and the Germans 500,000, but the wastage on the German side was increasing when the battle ended—a sign of declining morale which was supported by the first steady trickle of deserters. Worst of all, the lost German NCOs could never be replaced. Nor could the dwindling diet of the troops be improved.

1917—Year of Deepening Agony

UNRESTRICTED SUBMARINE WAR   The failure to gain a decision on land in 1916 led the German High Command to demand the unrestricted use of submarines to blockade Britain and put Germany's main enemy out of the war. Falkenhayn had strongly hinted at this course in his time. Now Hindenburg and Ludendorff demanded it, arguing that the Americans could not be more dangerous as a belligerent than as the uninterrupted supplier of the Allies, and the decision which brought the United States into the war was made on January 9, 1917.

Unrestricted U-boat warfare began on February 1. During the first week thirty-five ships were sunk in the English Channel and in the first three months 470 British ships were destroyed. The tonnage destroyed in February was 532,000 tons; in March 599,000 tons; in April 869,000 tons. Only 868,000 tons had been lost in the year 1915, and 1,236,000 tons in 1916. The threat to Britain was grave indeed, yet all the orthodox methods of naval warfare did little good, until convoys were instituted.[23]

For long the Admiralty resisted the new device with a half dozen good objections, but when in May 1917 the system was tried it proved to be one of the greatest inventions of the war. The convoy itself was a strong combat force; it was manageable and defensible. Losses dropped very rapidly and the huge

[23] Chambers, Grant and Bailey, *This Age of Conflict*, p. 77. Allied and neutral merchant ship losses during the war totalled 12,850,000 tons, 11,153,000 tons by submarines.—Hanson W. Baldwin, *World War I*, New York, 1962, p. 156.

American armies, with their supplies, were ferried over with microscopic losses.

NIVELLE'S CREEPING BARRAGE   In the West a new military star arose. During the last stages of the Verdun tragedy General Nivelle had devised the idea of a creeping barrage behind which the infantry would time its advance to the minute. At Verdun it worked, with a great saving of lives. Joffre was retired and Nivelle was made Commander-in-Chief of the French armies. He set out to win the war by applying the new idea on a broad front.

Nivelle had all the necessary qualities for persuading the governments to let him try where others had failed. He was "an outgoing man, affable, smiling, ever ready to discuss his operations." He "radiated power, wisdom and confidence." But he was also "given to towering rages and preoccupation with trifles" and he was under the influence of a subordinate who was dying of tuberculosis and was determined to win the war before he died. Nivelle mesmerized Prime Minister Lloyd George and became the toast of the town on a visit to London, where he distributed ten copies of his battle plan. Two copies were captured by the Germans in France.

Taking over a plan already in process for pinching off a big bulge in the Somme area, he declared that "victory is certain." Essentially the plan was like the others that had failed so dismally, and before it could be applied the Germans pulled the rug from under it by evacuating the entire bulge, 65 miles long and 25 miles wide, as the French should have done at Verdun. But in the process they did a fiendish thing. They vandalized the entire area, destroying the homes of 200,000 people, forests, orchards and every kind of communication. Even wells and reservoirs were poisoned.

This complete change of battle conditions made no difference to Nivelle. When Pétain objected, Nivelle was "livid" and the politicians smoothed his feathers, clearing the right of way for a new carnival of slaughter.

It began on April 16, eleven days after the devastating evacuation was completed. There was no longer any salient to pinch off, but Nivelle went ahead anyway pledging that if forty-eight hours proved the futility of his assault he would desist. But he persisted another ten days and France lost another 187,000 men. Some 11,020,000 shells had been fired, but over too many days and too much territory. The "creeping barrage" led only to slaughter. Nivelle then tried to blame others for the debacle before he was sent away to North Africa.[24]

FRENCH MORALE EXHAUSTED   Then the French Army revolted at the hopelessness of the carnage and the collapse might have put France out of the war. The evidence of failure, vacillation and incompetence in the command brought all the grievances of the *poilus* to a head. The wildest rumors of fighting in Paris spread. Some regiments tried to march on the capital and only a few loyal troops were available. By May 20 mutiny was widespread in the four armies which were on the offensive. Naturally, all attack stopped. Nivelle was replaced on May 15th by Pétain, who went among the troops everywhere, executing a few but redressing grievances and improving the soldiers' lot. He talked with the men of ninety divisions in one month. By late summer morale had greatly improved and two local operations were successfully executed in the autumn, both carefully planned to exclude any large casualties.

PASSCHENDAELE   The main brunt of the war during 1917 fell on the British. They now had ready in the field the great army which Lord Kitchener had created and expanded by volunteer methods from six divisions to seventy within twenty-two months, before his death on June 5, 1916. He was the one leader in any belligerent nation who from the start had planned for a three year war. Now in the third year Sir Douglas Haig aspired

---

[24] *American Heritage History*, pp. 207–11. Before the Nivelle offensive the Canadians took Vimy Ridge, the strongest position in Northern France, on April 9, 1917. Three thousand guns were used. Casualties exceeded 100,000 men.

to use Kitchener's great weapon to break through and win the war single handed, before the Americans arrived.[25]

On June 7, General Herbert Plumer exploded nineteen huge mines which had long been in place under Messines Ridge. The entire top of the ridge went skyward and with it six divisions of German troops. The ridge was occupied, and some additional ground. The attack was broken off when it exhausted its impetus seven days later.

By this time no reason for a "now or never" offensive remained. The submarine menace was met, French recovery was progressing and Russian disintegration was hopeless. Nevertheless Haig insisted on the Passchendaele offensive. He had explained on May 1 and 2 that his plan was to wear the enemy out by capturing ground through successive artillery barrages until finally "a moment will come when our advanced guards and cavalry will be able to progress for much longer distances until a real decision is reached."[26]

In his eagerness to gain the consent of a very reluctant Cabinet, Haig did not tell them: (1) that his engineers had warned that the chosen battlefield was a reclaimed marshland which would revert to a swamp if bombardment destroyed the drainage system; and (2) that his meteorological experts had warned that "in Flanders the weather broke early each August with the regularity of the Indian monsoon." Instead, Haig stressed the exhaustion of the German reserves which had already taken place and gave a definite assurance that he had no intention of entering into a tremendous offensive involving heavy losses.[27] In this fashion he overcame the deep reluctance and foreboding with which Lloyd George finally sanctioned the campaign.

Haig's vast preparations on the flat Flemish plain were spread

[25] B. H. Liddell Hert, *Why Don't We Learn From History?* London, 1944, pp. 13–14.

[26] Duff Cooper, *Haig*, London, 1935, Vol. II, pp. 102–3.

[27] Liddell Hart, *Through the Fog of War*, New York, 1938, pp. 335–36.

out on an open map upon which enemy bombers did heavy execution. On July 31 the great attack began. The next day the rains came and the guns bogged down, wheel to wheel, beneath the German airmen. In front, the guns at once created an "irremediable slough," except for the strong German pill boxes on the higher points. For the next hundred days Haig's men were thrown into this morass over which progress was impossible except along duckboards swept by German guns. Guns and tanks were engulfed and drowning was an ever present fate. The misery of life and death in the rain and mud made an unforgettable impression on the British people, one which partly accounted for the appeasement mentality when Hitler took the war path, and for British reluctance to open a second front on the Continent during World War II. After 1917 the Germans also regarded it as the culmination of horror, but they also made plans to avoid any such slimy fighting again.

The Passchendaele struggle went on until another 300,000 men had been sacrificed on each side. When the losses mounted and Premier Lloyd George came over to see what could be done about it, Haig told him that the poor physique of the captured Germans proved that the enemy was being exhausted, and he had the able bodied Germans removed from the prisoner cages before the Premier could get there to see them.[28] Finally, in November, the village of Passchendaele on one end of the coveted ridge was taken and the battle ended. Strategically nothing whatever had been gained and the next April all gains made had to be quickly evacuated.

A few days later the British made the first big tank attack at Cambrai, using 381 machines. The tanks surprised the Germans and put them to flight, but the infantry which might have exploited the break impressively had been lost in the Passchendaele mud.

CAPORETTO Meanwhile disaster had overtaken Italy. For two years General Luigi Cadorna had been trying to blast his way

[28] *Ibid.*, p. 356.

through the extremely formidable Isonzo river country to Trieste, which became a magnet to him as it perpetually eluded capture. He was the strong willed commander "who was to drive the Italian armies to their doom."[29] In the first two years of the war he had hurled his troops through eleven battles of the Isonzo, with nearly a million casualties, before the Austro-German offensive of October 24, 1917. In this long period no provision had been made for the comfort or entertainment of the troops. Cadorna was an autocrat and a bully who enforced the most rigid discipline through hierarchical channels. He dismissed the officers who reported growing disaffection. War weariness was rife behind the front. Socialist opposition to the war still continued. The Vatican had strong Austrian sympathies. Its peace note of August 1917 had condemned "the useless slaughter" and hinted at a compromise peace. Catholic chaplains in the Army were suspect.[30] Italy's preoccupation with Trieste had led to coolness between her and her allies and striking munition workers in Turin had been drafted as punishment and sent to the Caporetto front, where the enemy attacked.

As soon as the Germans appeared the Italians fled, drawing the reserves with them as they went, until great masses of deserters swept down the valleys, overwhelming any reinforcements and sucking an equal host of some 400,000 civilian refugees behind them. About 300,000 Italian troops had also surrendered.

To Cadorna's credit he did not lose his head and he shepherded the rout behind successive rivers until the Piave was reached, where he had earlier made effective defenses. Then a remarkable national revival occurred. Most of the men who had simply quit the war were reclaimed. Attention was at last given to their welfare, a great work of reorganization was accomplished and Italy's allies rushed to her aid with troops, relief organizations and supplies. The Allied premiers and war chiefs

[29] Baldwin, *World War I*, p. 62.
[30] Chambers, Grant and Bailey, p. 91; Cruttwell, p. 460.

met at Rapallo on November 4, 1917 and agreed upon a Supreme War Council, to sit at Versailles. This was the precursor of the final unity of command that was forced by events in 1918.

DISINTEGRATION IN AUSTRIA   On the other hand, the Austro-German victory at Caporetto could do little to revivify the rapidly decaying Hapsburg Empire. The majority of its peoples had no desire to die for it. For them the war was a dismal calamity unless it brought them a chance to win freedom. Political assassins killed the Austrian Minister-President, Karl von Stürgkh, as early as October 21, 1916. A month later the agèd Emperor Francis Joseph finally died at the age of eighty-six, snapping the last bond which was of any weight with his warring peoples. The young Emperor Charles did his best to stem the tides of disintegration. He even fired Conrad von Hötzendorf and called the long absent Reichsrat into session, only to find that it was a forum for Czech and Yugoslav demands for virtual independence. Even Austria and Hungary engaged in a bitter tariff war, while desertions of the other nationalities multiplied and embryo Czech and Yugoslav governments in Paris won Allied support for their aims.

PEACE MOVEMENTS   In March 1917 Emperor Charles opened secret negotiations with the French government through a couple of Bourbon princes, while Count Attokar Czernin, his Foreign Minister, made contact through Switzerland. But much as the Austrians wanted peace they could not get it. Even their victories over Serbia and Italy made it virtually impossible for the Allies to consider a separate peace.

Peace was in the air in 1917 in Germany also. On March 14, 1917, Chancellor Bethmann Hollweg suggested that the Prussian class voting system would have to be changed and in July the Kaiser came to the same point, just before the famous Peace Resolution came to a vote on July 19, 1917. Bethmann had resigned rather than carry out an order of the high command to block this demand of the Reichstag, passed by a vote of

212 to 126, that a peace of reconciliation with "no annexations and no indemnities" be negotiated. The new Chancellor, Georg Michaelis, promised to carry out the peace resolution "as I understand it," but Russian revolution and the wide open chance for decisive victory in the East enabled the generals to squelch the yearning for peace.

Both sides were weary and sick at heart during most of 1917. In November, Lord Lansdowne, the architect of the Entente Cordiale, urged publicly that the continuance of the war would "spell ruin for the civilized world."[31]

RUSSIA AND RUMANIA ELIMINATED   In December 1917 the new Bolshevik government of Russia signed an armistice with Germany, after two futile appeals to the Allies to accept a peace of no annexations and no indemnities, a defection which was partly balanced by the arrival of "the tiger" Clemenceau as Prime Minister of France, a flaming apostle of victory and revenge. It was President Wilson's speech of January 8, 1918, proposing his Fourteen Points, which really rallied the Allied world for the final ordeal and at the same time depressed the peoples of the Central Powers. The Germans, however, were buoyed up by the Treaties of Brest Litovsk with Russia, and of Bucharest with Rumania, both imperialistic settlements imposed on beaten foes which opened great vistas for the exploitation of vast areas in the East.

1918—The Year of Decision

These opportunities might well have led Ludendorff to decide to go on the defensive in 1918 and develop the great resources of the conquered East. All the war up to that time had proved that Germany would have been invincible had she remained on the defensive in 1914, especially in the West, even if she was

[31] R. J. Sontag, *European Diplomatic History, 1871–1932*, New York, 1933, p. 244.

determined to fight Russia. Germany's power was so immense that it could have withstood all assaults, particularly if the British blockade had been avoided. Now in early 1918 there was a new opportunity to let the very depleted Allies see what they could do in the West. Had Germany stood on the defensive, the French and British armies would hardly have accepted unified command and the Americans would have arrived more slowly. Doubtless it was too late to halt the dissolution of Austria-Hungary, but the chance of achieving a stalemate still remained. Some elements in the German General Staff argued that it was better to stand fast.[32] But Ludendorff was a gambler, and after the deceptive triumph at Caporetto he preferred to risk everything on one final throw in the West. He would be the one to break the horrible trench deadlock, now showing signs of yielding to new weapons, and achieve the decisive breakthrough. He also knew that disintegration born of hunger had begun in his forces and doubted that they had the spirit for a long defensive war.

LUDENDORFF'S GRAND OFFENSIVE   Ludendorff started with a superiority in numbers, some 3,000,000 men to 2,500,000, with half of his men in strategic reserves. He disposed of great forces but had no clear strategic plan for victory. The struggle, he said, "will begin at one point, continue at another and take a long time. It will be difficult; but it will be victorious." Probably he hoped so to batter the French and British armies as to break the war will of the peoples behind them.

The great German offensive began on March 21, 1918, practically destroying the British Fifth Army and inflicting 160,000 casualties. About 1500 square miles of territory were overrun. The British Cabinet reacted quickly with all the measures of aid at its command and on March 26, the entire Allied forces were at last placed under a supreme commander, General Foch, whose will to victory never flagged until the war was won.

The Germans used new tactics, such as organizing successive

[32] McPherson, *A Short History of the Great War*, pp. 309–10.

waves of attack and equipping small infiltration groups with all arms, even to small cannon. Their attack zones were organized to immense depth and in the four months after March 21 five great assaults carried them forward until the Marne was reached again and crossed in force on July 18.*

THE SECOND BATTLE OF THE MARNE But once more a great counter offensive had been prepared and it began on that day near Château-Thierry. As had so often happened before, some Alsatians deserted from the German army at the right moment, taking the German plans of battle to the French. Then having regained the offensive, Foch kept a many-sided advance moving with great skill for another four months, until the German armies had been hammered into a disorganized mass of several million men, still powerfully armed, still outside Germany's borders and capable of much resistance, but nevertheless defeated. Large numbers of the Germans were "spiritless, weary, middleaged men with a dull hatred of military life," while by November 2,000,000 fresh young Americans had arrived in France, at the unheard of rate of 10,000 a day.

In his final bull rushes Ludendorff had taken 225,000 prisoners, 2500 guns and had inflicted a million casualties, only to suffer in turn the loss by capture of 360,000 men, 6200 cannon and 39,000 machine guns, plus a million casualties of his own.[33]

THE COLLAPSE OF AUSTRIA While Germany was being battered into submission in the West the Austrians had tried to produce another Caporetto on the Piave in June, an offensive which broke down disastrously, and on October 24 the Italians had their revenge in the Battle of Vittorio Veneto which converted the Austrian armies into fleeing contingents of Magyars, Czechs, and South Slavs, all fighting at every rail head for the trains to take them home. The Emperor Charles tried to make peace on

---

* This was the date of the author's arrival in France as an American soldier, though he was never able to convince his students that there was a close relation between this event and the final German retreat which began that same day.

[33] *The Memoirs of Marshal Foch,* Garden City, 1931, p. 492.

September 14, and on October 16 he issued a proclamation transforming Austria-Hungary into a federal state, with full autonomy to the various nationalities—except that the Hungarians clung to all of their subject peoples. To the end they frustrated the solution which could have saved the Empire and prevented the First World War had it been applied before the crime of Sarajevo. In November 1918 the entire Empire fell apart. Even Austria disclaimed Charles and organized a republic.

The War in Retrospect

Thus ended in November 1918 the attempt to bolster the waning Hapsburg Empire by war, and to defend and extend the European hegemony of Germany while it was still valid. Nothing had gone according to plan. Immense victories had been won and vast territories gained and lost by the German champions of authority. On their side the generals had had full sway, and of them all only Falkenhayn had shown any grasp of the political realities.

On the side of the Entente the generals had also had their day, usually resenting warmly the efforts of the civilian ministers to provide them with new weapons and chafing at the efforts of the civilian heads to prevent the immense wastage of lives. Yet on the whole the Entente powers retained very considerable control of the military men and it was the despised democracies which mustered the endurance and resiliency necessary for victory. Even then they might have failed without the powerful aid of the sea blockade which wore down the Central Powers while it enabled the resources of the world to be employed by the Allies.

At length the slaughter ended, after ten million men had fallen in battle, after twice that number of civilians had died of privation and influenza, after a wealthy and prosperous continent had been reduced to a poverty that was to appear plenteous after the Second World War. In 1918 wealth to the value of nearly $400,000,000,000 had been squandered in war, because the world had no machinery capable of mediating the squabbles of the governments and dynasties—or of curbing their ambitions.

The killing of an Archduke had started it, and when the carnage was over the Hapsburg, Hohenzollern, and Romanov dynasties had all been deposed and ended. Red revolution had swept through the vast realms of the Tsar, an event which was to haunt the conservatives of all lands for many a year. Vast forces had been loosed which no man could thereafter confine.

The desolation and suffering was also so vast that it did not seem credible that another such calamity could be permitted to occur. If there was any sanity left in mankind surely men and statesmen of good will would draw together to build solid bulwarks against the return of a deluge so devastating.

THE TREATY OF VERSAILLES In total contrast to the German drive for annexations, indemnities and economic overlordship, Wilson worked throughout the war for a peace of reconciliation and of self determination for all peoples. Afterwards there was an outcry from American liberals that he had made concessions from his principles to our allies. Yet by comparison with the German dominated Europe which was so narrowly averted, the new Europe was a sea of freedom, with Germany herself still a great power. When compared with the kind of peace she would have imposed, the treaty was one of Wilson's greatest monuments.

In 1914 Professor Paul T. Birdsall published a landmark study of it, long before Fritz Fischer had supplied the overwhelming details, describing the "German mastery of Europe and world power of menacing proportions" which we barely escaped. He concluded that "The record clearly shows that on every major subject but that of reparations" the treaty would have been worse had Wilson not been in Paris.[34] It was a blend of his principles and the demands of sorely wounded victor peoples, but the League of Nations was to be always a means of administering and mitigating it, in the interests of the established peace.

[34] Paul Birdsall, *Versailles, Twenty Years After,* pp. 2-3, 19, 295.

VIII. The Deadly Spiral of Destruction in Our Century

———◆———

Throughout all the slaughter and suffering, the barbarities and wastes of the war people everywhere knew that there had been a pitiful failure of civilization. The life of the Western world, which had been so bright with assurance of progress in the early years of the twentieth century, had been plunged into chaos and uncertainty, into death and despair for countless millions in the bosom of the continent that ruled most of the world. The endless horror went on, too, for four years and of course it could not be endured without clinging to some hope, the obvious one that out of it all would come a world in which such a stupid, frightful catastrophe could not recur. This meant some kind of world organization to keep the peace, or at least to ward off the worst effects of blind national rivalries.

Everyone who lived through the period as an adult, as I did, knew the depth of that yearning and no true historian can fail to find it. It is clear to Barbara Tuchman that the war could not be sustained without hope "that it could never happen again," and that after it "the foundations of a better ordered world" would be laid. "Nothing less could give dignity or sense to monstrous offensives in which thousands and hundreds of thousands were killed to gain ten yards and exchange one wet-bottomed trench for another."[1]

In the United States, President Wilson was only one of the

[1] Barbara W. Tuchman, *The Guns of August*, New York, 1962, p. 439.

multitudes who saw the compelling necessity of organizing the peoples against such insane deluges of destruction. As early as January 1915 a group of thirty national leaders began work on the problem in New York City and their discussions led to a distinguished assembly in Independence Hall, Philadelphia, on June 17, 1915, which formed the League to Enforce Peace. It was headed by Republican ex-President William H. Taft and soon became the greatest educational organization which the country had ever known, with branches in nearly every Congressional district. Its second national convention, on May 17, 1916, was greeted by the *Washington Star* as "the largest and most distinguished gathering of a voluntary character that ever assembled in this city." The 2000 delegates contained the élite of the nation, including its business leaders. Some 96 percent of our Chambers of Commerce had voted "that this country take the initiative in forming a league of nations" and 64 percent were for military enforcement of mediatory decisions.[2]

The May 1916 League to Enforce Peace Assembly was notable also for strong support for its central principle by both Senator Henry Cabot Lodge and President Wilson. Speaking first, Lodge emphasized that he knew all the difficulties, "the obstacles." He knew "how quickly we shall be met with the statement that this is a dangerous question." He anticipated all the arguments about entangling alliances, but the next step was "to put force behind international peace. We may not solve it in that way but . . . it can be solved in no other." Then Wilson rose and stated his support for "an universal association of nations" to prevent war in violation of treaties or "without warning and full submission of the causes to the opinion of the world."[3]

[2] D. F. Fleming, *The United States and World Organization, 1920–1933*, New York, 1938, pp. 11–13. Similar organizations were formed in Britain and Holland.

[3] H. C. Lodge, *The Senate and the League of Nations*, New York, 1925, pp. 131–32; *Messages and Papers of Woodrow Wilson*, New York, 1924, Vol. I, p. 275.

The Defeat of Wilson and the League of Nations in the United States

Thereafter Wilson never wavered in working for a league of nations, but in the election of 1918 his appeal for a Democratic Senate, to assist in making peace, lost by the narrowest possible margin—one vote in the Senate—and when the new Senate met in May 1919 his opponents organized the Senate and its Committee on Foreign Relations under the leadership of Lodge who packed it, over the protests of Taft, with irreconcilable opponents of the league proposal. Soon after the 1918 election the new Senate leaders strongly opposed Wilson's personal participation in the peace-making in Paris, to begin early in 1919. Nevertheless, he went and in a series of evening meetings of the League of Nations Commission, after the main sessions of the Conference in the day time, managed to secure the Covenant of the League of Nations and to make it a part of the treaty of peace, much to the chagrin of his enemies at home who knew it would be much more difficult to reject the entire treaty than it would be to defeat the Covenant alone.

It was not easy to secure agreement on it at Paris, since our Allies were more concerned in making the territorial settlements and in collecting reparations from the defeated Germans, but it was accomplished, and this was the first requisite. Without the League Covenant no new beginning could be made, and it is difficult to believe that it would have been born without the vast personal prestige and authority of Wilson on the spot. His great messages as a war president had reverberated to the ends of the earth, carrying into deserts and mountain fastnesses his call for the self determination of peoples and a better future safeguarded by a league of nations. In the end, it was to him that the Germans had appealed for peace and it was to be made on the principles which he laid down.

At Paris he secured the adoption of four amendments to the Covenant, the changes most generally urged in this country. He did not consider any of them necessary, but to meet objections he engaged in a long grueling fight in the Commission to secure explicit recognition of the Monroe Doctrine which did not end in success until its last meeting on April 11. This is pertinent to charges that he would do nothing to satisfy critics of the League.[4]

THE PLAN OF OPPOSITION   To prevent Wilson from achieving great success in the peace conference, which they believed would keep his party in power for a generation, was no small undertaking. However, the Republican leaders in the Senate moved promptly to block him. On December 3, 1918, Lodge outlined in a letter to former Senator Albert J. Beveridge the plan of campaign that was eventually to be successful. It would be a mistake, he wrote, either to admit that the League was a good thing or to meet it with a flat denial. The thing to do was "show up the impossibility of any of the methods proposed" (to *be* proposed). His own judgment was that "the whole thing will break up in the conference," but "if any practical League" resulted, "then our issue is made up and we shall win." They would begin by pointing out the dangers, but to forestall the necessity[5] of defeating the treaty of peace Senator Philander C. Knox introduced a resolution in the Senate, on the same day, declaring that any project for a league of nations should be postponed for consideration "if and when at some future time general conferences on those subjects might be deemed useful."[6]

[4] D. F. Fleming, *The United States and the League of Nations, 1918–1920*, New York, 1932 and 1968, pp. 182–89. In this book I tried to make a full record of the struggle which resulted in our abstention from the League of Nations. It is to be republished in late 1966 or early 1967 (Russell and Russell, New York).

[5] Claude G. Bowers, *Beveridge and the Progressive Era*, Boston, 1932, pp. 500–1.

[6] *Congressional Record*, Vol. 57, Pt. 1, p. 23.

In mid-December Lodge and Theodore Roosevelt held a conference in New York at which they planned in detail to attack any constitution for a league of nations which Wilson might achieve with amendments and reservations. Their planning was so detailed that afterward Roosevelt's sister, Mrs. Douglas Robinson, who was present, wrote that they "went over every one of the reservations during a session of three hours, changing and deciding on this one and that and finally every one of them was O.K'.d."[7]

CAMPAIGN FOR POSTPONEMENT Pursuing their demand that nothing should be done about a league of nations under Wilson's leadership, and while humanity so poignantly recognized the need for it, Knox and Lodge opened a campaign for postponement in the Senate on December 14 and 21, 1918. Lodge actually protested against "trying to provide against wars which may never be fought" and warned that any "extraneous" provisions of the treaty "would surely be stricken out or amended, no matter how many signatures" there might be on the treaty. Then after the Covenant had been adopted in Paris, on February 14, 1919, and greeted with overwhelming approval in this country, Lodge found uncertainty clouding it "from end to end" and Knox uttered perhaps the most presumptous and imperious demand of all time: "Let us have an end of this!"

To enforce his ultimatum, he drew up a written statement demanding that the peace conference put aside the Covenant until after the treaty had been made, and slightly more than a third of the senators, all Republicans, signed the manifesto, i.e., enough to defeat the treaty in the Senate.[8]

Yet Lodge believed that any attempt to defeat the Treaty and the League by a straight vote would be "hopeless," and

[7] Fleming, *The United States and the League of Nations, 1918–1920*, p. 72. Of course the Covenant was not yet written, but the two planners succeeded in anticipating what it would contain so well that, writing in *The New York Times* on October 29, 1920, she thought the much debated reservations had actually been written in her brother's hospital room.

[8] *Ibid.*, pp. 153–71.

on April 29 he said that "there was only one thing to do and that was to proceed in the discussion of the treaty by way of amendment and reservation."[9] This procedure began as soon as the treaty was laid before the Senate, on July 10, 1919, and after adopting fifty amendments the Committee decided, on August 21, 1919, to hold hearings indefinitely, providing a forum for all who had war-born grievances.

As they proceeded and promised to go on for a very long time, Wilson made his decision to appeal personally to the people of the West, who had provided his victory in 1916. Leaving the White House on September 3, plagued by severe headaches, he made thirty-seven addresses in twenty-two days which increasingly moved his great audiences deeply. Heading a dozen wearying parades, he traveled 8000 miles to the Pacific and back to Kansas before a partial paralysis forced him to return to Washington, a semi-invalid for the rest of his life.

Thereafter, the cause of the League was largely leaderless. On September 10 the Committee submitted its report proposing fifty-odd amendments and many reservations. The second reservation listed and forbade every conceivable kind of enforcement action under Article 10 of the Covenant, the central article, "except by action of the Congress of the United States." Article 10 read:

> The Members of the League undertake to respect and preserve as against external aggression the territorial integrity and existing political independence of all Members of the League. In case of any such aggression or in case of any threat or danger of such aggression, the Council shall advise upon the means by which this obligation shall be fulfilled.

This was as small a pledge as the governments could make if there was to be hope of controlling future wars, but it was too much for those intent on defeating either Wilson or the League.

[9] Lodge, *The Senate and the League of Nations,* p. 147.

In one minority committee report Republican Senator Porter J. McCumber of North Dakota regretted that "No matter how just may be any antagonism against President Wilson, the aspirations and hopes of a wounded and bleeding world ought not to be denied because, under our Constitution, the treaty must first be formulated by him." McCumber could not "understand why a country whose whole history has been devoted to the advocacy of the peaceful settlement of international disputes is suddenly to have its policy reversed."

Nor could millions of other anguished citizens. Yet the struggle to defeat the League, controlled by its opponents, continued all through the autumn, arousing the fears of many unconverted isolationists.

RESERVATIONS VOTED   From October 16 to November 7, 1919, the fifty direct amendments were all debated and voted down. During the next two weeks enough of the Republicans who wanted the League in some form, plus a few Democrats who opposed it in any form, combined with the organization Republicans to provide majorities for all of the fourteen committee reservations and, on November 19, the treaty was defeated, both with the reservations and without them, by approximately 40 votes for to some 55 against, the sixteen "Irreconcilables" swinging over from one vote to the other.

During the four months that the treaty was debated, the fears of entanglement, loss of sovereignty and getting mixed up in other people's quarrels, that were voiced so long and loudly, affected many Americans, but they did not spread to any other country in the world. The other nations, including those in Latin America, continued to ratify the Treaty and the Covenant. Only the greatest surviving belligerent of the sad catastrophe, emerging as incomparably the strongest power in the world, refused to have any part in what Senator Frank B. Brandegee of Connecticut called "this contraption," the effort of many nations to ward off another deluge. The other peoples all flocked into the League of Nations, bewildered and troubled by the spectacle of the great leader suddenly torn by partisan war and selfish turning inward. Many hoped that the Americans would soon recover from their great relapse and resume their indispensable role.

At home a vast company of those who had comprehended the war in all of its enormity suffered deeply. It did not seem believable that the great hope which had been held so high during the war by virtually all of our leadership, official and unofficial, should be so suddenly disavowed. It seemed impossible that the greatest calamity ever brought by men on themselves should generate no remedial measures, no bulwark against a recurrence. This feeling was so strong that a massed body of official leaders of twenty-six great national organizations, whose combined membership totalled 20,000,000 voters, called on Lodge, urging ratification on a basis "that will not require renegotiation"—a vitally important point, as will be explained below.

Other pressures, especially from the mild reservationist senators, forced a bi-partisan conference of nine senators, meeting first on January 15, 1920, which seemed at times to be near agreement on compromise reservations. Wilson had agreed in November to five reservations proposed by the Democratic leader, Senator Gilbert M. Hitchcock of Nebraska, and he now accepted the reservation concerning acceptance of a colonial mandate. On his side, Lodge received a powerful assist from Viscount Grey, the former Sir Edward, then British Ambassador to Washington, who returned to London to advocate strongly that the reservations should be accepted. Granting the Americans their fears would do no harm in practice.

THE TREATY DEFEATED However, the Irreconcilables threatened Lodge with loss of his leadership if he yielded. Wilson continued to believe that the Lodge reservations would nullify our membership in the League and another long debate resulted in final defeat of the treaty, on March 19, 1920, the reservations having been stiffened and a 15th added calling for

self determination for Ireland. On the final vote the Southern
Democrats, loyal to Wilson, were joined by 15 Irreconcilables to
prevent a two-thirds vote for the reservations and the treaty
was defeated 49 for ratification and 35 against. This tally spelled
defeat for everyone except the bitter enders—even for Lodge
who, feeling the tide running toward salvaging the League in
some form, had been confident that he could secure Senate
approval with his reservations and put upon Wilson the onus of
refusing to ratify his own treaty.[10]

WOULD THE RESERVATIONS HAVE BEEN ACCEPTED ABROAD? The
original fourteen reservations, tailored to match in number the
Fourteen Points of the President's peace program, began by
talking about withdrawal from the League by a majority vote
of Congress. Then they went on to forbid any action under the
key Article 10 unless by act of Congress; to forbid the acceptance of a colonial mandate by the President; to make a long
list of "domestic questions," including the traffic in women and
children, which the League should let alone; to put the Monroe
Doctrine "wholly outside the jurisdiction of the said League";
to disavow any assent to the Shantung settlements in the Treaty;
to arrogate to Congress, in a specification seventeen lines long,
full control over the appointment of every conceivable U.S.
representative in the League; to forbid the Reparations Commission to regulate commerce with the United States without act
of Congress; to disavow contribution to any conceivable League
expenses except by act of Congress; to provide for cancellation
of any League arms limitation agreement in the name of self
defense; to forbid economic sanctions by the League from
affecting the citizens of an offender outside his own borders,
especially in the United States; to assert control of Congress over

---

[10] Lodge's memoirs demonstrate amply his single-minded determination
to defeat Wilson. See Lodge, *The Senate and the League of Nations*, pp.
212, 218–19, 226. He states that "a correct analysis of Mr. Wilson's probable attitude was an element of vital moment to me," and says on the last
page of his book: "I made no mistake in my estimate of what President
Wilson would do under certain circumstances."

any U.S. membership in the International Labor Organization; and to question our liability for any act of the League concerning which the British Dominions (Canada, Australia, etc.) had voted. Then the call for Irish self determination and membership in the League was added at the last moment, in spite of Lodge's chagrin about affirming the Wilsonian principle of self determination.[11]

Obviously framed to strike at President Wilson by attempting to limit his powers to represent us in the League and to fortify those of Congress, they carried an equal impression of hostility to the League itself. Some were clearly unnecessary and some harmless, but others seemed to nullify our membership in the League, especially to Wilson who had struggled so many months to get the provisions of the Covenant and the Treaty. He agreed to the four Hitchcock reservations and some of the chief points of dispute, but as Lodge anticipated, he would not yield on Article 10, the key obligation. Nor could anyone deny that the Lodge reservations cast a cloud of distrust, doubt and negation over the great attempt to create a league of nations.

Would they have been accepted if presented to the other League members? Their creators assumed they would be, and sought to provide that silence for a certain period would give consent, but the assumption that the mighty United States could have a long set of suspicious provisos that no one else thought necessary strains credulity. Any one of many Latin American governments might have rejected the reassertion of the sanctity of the Monroe Doctrine, greatly expanded under Theodore Roosevelt and resented accordingly. Any other parliament would have had the right to reject all of the reservations, and several might have proposed a list of their own.

Finally, one reservation struck directly at Japan and another against the votes of our sister British Dominions, the votes which certified their new nationhood. One also mixed openly in British

[11] The reservations are considered at length in Chapter 17 of *The United States and the League of Nations, 1918–1920*.

internal politics. Would thirty-three other governments have kept silent in sorrowful tolerance of the Senate's animosities and fears? Yet all along the Treaty and the Covenant had been multilateral treaties which, once agreed upon, could not be altered without the consent of all the signatories. All that was necessary was for *one* of them to reject *one* reservation, and Canada flatly stated that if the other nations accepted the reservation aimed at her vote in the League she would withdraw.[12] Years later, when the Senate itself asked the forty-eight members of the World Court to accept its reservations affirmatively the governments of five tiny states did so. Most of the forty-eight did not even reply.[13]

No other government in the world proposed reservations to its entry into the League. There was real debate in Switzerland, but the Federal Council assessed Article 10 as "not a very heavy obligation" and the parliaments of the mature Scandinavian countries approved the Covenant by overwhelming votes.

SHOULD WILSON HAVE ACCEPTED THE RESERVATIONS? In later years a tendency grew up to blame Woodrow Wilson himself for the failure of the Treaty in the United States. It was said that before the Senate voted on it for the second time, on March 19, 1920, he should have told his supporters in the Senate to accept the Lodge reservations. It was "the supreme act of infanticide" said Professor Thomas A. Bailey in 1945, and in 1956 Professor Arthur S. Link, Wilson's official biographer, agreed that his failure to do so was "an error of tragic magnitude." With his own hand, he said, Wilson removed "the corner stone of his edifice of peace."[14]

[12] *Current History*, April, 1920, p. 29.

[13] An account of our effort to become a member of the World Court under Senate reservations may be found in my book, *The United States and the World Court*, New York, 1945 and 1968.

[14] Thomas A. Bailey, *Woodrow Wilson and the Great Betrayal*, New York, 1945, p. 277. Bailey also wrote a fine companion volume, *Woodrow Wilson and the Lost Peace*, New York, 1944. These volumes are an outstanding contribution to the history of our failure to make peace after World War I.

These crushing judgments involve a decision that, after all, the reservations did not matter and that the millions of words spoken and written about them cancelled each other. They involve a finding that Wilson's heroic crusade to get a permanent bulwark against the return of another deluge of devastation—the greatest effort of its kind in history—had to end in the grudging, suspicious acceptance by his own people of a seat in the League of Nations very close to the door. Was it really the fault of the man who gave his all for a desperately needed step forward that the greatest of the nations failed to supply the powerful leadership which the League of Nations was certain to need?

SEPARATE PEACE The 15 reservations were not infectious outside our country, but they contributed, along with other factors, to the election of amiable Senator Warren G. Harding to the presidency in 1920. By addressing half of his speeches to the anti-league sentiment and half to the multitudes of pro-league Republicans he kept both wings of what was still the majority party in line.

On April 12, 1921 President Harding declared that "In the existing League of Nations, world governing with its super powers, this Republic will have no part," and on August 25 an unknown member of the State Department signed a separate treaty of peace with the defeated Germans. The ceremony lasted two minutes and no one was present. The treaty rearranged the Treaty of Versailles in such a manner that Senator William E. Borah, one of the Irreconcilables, found that "whatever comes to us must come free, without the discharge of any responsibility or obligation on our part. The execution of the Versailles Treaty, whether it be expensive in treasure or blood, we step from under."[15]

See also Arthur S. Link, *Wilson the Diplomatist*, Baltimore, 1957, pp. 153–55.

In 1968 Link was midway in editing a monumental edition of Wilson's papers, interrupting his multi-volume biography of Wilson.

[15] D. F. Fleming, *The United States and World Organization, 1920–1933*, New York, 1938 and 1968, p. 50.

Divided World Leadership

EARLY LEAGUE SUCCESSES   Then to the surprise of many in the
U.S.A. the League of Nations lived. By 1921 its membership
had grown to thirty-three, and a decade later to fifty-five. No
invited neutral state failed to join. In its early years, too, it
assisted in settling disputes over the Aaland Island, Upper
Silesia, Albanian boundaries, Vilna, a Greco-Bulgarian boundary
clash and Mosul. It was the center also of a long, anxious
search for the security which all had hoped to find in the League,
but which was not felt in the absence of the United States.
There were Franco-British security negotiations and debates on
the application of Article 10 and the interpretation of Article 16.
There was a comprehensive Draft Treaty of Mutual Assistance
which did not succeed and the famous Geneva Protocol which
also failed, before the Locarno agreements at last brought Germany into the League and seemed to give strong assurance of
security in West Europe.[16]

In the fields of world health and labor problems the corresponding arms of the League had notable success. By 1927 a
leading student of contemporary affairs wrote that as an in-
stitution the League had evolved slightly, "but as an idea and a
(meeting) place its expansion has been well-nigh incredible."
He added that "Only in the United States does the opposition
to the League of Nations successfully hold its ground."[17]

This was sadly true. Its opponents had assumed at first that
it would die in our absence and they hoped it would. In the
early years every kind of recognition was withheld from it, but
eventually unofficial American "observers" began to appear at
League conferences. After refusing any part in arms traffic reg-

[16] *Ibid.*, pp. 180–218.
[17] Frank H. Simonds, *How Europe Made Peace Without America*, New
York, 1927, pp. 267, 373–74, 376–80, 386.

ulation meetings for three years the American Minister to Switzerland came, to be advised and to receive information. The U.S. felt compelled also to join in a League conference to control the opium traffic as early as 1923, though our delegate, Representative Stephen G. Porter, began with an ultimatum about how to proceed and then stalked from the room.

WASHINGTON NAVAL TREATIES In 1921 the Harding administration called a peace conference of its own which met in Washington from November 12 to February 6, 1922, to deal with the naval building race between the U.S. and Britain and between us and Japan. These problems seemed urgent since our two rivals were bound together by the Anglo-Japanese Alliance of 1902, which had been very useful to both parties. To get the alliance abrogated a Four Power Treaty between the U.S., Britain, Japan and France was agreed upon, providing that all would respect the *status quo* in the Pacific and promise to consult if it were threatened.

Then Japan was induced to sign a treaty restoring Shantung to China, and a Nine Power Treaty guaranteeing her against future interference from Japan. Finally, a Naval Limitation Treaty was made in which Britain conceded full parity to us and Japan accepted an inferior 10:10:6 ratio. Best of all, the number of dreadnoughts that each navy should have was specified. Some partly built ships were scrapped and much money saved. This was an event in human history. However, the Washington treaties were made outside the League and did nothing to strengthen the main structure upon which future peace depended. They were approved by the Senate, after Harding—no longer a senator—had pleaded with the Senate that "Either these treaties must have your cordial sanction, or every proclaimed desire to promote peace and prevent war becomes a hollow mockery." Democratic votes supplied the two-thirds majority.

The ensuing costly race in cruiser building embarrassed the Coolidge administration, which called a conference of the naval powers in Geneva, June 20, 1927. France and Italy did not attend. When the big three met, Britain and the U.S. could not agree to extend the 10:10:6 ratio to cruisers. However, in 1930 another naval conference was held in London which, after three months of deadlock on the question of consultation in case of trouble, at length agreed upon a treaty between the big three, conceding cruiser parity to the U.S. but mainly on a light cruiser basis, and a 10:10:7 ratio in cruisers was won by Japan, with parity in submarines.[18]

WORLD DISARMAMENT CONFERENCE By this time the great World Disarmament Conference for which the League had been working since 1920 was near. In September 1931 the United States joined in the preparation discussions in a consultative capacity, and the U.S. accepted full membership in the conference itself, which finally met on February 2, 1932, as Japanese aggression in China, spreading from Manchuria, was hammering a large section of Shanghai into dust. By this time German impatience over the long delay in the Allied promise at Versailles to disarm was rising and Hitler was in the wings. The faltering German Republic, hard hit by the disastrous economic depression, badly needed a success in equalizing armaments, but every nation's weapons proved to be strictly defensive to it and highly offensive to others.

To break the deadlock the American delegation proposed the Hoover Plan which called for a reduction of all armies, battleships and submarines by one-third and the abolition of all tanks, large mobile guns, bombing planes and chemical warfare weapons. But the mathematical bombshell method of attack which had succeeded in the Washington Conference now failed, even though Secretary of State Stimson went to the great conference in Geneva. Neither the British nor the Japanese were ready to cut their forces steeply again and too many political

[18] Fleming, *The United States and World Organization, 1920–1933,* pp. 79–111, 88–91, 360–71.

considerations were ignored, as the Nazis increased their strength in the Reichstag on July 31st from 107 seats to 226.

At long last, Secretary Henry L. Stimson declared on August 8, 1932, that when pacts were threatened with violation consultation was inevitable, but on August 29 Germany withdrew from the Conference, with some hope of returning if her right to equality in arms was granted. Thereafter other plans and formulas were debated in the Conference, which continued to meet until October 1933, when the final resignation of Nazi Germany from the Conference and from the League turned all energies toward armament.[19]

For several weeks I personally watched the failure of the Conference, from its galleries and corridors, oppressed by the feeling that this major effort at disarmament had come too late. I wrote later, that it had never been a practical proposal, unless the Anglo Saxon powers would assume some degree of responsibility for world order, and after our abstention from the League the British would not attempt in its crises to carry the load. This also was the conclusion of analyst Frank Simonds, who wrote that "The American rejection of the Treaty of Versailles had resulted in the complete disorganization of the whole system of international peace and order founded upon the League of Nations."[20]

WAS OUR FAILURE TO LEAD DECISIVE? It is often said that the League of Nations might or would have failed in its great purpose even if the United States had been a member, and this is quite possible. Indeed, if our Government had acted as national governments usually act, the failure would still have come. But the great regret will always linger that the United States did not *try* to support the League system, much less to lead it, until it was far too late. It was our leadership, too, that was desperately required. With the other big governments

[19] *Ibid.*, pp. 371–88.

[20] Frank H. Simonds, *American Foreign Policy in the Post War Years*, Baltimore, 1935, p. 105.

destroyed or badly crippled—either in defeat or victory—real leadership could come only from us, the great undamaged victor. If we had led the League from the start, all of the presumptions would have been for success, instead of failure. The aggressive governments which soon came to challenge and disrupt the League would have had to count on a far different situation, one in which governments like the British and the French would in all probability have lined up behind our leadership. Certainly the great rank and file of governments would have done so. My most enduring impression from sitting for many weeks in the halls of Geneva, both during the Manchurian and Ethiopian crises, is of the delegates of the small and middle sized powers trooping to the platforms again and again to make it clear that they wanted the law of the League supported, and that they would do what they could to defend it. Of course they were weak individually, but if led by the great powers their strength would have been real.

Wherever one looks, the absence of the great leader was a huge factor, if not the decisive one. "Every student of disarmament knew," said one of the American newspaper correspondents on the scene of the Disarmament Conference, "that there could never be disarmament without security, and that there could never be security without a strong League of Nations, where every country, great or small, could be sure that the navies of the United States and Great Britain were not instruments of national policy, but the policemen of an organized world community."[21]

POSTWAR RECONSTRUCTION In 1933 the world was still disorganized from the great economic depression which had afflicted all nations. Its coming at the top of the period of our return to non-entanglement in the politics of the world had puzzled many isolationists.

At the end of the war there was no question about what had

[21] John T. Whitaker, *And Fear Came*, New York, 1936, p. 127.

to be done. The amount of wealth consumed by it was beyond all human imagination. In Europe hardly a nation was able to survive the terrible winter of 1919 without our help. Some 400,000,000 people were threatened with disaster. However, our economy was geared up to an undreamed-of pitch of productivity and it was able to furnish food and clothing throughout the vast war-torn area, approximately in proportion to the need. Those who had any credit left were required to pledge it, to the extent of some $500,000,000, but beyond that the U. S. Treasury financed an additional two billion dollars' worth of supplies. Our contribution was magnificent, though it also prevented a great glut and crash of prices in this country.

Then the League of Nations took up the work of resettling 1,400,000 homeless Greeks expelled from Turkey, the repatriation of 427,000 prisoners of war, alleviating the lot of millions of refugees scattered over Europe, assisting Bulgaria with a loan for the settlement of refugees, aiding Hungary with a $50,000,000 loan and establishing the small new state of Austria with a gold loan of $170,000,000. American financiers contributed to these loans and the United States quickly went on to become the world's banker.

BOOM AND COLLAPSE Continued surpluses of American exports were financed by accepting and actively seeking bonds, until the accumulation of these beautifully lettered documents became almost a national mania. In the 1920s our private loans to foreigners aggregated a billion dollars a year. A great part of them went to Germany, but Latin American dictators were scandalously supplied. The trade of the world was financed in this manner and American prosperity was high except in the rural areas, which were pinched by low prices for their products. Farm subsidies were rejected repeatedly, but tariffs were raised, in spite of a grave warning by 1028 economists, to keep out the foreign goods which might have alleviated the plight of the farmers.

During the years of the great prosperity 4817 banks failed, mainly in the rural areas, but dizzy corporate structures were piled up on one another and by 1927 a great bull market was under way in Wall Street in which the prosperous and many others gambled until the great crash on October 23, 1929, the effects of which soon spread around the world. Funds from all parts of Europe had been sucked into Wall Street to share in the winnings, straining currency systems at home. Then the great flood of American loans to all the world was suddenly cut off. First the great Kredit Anstalt Bank in Vienna had to be bailed out. Then the Young Plan for financing German reparations to the Allies, and indirectly Allied war debts to the United States, collapsed and there was a world run on Germany, as nearly six billions of foreign investments tried to escape. This necessitated the Hoover moratorium on all inter-governmental debts, but that did not prevent a great run on London which large credits from abroad did not stop. On August 28, 1931, Britain abandoned the gold standard, but still the flight from sterling continued.

The crisis was racing around the world like a virulent epidemic. During 1930 and 1931 it was the primary, though not the sole cause of eleven revolutions in Latin America. The cloud of creditors which had devoured London's gold then flew to New York, where a silent nation-wide run on the American banking system was taking place. In the fourth quarter of 1931, 1055 banks closed and 7316 businesses acknowledged bankruptcy. This went on until March 4, 1933, when the Governors of New York and Illinois issued virtually simultaneous proclamations closing the banks and soon every bank in the nation was shut, as Hoover's presidency came to an end, along with the period which Harding had called "Normalcy," during which all foreign political entanglements were sternly eschewed.[22]

[22] Fleming, *The United States and World Organization, 1920–1933,* pp. 317–60.

The Failure of Britain and France
to Lead the League

The great world depression created the conditions of desperation in Germany in which Hitler's fascist party could seize
power and weakened the democracies for resisting earlier aggressions by Japan and Italy through the League of Nations.

MANCHURIA, 1931 The first trial of strength came with Japan,
which isolationist Washington seemed to have disciplined so
successfully, though the lesser naval strength conceded to her
really turned naval control of the Orient over to her when
logistics are considered, unless the American and British navies
were combined against her. This was made virtually impossible
by American abstention from the League.

When Japan began her aggression in Manchuria, on September 18, 1931, the League Council was in session and it favored
a quick inquiry. As Japan seemed about to accept, Secretary of
State Stimson told the Japanese that he opposed the commission
of inquiry and the Japanese stiffened on September 23. Apparently frantic messages from Geneva during the night led
Stimson to try to undo the mistake the next day, wrote Clarence
Streit to the New York Times, but "irremediable psychological
harm had been done and the favorable moment had gone forever." Stimson had erred not from any lack of good will but
from lack of experience in Geneva. He promptly wrote strong
notes to Japan, but to no effect. The Japanese military leaders
knew that he would not be able to concert strongly with the
League to restrain them. He did try to maintain liaison. Our
Swiss Minister sat in the antechambers of the League while it
wrestled with the problem, and on October 4 an American note
urged the League "to assert all the pressure and authority in its
competence," as the Japanese bombed Chinchow to drive the
Manchurian government out of the country.

As early as September 24 our Consul, Prentice Gilbert, had been authorized to sit with the League Council in a consultative capacity and, over Japan's protest, he did so at four meetings, but only to get the League members to "invoke" the Kellogg Pact, which had no enforcement machinery.[23] Then, after Japan had invaded North Manchuria, U. S. Ambassador to Britain Charles G. Dawes was ordered to go to Paris with authority to sit with the Council. A man of great prestige, General Dawes did not choose to do so. Instead, he established himself in a hotel across the river from the Quai d'Orsay in Paris, where the Council was meeting, and dealt with the League as a coordinate power, avoiding completely that "town meeting" and calling selected members from it over to see him. The Japanese and Chinese members were frequently summoned and after he thought he had about settled their differences he sent word to the Council that he was coming over to make a speech, just as it was ready to adjourn its round of November sessions. The consternation of the Council was relieved by Stimson's decision to cancel the speech, but nothing was done to stop the renewal of Japan's advance in Manchuria.

Feeling that *something* must be done, Stimson issued, on January 7, 1932, a declaration refusing to recognize any situation or treaty (conquest) which might be made in violation of the Kellogg Pact. Though it was toothless, Stimson at least showed our complete disapproval of Japan's acts, the next of which was a big landing and attack on the Chinese part of Shanghai, with bombers, artillery and troops, horrifying the world with its first glimpse of what was in store for its cities.

As the peoples watched aghast, the United States and Britain, supported by France and Italy, presented a five-point peace proposal to Japan, which was promptly rejected. By this time the British government had decided to stay close to Japan.

[23] No one who had not lived through the years of hating the League could understand how near "sitting with" the League Council, its high political organ, was to the unpardonable sin.

Foreign Secretary Sir John Simon presumed to speak for the United States in the Council and repeatedly urged that body not to interfere with the efforts of the big powers to negotiate. In their anguished frustration the twelve non-belligerent members of the Council addressed an appeal to Japan to recognize her obligations under the Covenant. The diplomatic pressure on Japan was unprecedented, but Stimson failed after four telephone talks with Simon to persuade him to invoke the Nine Power Treaty, which was being violated as clearly as a treaty could possibly be. Sir John would say neither yes or no.

Blocked in London, Stimson wrote a letter to Senator William E. Borah, Chairman of the Foreign Relations Committee, in which he reviewed all of the applicable treaties, trying at least to set the record straight. Stimson did what he could from his lonely eminence outside the League of Nations, but he could not do what the United States might have done from the inside after years of leadership in the League.

The great powers having failed to deter Japan, the League Assembly took up the question on March 3, 1930 and struggled with it another year. Headed by courageous Assembly President Paul Hymans of Belgium, the representatives of the smaller states did their best, but the British Government was "literally in a blue funk" at the prospect of sending its fleet against Japan, especially after the provisions of the Washington Naval Treaty had made their Hong Kong naval base obsolete and Japan supreme in Asiatic waters. France also, mindful of her own imperialistic operation in Indochina and of an informal entente with Japan, was no more inclined to move. Only the combined American and British fleets would have made an adequate power base for disciplinary action against Japan and President Hoover was by no means ready for that, even if Britain had been.

The other obvious core of power for upholding the function of the League would have been action by the two great-power neighbors of Japan, the U.S.A. and the U.S.S.R., but the Soviet

Union, as a state with a pariah social system, was not yet a member of the League. For that matter, too, the naval treaty had made our Manila naval base obsolete. The lesser nations therefore did what they could in the Assembly. On March 11, 1932, they supported strongly the Stimson doctrine of non-recognition of conquests and set up a Committee of Nineteen to deal with the crisis.

The Assembly also fostered the Lytton Commission of Enquiry, which had been belatedly authorized on December 10, 1931. After work in the Far East it made a notable report, on September 4, 1932, which defended the sovereignty of China in Manchuria and suggested ten conditions for a settlement. The report was considered in the Council in November under the presidency of de Valera of Ireland, whose mild firmness (I observed) was more than a match for the belligerence of Japan's Matsuoka. Back in the Assembly, in December, the small powers made their feelings clear, but the imposing figure of Sir John Simon opposed any action and pleaded for "conciliation."

Then the Lytton Report was referred to the Committee of Nineteen which presented a long report that was the basis of an Assembly resolution, February 24, 1933, which so clearly and firmly condemned Japan's conduct that Matsuoka walked out and Japan finally withdrew from the League on March 27, 1933.[24]

Thus the first great test of collective security ended in failure. Measured by the long, slow growth of international law a great advance had been made. The acts of a great power had been examined and condemned by a world assembly of the nations but, gauged by the desperate need for much more which World War I had revealed, the failure was sad and decisive, for we did not have time for the League to build slowly on precedents. Other strong governments were disgruntled with their post-war

[24] Fleming, *The United States and World Organization, 1920–1933*, pp. 392–456.

lot, ready to plunge into aggression if Japan succeeded. With the weapons of destruction increasing in destructiveness, we could not afford even one successful defiance of the League's saving purpose.

ETHIOPIA, 1935   Just as soon as it was evident that the League was not going to restrain Japan, Mussolini began to plan actively the conquest of Ethiopia. In the spring of 1932 enormous construction work on the roads and ports of an adjoining Italian colony began and October 1935 was set as the unalterable date when the conquest would begin.[25] On December 5, 1934, the necessary incident was provoked at the Wal Wal wells, about a hundred miles inside Ethiopia. In January 1935 the Ethiopian delegate to the League tried to invoke Article 15 of the Covenant, but the Secretary General, a Frenchman, and Sir John Simon took the document from him and put it in the waste basket.[26]

The incident signalized the determination of the British Conservatives not to be embarrassed by any new talk of League of Nations sanctions. Some of them had sympathized strongly with Japan, as fellow imperialists, when she cracked down on upstart Chinese nationalists who sought to build and operate their own railroads. Now they would have no nonsense about opposing Italy in Ethiopia—unless she reached for too much. They had accepted the League as a tool of the Foreign Office, but not as something which could give direction to it. On their side the French had always regarded the League as merely another weapon to prevent a German resurgence and Premier Pierre Laval was wholly intent on securing Italy as an ally for this purpose.

Accordingly, the two governments united to stall and postpone action by the League against Italy through successive Council meetings on March 16 and April 15. Finally, world

[25] George Martelli, *Italy Against the World,* New York, 1938, pp. 41–48.
[26] Whitaker, *And Fear Came,* p. 247. The author knew Whitaker well, in Geneva at the Autumn 1935 Sessions of the League, as a wholly reliable representative of the *New York Herald Tribune*.

opinion forced the two to produce a Council resolution, on May 25, 1935, setting up a time limit of three months for the completion of arbitration proceedings (and of Italy's huge military preparations).[27]

While these farcical proceedings dragged on, there was one of the most remarkable risings of public opinion in Great Britain which ever occurred in any nation. The League of Nations Union, with a million dues-paying members, was supported by thirty-eight other organizations in conducting an unofficial national plebiscite, to counter the effort of Tory newspapers to take Britain out of the League and to force it to act in the Ethiopian affair.[28] By June 1935 the ballots of 11,640,066 voters had been signed, verified and carefully preserved, or 38.2 percent of the possible voters. This remarkable result of house to house visitation, surely the greatest poll ever undertaken anywhere, showed 96 percent in favor of remaining in the League, 86.8 percent for economic sanctions and 58.7 percent of those who voted in favor of military sanctions.

This unheard of rising of the voters compelled the British Government to appear to move in the League for sanctions against Italy's aggression. Sir John Simon, who found it wholly "mischievous to ask the opinion of uninformed persons on such intricate matters of peace and war" was dropped as Foreign Secretary and replaced by Sir Samuel Hoare.[29] He at once began to try to buy off Mussolini with slices of Ethiopia. Anthony Eden went to Rome late in June with an offer of part of Ethiopian Ogaden. This was rejected indignantly. Most government speeches were of the stand-by-the-League variety, but

[27] The League of Nations, *Official Journal*, XVI, June 1935, p. 640.

[28] Dame Adelaide Livingston, *The Peace Ballot, The Official History*, London, June 1935, pp. 9–108; *The National Declaration on the League of Nations and Armaments*, London (King and Jarrett), 1938, p. 16.

[29] *The New York Times*, June 28, 1935. National leaders bent on imposing their will on the people at home, or others abroad, are always sure that they have the inside information on which policies and action can be based.

financial and commercial interests were violently opposed to the whole idea of sanctions as dangerous to business.[30] Therefore, a second offer of Ethiopian resources was made by Britain and France to Italy on August 15 and rejected by her on the 18th. Then a third offer adding the Danakil region was made on September 18, through a League Council Committee. This, too, was promptly rejected.

This left London and Paris with no choice but to appear to apply some League sanctions against Italy. To the imperialists who dominated both governments nothing was more distasteful and ridiculous than for the two greatest imperialist powers to levy sanctions in behalf of the half-savage Ethiopians against another imperial power. Yet the British people had spoken thunderously, and from nearly every League country, and others, appeals and demands poured into Geneva for the application of the Covenant. Ten thousand telegrams were received in three days as the Council met in September and as the Assembly convened on September 9, 1935, the eyes of the world were upon it.

Driven to do something, Hoare and Laval met on September 10. In Laval's words, "We found ourselves instantaneously in agreement upon ruling out military sanctions, not adopting any measure of naval blockade, never contemplating the closure of the Suez Canal—in a word, ruling out everything that might lead to *war*." (Italics added.)[31] So, it having been agreed that nothing effective would be done to restrain Italy, Hoare made his famous speech in the Assembly the next day in which he said resoundingly that the British government "will be second to none in their intention to fulfill within the measure of their

[30] *The New Statesman and Nation,* August 31, 1935; The London *Daily Herald,* May 8, 1935.

[31] Helen Hiett, "Public Opinion and the Italo-Ethiopian Dispute," *Geneva Special Studies,* February 1936, Vol. VII, No. 1, p. 4.

Government spokesmen, determined not to use the League to regulate or forestall war and conquest, were always quick to label any police action by the League as "war."

capacity the obligations which the Covenant lays upon them." Bowing plainly to the British peace ballot, he declared that his country stood for "the collective maintenance of the Covenant in its entirety and particularly for steady, collective resistance to all acts of unprovoked aggression." Then Edouard Herriot and Paul Boncour, two French Cabinet members who were staunch friends of the League, labored with Laval for two days to induce him to make a strong statement, which he eventually did in a manner which obviously carried no conviction.[32]

On September 26 the Council agreed that Article 15 was applicable and set up a Committee to report under it. On October 2 Mussolini issued a fierce war cry to the Italian people and began the invasion of Ethiopia the next day. On October 7 the Council declared Italy to be an aggressor and, on the 11th, fifty of the fifty-four states represented in the Assembly endorsed the Council's verdict.

Meanwhile, for many months a *de facto* arms embargo against both Italy and Ethiopia had been in effect, penalizing Ethiopia fatally, since she had no arms industries, and on October 5 President Roosevelt made the embargo official for the United States, shutting off all arms to Ethiopia. The League sanctions levied a boycott on the importation of Italian goods and placed an embargo on certain exports to Italy, but not on manufactured iron products or oil.

If the world had been back in the eighteenth century this would have been another big step forward, but in 1935 it meant another failure for the League which struck deeply into the hearts of all those who knew that balance of power politics had produced World War I. This feeling was so strong that the Committee of Eighteen moved to extend the sanctions to cover oil and other sinews of war, though there was uncertainty as to whether the United States would cooperate in an oil sanction

[32] My Geneva diary shows that the time of his speech was announced and postponed repeatedly while it went through many drafts.

and American oil shipments to Italy were rising rapidly. Laval postponed this action repeatedly, and finally, on December 9, to ward it off entirely, Hoare and Laval made their fourth offer to Italy, greatly enlarging the areas of Ethiopian territory to be annexed by Italy or administered by her. However, this scheme quickly leaked to the press from Paris, on December 9, and such a storm of indignation swept the world, especially in Britain, that the British Government had to disavow it, but the oil sanction had been killed. Thereafter, Foreign Secretary Anthony Eden, who had succeeded Hoare, pressed for the oil sanction in Geneva while Laval continued to reject it until Ethiopia was conquered.

When the Assembly met on July 4, 1936, to formally repeal the sanctions against Italy, a deep "silence fell over the Assembly, the press and public galleries" and this brooding silence "lasted a quarter of an hour."[33] Their forebodings were quickly verified, for only one hour later the Nazi President of the Danzig Senate mounted the rostrum to demand the termination of the League's jurisdiction over the Danzig Free State. He insolently gave the Nazi salute to Anthony Eden and thumbed his nose at the press and public galleries. The way was now wide open for Germany, the greatest of the three rampant aggressors, to go as far as she liked.

The path of German aggression had been further cleared, though this was not so evident at the time, by a snap election which the British government had called for November 14, 1935, at the top of the time when it seemed that the League was moving to restrain Italy, to get a new lease of power on a platform of standing strongly behind the League. Pushing this line to the limit the Baldwin government won what was perhaps the most dishonest election ever conducted in any democracy. It got a majority in the House of Commons of 431 to 184, so huge that the Cabinet had a free hand during all the coming

[33] Clarence Streit, *The New York Times,* July 5, 1936.

disasters of appeasement. Three weeks after the election of
November 14, 1935, the Hoare-Laval deal gave the league its
final blow.

The Appeasement Slide into World War II

The floodgates were now wide open, releasing torrents of vindictive and vengeful aggression and carrying humanity swiftly into
World War II. In all the world there was no important government that was willing to raise a hand against a greater doom
than World War I, except the Soviet Union which had not been
brought into the League of Nations until September 18, 1934,
on the initiative of the one enlightened rightist French statesman,
Jean Louis Barthou. Ceasing years of scoffing against the League
as an outcast, Stalin said that if the League of Nations has
only the tiniest desire "somewhere to slow down the drive
toward war and help peace, then we are not against the
League."[34]

Russia feared a Hitlerian eruption, probably combined with an
attack by Japan. The French, driven by fear of Germany, had
somewhat equivocally made a new Franco-Soviet Pact, but in
both France and Britain the rightist forces had an aversion to
Soviet Communism that was far greater than their fear of
Fascism, Italian, or German. It, after all, allied itself with them,
though at a distasteful price, and Hitler promised loudly and
often to end the Communist "menace" once and for all.

THE RHINELAND MILITARIZED, 1936 So when Hitler smashed
both the Versailles Treaty and the much vaunted Locarno Pact,
by marching into the demilitarized Rhineland on March 7, 1936,
he knew better than his terrified generals that there would be
none to say nay to his still weak military forces. Seeing that
Mussolini had won Ethiopia, he went ahead in full confidence

[34] *The New York Times,* December 28, 1933.

that he also would be appeased. In France the Government was disposed to use its still superior army to defend the European Order which World War I had created, but the British Government was adamant. Fortified now by unlimited power but still bruised by "the accursed matter of Ethiopia," it would not hear of any move against Hitler. Consequently, he was allowed to close his back door against the West, to furiously fortify the Rhineland and make ready to pick off his small neighbors in Central Europe, one by one, on his way to bigger things. He was also free now to turn back and attack France and the Low Countries if he wished, which he did four years later. The ability to deprive him of all this mobility, and most probably to speed his downfall, was firmly thrown away by London and Paris in the 1936 Rhineland crisis.

While this happened the United States was aloof from the abhorred European politics. "By a curious logic" the inevitable European chaos which resulted from renewed isolation was then used as "a further foundation for isolationist argument."[35]

SPAIN STRANGLED, 1936–1938 Then the British Conservatives determined to do nothing further to oppose the Fascist aggressors. In France the corresponding groups, many of which openly preferred "Hitler rather than Blum" heartily agreed. Yet the Socialist leader Léon Blum was Premier when the Spanish rightists rebelled in Spain in July 1936 against the effort of the Spanish Republic to bring Spain, with her four privileged ruling classes, out of the fifteenth century. However, the Blum government, caught between the wrath of its rightist groups and its need for British support against the ring of ruthless Fascist powers closing around France, did not dare, except intermittently, to give the Spanish Republic the aid which it had every legal and moral right to send. Instead, it went along with the British government in calling twenty-seven European states away from Geneva to form a Non-Intervention Committee in

[35] Paul Birdsall, *Versailles, Twenty Years After,* New York, 1941, p. 307.

London which resolutely held a blanket of high impartiality over the tragedy in Spain until the Republic was strangled to death beneath it.

The agony lasted nearly three years, during which time Germany sent every kind of aid to the Franco forces; and Italy sent scores of thousands of troops, while the democratic powers practiced non-intervention; that is, an illegal neutrality which prevented the legitimate Spanish government from getting the arms it required for survival. Only the Soviet Union sent aid, belatedly, and part of that was sunk by piratical Italian submarines. The United States hastened to impose an arms embargo against sending arms to a civil war, completing its barricade of neutrality laws, behind which it would be isolated and safe during the coming holocaust.[36]

AUSTRIA SACRIFICED, 1938   Then it was Austria's turn to be seized by Hitler in March 1938, after British Prime Minister Neville Chamberlain had publicly condemned "the shams and pretences of sanctions" and declared that "We must not try to delude small and weak nations into thinking that they will be protected by the League against aggression." His was the government which had obtained an impregnable lease of power in November 1935 on a platform of "Stand by the League!" and "Our Word Is Our Bond."

However, the Austrian government did not cooperate in a quiet Nazi take-over but tried instead to avert it by a plebiscite which was frustrated by a brutal invasion of Hitler's troops.

This disturbed Chamberlain's plans for peaceful satisfaction of Hitler's ambitions. On November 26, 1937, he had written about the Germans that "of course they want to dominate Eastern Europe" and he had concluded that Britain should say to Germany: "give us satisfactory assurances that you won't use force to deal with the Austrians and Czechoslovaks, and we will give

[36] However, the percentage of Americans favoring the Spanish Republic increased from 65 percent in February 1937 to 76 percent in December 1938.—*Public Opinion Quarterly*, October 1939, p. 600.

you similar assurances that we won't use force to prevent the changes you want, if you can get them by peaceful means."[37]

CZECHOSLOVAKIA DISMEMBERED, 1938 It followed inexorably that since the Austrian affair had been repulsive the Czechs must submit to dismemberment without provoking Nazi violence, which had the highly dangerous disadvantage that it might arouse France to honor her alliance with the Czechs, in which case the Soviet Union gave every indication of keeping her conditional alliance with Prague. If developments went that way, another eruption of British opinion might even force London to take a hand in what would then be a big conflict.

Therefore Chamberlain rejected Russia's request for a conference on March 24, 1938, in a speech which, amid much obfuscation, revealed his plan to bring such pressure to bear upon Czechoslovakia that the French alliance with her would never become operative. This involved making it plain to France, which he did on April 28, that "in no circumstances would Britain give immediate support to either France or Czechoslovakia," and "from that moment the French, consciously or subconsciously, wrote off their own obligation" to Czechoslovakia.[38] On May 10 Chamberlain announced to the world that neither France, Russia nor Britain would fight for Czechoslovakia, and pushed his plan for a Four Power Pact with the Fascist duo that would exclude Russia.[39]

Ten days later heavy German troop concentrations on the Czech frontier precipitated an intense crisis. The Czechs partially mobilized and London and Paris had to warn Hitler firmly and repeatedly before he subsided bitterly. Under the sudden whip of fear the appeasers had done what they should, but they resolved resentfully that the Czechs should never stand up

[37] Keith Feiling, *The Life of Neville Chamberlain*, New York (Macmillan), 1946, p. 333.

[38] J. W. Wheeler-Bennett, *Munich, Prologue to Tragedy*, New York, 1948, pp. 50–51.

[39] G. E. R. Gedye, *Betrayal in Central Europe*, New York, 1939, pp. 390–91; Wheeler-Bennett, pp. 52–53.

again. Hitler wanted 3,000,000 Germans in Czechoslovakia—people who had never been in Germany—along with her great ring of mountain defenses, and his allies in London and Paris agreed that it would be good Wilsonian doctrine to give them to him. In late July Lord Runciman was forced upon Prague as a "mediator" in a speech by Chamberlain to the House of Commons, which was "as remarkable an example of prevarication as that chamber can ever have heard." He lied brazenly in saying that the Czechs had asked for a mediator and that the government had no responsibility for it.[40]

The heart breaking story of the ruthless dismemberment of Czechoslovakia by her democratic allies and friends must be greatly shortened here. That she was one of the finest democracies in the world, the best fruit of World War I, mattered not an iota to the British government, though half of the French Cabinet did suffer acutely over what they joined in doing. The surgery was performed without any anesthetic at the Munich Conference in October 1938. At last Chamberlain got his cherished association with the two Fascist dictatorships, after he had flown over twice to propitiate Hitler. Under the most extreme pressure the Czechs were forced by their allies to submit—without using their great fortifications, fine air force and splended army of 1,500,000 men—to all the sadistic horrors of the Nazi occupation—beatings, plundering, raping and insults, before a few months later their whole country was engulfed by an even worse German terror.[41]

MUNICH'S CONSEQUENCES For France the Munich sacrifice was doubly deadly. She was doomed now to suffering the rapid spread of the moral rot that had been so evident during the massacre of the Spanish Republic, and she had lost her last

[40] Wheeler-Bennett, pp. 70–77.

[41] It was my melancholy fortune to watch the crucifixion of Czechoslovakia from London during the Munich period. During it I heard many expressions of willingness by ordinary people, those who would have to face the German bombs, to stand up then to Hitler and all that he meant.

chance to fight, with powerful allies in the East. Now she must wait for her own conquest, in Hitler's own time.

For Russia, too, the consequences of Munich were catastrophic. All of her efforts since 1934 to form a common front with the Western powers against the obvious explosion of German *furor Teutonicus* had been rejected. Now excluded from Munich, she saw the great Czech bastion destroyed and the way opened wide for German conquest in the East, as far as the wheat of the Ukraine, the oil of the Caucasus and the minerals of the Urals—all of which Hitler had publicly and frequently coveted. No deduction was open to them except that the iron determination of the British government had paved Hitler's way to the East. Obviously the Soviets had to survive as best they could, yet it was to be another year, as Hitler was poised for the destruction of Poland, before they finally agreed to the Nazi-Soviet pact of August 23, 1939, which turned Hitler back upon the West for nearly two years and nullified the perennial hope of the appeasers that he would leave them alone while exhausting Germany on the plains of Russia.[42]

For the United States and the world the Munich Conference was the second great turning point of this century, following inexorably the refusal of the United States in 1920 to help administer and enforce the peace after World War I. When it was all over, too, it was crystal clear that the Munich men, building upon our abdication, had achieved the exact opposite of the result they desired. Instead of seeing Hitler's unlimited appetites sate themselves in the East, they saw his Germany wax so mighty that even the combined power of the United States and the Soviet Union could barely accomplish her defeat. Then after Stalingrad, in late 1942, the slow but dogged return

[42] I have written an extended account of the Soviet-German truce, 1939–1941, in Chapter VI of my book, *The Cold War and Its Origins, 1917–1960*, New York, 1961. My research time from 1946 to 1960 was devoted to this book. Volume I covers the period 1917–1950; Volume II, 1950–1960.

of the Russian armies carried them through Eastern Europe to Vienna and Berlin without the West being able to muster the desire or the will to stop them. Hoping to see Soviet Communism wrecked, the Munich men had made it necessary for all the resources of the world to be mobilized through another eternity of carnage in order to destroy the raging Fascist trio. Then the world was left divided between the Soviet colossus and the American giant.

This, too, was not to the liking of the giant, but it had been made unavoidable by the American-British decisions to fight a peripheral war in North Africa and Italy, while the Russians absorbed the terrible and successive impacts of the German armies through five years and drove them back into the heart of Europe.

POLAND, 1939   During the year, after Munich, Germany occupied the rump of Czechoslovakia, on March 15, 1939, causing a great revulsion of opinion in Britain which led London to inquire two days later about Russia's attitude, but when Moscow proposed an immediate conference of all the threatened states the British again thought this "premature." Hitler's action on March 16 in giving the tip of Czechoslovakia to Hungary was clear evidence that he was going to clean up the West first, and finally, on March 31, London threw out a guarantee of Poland's independence, but the Polish colonels and landlords, gorged by White Russian and Ukrainian lands, could never be brought to accept Soviet aid. This was warmly understood in Downing Street, which had equal sympathy with the desire of the semi-fascist little Baltic states—Latvia, Esthonia and Lithuania—not to be defended by Russia. Yet these states, with their German landlords, were certain avenues of German fifth-column penetration—up to Leningrad. In London the same men whose hearts had been flinty during the destruction of the Spanish, Austrian and Czech democracies now fully understood how the Baltic leaders felt. So, fearing any expansion of Soviet boundaries, they actually invited Russia, on May 9, 1939, to give a unilateral guarantee to Poland and Rumania and added the astounding proviso that it should go into effect only on the decision of the British Government.

After this supreme exhibition of effrontery, reports began to come in of German-Soviet negotiations, but Chamberlain's eye ranged over the entire globe to find reasons against an alliance with Russia. People in French Canada, in the Balkans, or the Spanish fascists might not like it. Deeply alarmed cries were welling up in Britain and in the House of Commons for a Russian alliance, but Chamberlain could not hear them, even though a British Gallup poll showed 92 percent for alliance with Russia. It was not until July 6—three months before Hitler's deadline for the Polish kill—that London agreed that the Baltic states should be guaranteed, but in the same months the British were making cartel agreements with the Germans, shipping $25,000,-000 of Czech gold to them and offering a possible loan of five billion dollars.

It was not until July 31, 1939, that Chamberlain could bring himself to name the all important mission to negotiate the military alliance with Russia for which his people were pleading. Then, on August 5, he sent them on a slow Baltic boat to Moscow, as Poland's last days ticked away on Hitler's clock of doom. When these obscure Anglo-French delegates finally arrived in Moscow it transpired that once again they had no power to conclude an agreement, and on August 23 the Soviet leaders yielded to great pressure from Berlin and accepted a Non-Aggression Pact with Germany and other treaties which gave them back a 200-mile strip of the territories lost in 1918—including the Baltic States, eastern Poland and Bessarabia—and as events proved, two years' time in which to prepare for Hitler's assault on them. Then London and Paris resurrected the League of Nations for its final act and the Soviet Union was expelled from the League for attacking Finland in order to push her guns out of range of Leningrad. Hearts that had never felt for dying democracies when smothered by fascist conquest now bled for the Finns in conflict with Communist Russia.

CLASS INTEREST VS. NATIONAL SECURITY Wheeler-Bennett summed up the inner explanation for the entire tragedy of appeasement when he observed that French conservatism began early to "waver between class interest and national security." This was equally true of the British Tories,[43] and of many American conservatives. What they all conceived to be class interest paralyzed the defense of national security through long years when it was increasingly menaced by the most open and terrible threats, until at last the fascist dictatorships were uncontrollable and everybody had to unite against them in another four years of far more destructive war than had scourged the world in 1914–1918. If proof of the power of Western conservative bias during the appeasement period were needed, it is to be found in the wholehearted and extravagant eruptions of sympathy in the U.S.A., Britain and France for Finland when attacked by Russia. Indeed, London and Paris forgot about their declared war with Germany, which they were complacently sitting out behind the Maginot Line and the English Channel, and after sending large amounts of scarce munitions to the Finns they were actually at the point of waging war with the Soviet Union when Finnish resistance finally collapsed.

World War II

The Finns had fared much better against the half-hearted Russian attack than the Poles had against the raging fury of Hitler's assault on Poland, in which Hitler's Germany destroyed Poland virtually in a single day, as a million troops swept over her from a giant semi-circle while 5000 bombers from the same

[43] Wheeler-Bennett, *Munich, Prologue to Tragedy*, p. 94.

three sides bombed and machine gunned the cities and every-thing that moved outside them.[44]

The German assaults on Denmark, Norway, Holland, Bel-gium, and France did not come until April and May 1940, when German power rolled over them, a little less barbarously perhaps than in Russia and Poland, and only the heroic work of Britain's airmen defeated the Luftwaffe and enabled Britain to survive as a staging base for nearly four years of gruelling Allied effort to defeat Germany, Japan and Italy.

Though they aided the British strongly after May 1940, the Americans had clung formally to the neutrality which Woodrow Wilson's enemies had led them back into until a big segment of their fleet was sunk by the Japanese without warning on December 7, 1941, and they were soon at war with all the Axis powers.

So it was all to do over again, only on a bigger and more barbaric scale. The unlimited greed of the Japanese warlords had to be opposed after all, "with force." The abhorred League of Nation's sanctions, which would never have needed to be ap-plied by a strong league and which would have cost only limited fighting in 1931 or 1935, were now superseded by unlimited, savage fighting all around the world. The crippled U. S. Navy had to fight years of desperate war all over the Pacific Ocean.

ENORMOUS LOSSES TO U-BOATS AGAIN   In the Atlantic another and bigger fleet of German submarines—built, unbelievably, by permission of the 1935 Anglo-German Naval Treaty—was ready for action again. Early in January 1942 the U-boats were sinking ships at the mouths of the St. Lawrence and the Mississippi Rivers and along our coasts. By June 2,250,000 tons of shipping

[44] When Italian Foreign Minister Ciano talked with his allies, Hitler and Ribbentrop on August 11–13, he wrote in his diary about the attack on Poland: "The decision to fight is implacable. . . . I am certain that were the Germans given much more than they ask they would attack just the same because they are possessed by the demon of destruction. . . . Hitler has decided to strike and he will."—F. L. Schuman, *Soviet Politics at Home and Abroad*, New York, 1946, p. 376.

had been sunk and in that month 145 ships were lost. Ships were being destroyed faster than they could be built, compelling a vast air and sea hunt all over the North Atlantic. In the first half of March 1943, half a million tons were sunk, most of it in convoy, but in May 41 U-boats were destroyed.

During the entire Atlantic war a total of 782 German submarines was sunk, but the toll they took is almost beyond the ability of the human mind to measure. In each of the years 1940 and 1941 they sank more than 4,000,000 tons of Allied shipping. In 1942 this huge total was doubled. In the entire war the U-boats sent to the bottom 23,351,000 tons of shipping, but twice this tonnage was built during the war.

The loss of wealth was incalculable, yet it had an economic effect which a great many people enjoyed. There was no danger of over production of goods of any kind. The "market" was insatiable. Any conceivable surplus of goods was quickly disposed of by German torpedoes. There was no controversy about the distribution of surplus food and manufactures among Americans who could not afford to buy them.

CARNAGE AND DEVASTATION IN THE U.S.S.R. The heroism and hardship of our sea fighters, and those of our Allies, could never be measured. This is true also of what the Russians had to endure on land in this war which should never have been permitted to happen. In 1941 and 1942 the Germans hurled the vast bulk of their armies into Russia and had about 200 divisions emasculated, yet in 1943 they could still keep 218 divisions in the Soviet Union and 199 in 1944.

In the North, Leningrad was closely invested by German armies on one side and Finnish on the other. The Germans used 6000 cannon, 4500 trench mortars, 19,000 machine guns, 1000 tanks and an equal number of planes against the city, together with 600,000 troops, but it survived an epic siege of twenty-nine months, sometimes entirely surrounded, at others able to open a window across the ice of Lake Ladoga. In spite of constant artillery attack and a huge death rate from starvation rations, the city kept up some industrial production and eventually took a large hand in its own liberation.

In the center the German armies got within sight of Moscow, only to be turned back, and in the South they were decisively defeated at Stalingrad late in 1942, the turning point of the war on land. For four years the great armies ground back and forth across the face of Russia and the Germans used every known device to degrade as *Untermenschen* the eighty million people in the lands they occupied. They destroyed, completely or partially, fifteen large cities, 1710 towns, and 70,000 villages, depriving 25,000,000 people of shelter. They demolished 31,850 industrial enterprises, 65,000 kilometers of railway track, 56,000 miles of main highway, 1135 coal mines and carried off 11,300 electric generators. In the rural areas the figures were just as enormous and some 250,000 cultural institutions, such as schools, libraries and hospitals, were destroyed.[45]

GENOCIDE IN POLAND The Poles, upon which the Nazis had first been able to vent their full destructive capacities, suffered from both sides. Before the Germans attacked Russia the Soviets had forcibly deported 1,500,000 Poles into the interior of the Soviet Union. All of the upper classes, and everyone who might conceivably be a danger to the Soviet regime, were deported in endless trains of freight cars, in bitter heat and cold. Most of them were taken to slave labor camps and after they were amnestied in 1941 they brought back tales of horror which deepened the rift between the two peoples.[46] Later, in 1943, 10,000 Polish officers were found buried in the Katyn Forest and the weight of evidence pointed toward Russian guilt.

On their side, the German Nazis had openly set out to destroy the Polish nation. Proclaiming the Slavs to be inferior peoples, really sub-human, the Nazis had freely stated their intentions

[45] Statement of the Extraordinary State Committee, *Information Bulletin*, Embassy of the U.S.S.R., Vol. V, No. 106, October 11, 1945, pp. 1–12.

The Russians estimated their human losses in killed as some 13,000,000, but afterwards Western demographers put the figure at 20,000,000 at least.

[46] See *The Dark Side of the Moon*, New York, 1947.

to depopulate an area in Europe, mainly toward the East, big enough to hold 250,000,000 Germans, as fast as they could be bred by any and all means. In Poland, too, they had driven the Poles into a small central rump called *Gouvernement Poland*. The Germans made as much progress toward destroying the Poles as they could in the time allowed. They caused the death of 8,000,000 Poles, killing 700,000 in Warsaw alone. In their murder camp at Majdanek they burned more than a million people, mainly Jews, but including Poles and Russians.

The Germans also seized and deported a million Poles for slave labor in Germany and seized Polish girls for their military brothels. Libraries were destroyed and every effort made to wipe out Polish culture and reduce the surviving Poles to helots. Only the defeat of Germany prevented the total enslavement of the Poles.[47]

EXTERMINATION IN GERMANY   In Germany itself human bestiality sank to its ultimate depths. There at the Auschwitz murder camp alone more than 4,000,000 people—men, women, and children—were killed and burned. Doctors performed horrible experiments on living people that were gravely discussed by the eminent medical societies, bankers "stuffed their vaults with dental gold extracted from the teeth of murdered Jews" and lampshades made of their skins were displayed in German homes. Millions of slave laborers were seized in many parts of Europe, but especially in the East, and great numbers of these

[47] See the record of Odd Nansen, son of the famous Norwegian explorer, who was a prisoner in Sachsenhausen, in his diary *From Day to Day*, New York, 1949; Simon Segal, *The New Order in Poland*, New York, 1942; and Arthur Bliss Lane, *I Saw Poland Betrayed*, Indianapolis, 1948, pp. 158, 214.

By comparison the Russians were heartless in their deportations and ruthless in destroying political opposition, but the books detailing their crimes do not describe the use of mass slaughter as a political weapon, or any instances of "the purest sadism, of a craving for the sight of pain, the display of power, the exercise of hate" which Nansen observed (p. 386) and millions of others experienced at the hands of the Germans.—See Lane, *I Saw Poland Betrayed, The Dark Side of the Moon*, and Mikolajczyk, *The Rape of Poland*, New York, 1948.

were worked "literally to death" by German farmers and industrialists.[48]

The Germans hauled out of Russia and East Europe everything portable and destroyed that which was not. In West Europe the German business partners of the Nazis seized some 25 billion dollars' worth of properties, big and little. Germany swam in the plenty that Hitler had promised, his conquests defeating the British blockade which had finally strangled her economy in World War I.

RED REVOLUTION IN CHINA In the Far East the Japanese army staged a spectacular rape of the city of Nanking, an example of frightfulness hardly needed to speed the departure of the Chinese Nationalists up behind the Yangtse gorges where their government rotted while the Chinese Communists organized the countryside in North China, cooped up the Japanese in the cities and towns and laid a firm base for defeating the Kuomintang after Japan's surrender. Then the rapacious post-war conduct of the Nationalists forever removed the "mandate of Heaven" from it. American forces ferried nearly 500,000 Nationalist troops into North China and Manchuria but the hostility of the Chinese people forced them out. Then two myths grew up in the United States: that our Chinese experts who had rightly predicted Communist ascendancy were somehow guilty of it; and that Chiang Kai-shek failed because at some time we did not aid him enough.[49]

MASS SLAUGHTER IN GERMAN AND JAPANESE CITIES While the troops of our enemies were wreaking havoc upon vast populations we ourselves learned well how to bring death, devastation and lingering suffering to the people in their homelands. In

[48] Kenneth Davis, *Experience of War,* New York (Doubleday), 1965, p. 625. This is an outstanding history of World War II from the American standpoint.

[49] In my book, *The Cold War and Its Origins, 1917–1960,* Vol. II, pp. 543–88, Norman L. Parks, one of my esteemed colleagues, has provided a fully documented account of what did happen in China during and after World War II.

their frustration over Hitler's conquests the highly competent Royal Airforce first worked out something called "strategic bombing." The idea was to "de-house" German workers and wreck their war industries by using the bombers that were now available. Raids by 500 or 1000 planes, all carrying big bombs, were now feasible. So the raiding began, in which we joined after 1941. The bombers did so well at Hamburg that a great fire storm was created and 60,000 people were roasted alive, but five months later 80 percent of the city's productive capacity was restored. Some 3,600,000 homes were ruined in Germany but war production continued. In East Germany the lovely city of Dresden, crowded with refugees, was destroyed late in the war and 50,000 people killed. Eight other large cities were subjected to heavy "area" attacks, yet together they contained only three big war plants. Saturation bombing—all over a city—was developed, as estimable military men ticked off the list of German towns that were to be destroyed each week until sixty German cities had been ruined, and many more towns. From these emerged afterward the pitiful legions of people without arms, legs, or eyes; with twisted faces and scarred bodies—those doomed to live on only partly alive.

Yet subsequent careful studies by the U. S. Strategic Bombing Survey showed that German war production *increased* until mid-1944, when the Allied armies closed in on Germany and when selective bombing of rails and oil plants was finally done. Then eminent British war critics concluded that Churchill's use of the resources of his country "to make the enemy burn and bleed" had delayed the invasion of Germany and prolonged the war by a full year. The prodigious bombing had "no positive yield whatever," though it cost our side 150,000 of its finest young air men.[50]

Of course the crushing answer to these conclusions is: "We had to *do something,* didn't we? Given our proven inability to learn any saving lesson from succeeding orgies of destruction,

[50] *Ibid.,* Vol. I, pp. 403-5.

the affirmative answer to that question will one day end our alleged civilization. We *must* maintain a power base in South East Asia. And must we not "do something" about China's nuclear installations, even if a war that would kill 100,000,000 Chinese people resulted? Pending the final human decision of some questions like this, we did learn in Japan how to end a war. In 1945 we had great quantities of improved fire bombs, and we used them with spectacular effect on Japanese cities. On the night of March 9–10 General Curtis LeMay was able to send 334 giant B-29s to drop 2000 tons of incendiaries on "the highly inflammable heart of Tokyo," raising a fire storm more terrible than Hamburg's. Looking down on a tossing sea of flame our airmen found the "unpressurized cabins of their planes filling up with a strange red mist, permeated by a stink of burning flesh so strong that it caused many a man to vomit." About 100,000 people were burned to death or suffocated. Some seventeen square miles of "the most densely built-up city in the world were utterly devastated, leaving a million and a half people homeless."[51]

Did this indescribable horror end such holocausts? No. General LeMay having congratulated himself and having received warm congratulations, then proceeded to gut other Japanese cities, two to four at a time, in raids two or three days apart. Before the war ended his bombers had hit 69 Japanese cities and burned to death twice as many people as had died in all of Japan's forces during the war.[52] By midsummer 1945 the cities of Japan were half destroyed, her navy virtually finished, her air force knocked from the skies. The July headlines show that she was virtually helpless, yet there was fear that her troops might cause us large casualties in bitter-end fighting when the time came to invade in November.

ATOMIC HOLOCAUSTS   This was the principal reason advanced,

[51] Davis, *Experience of War,* pp. 639–40. He cites for "a graphic and detailed account of this most devastating air raid in history" Martin Caiden's *A Torch to the Enemy,* New York, 1960.
[52] *Ibid.*

then and since, for using our first two atomic bombs upon Japanese cities—"Little Boy" made of Uranium-235 and "Fat Man" made from plutonium. A strong majority of the scientists who had made the bomb possible were opposed to its use on a city and those who were in Chicago managed to take a poll which was considered in Washington on July 23, 1945. An urgent message having come to scientist Arthur Compton asking for its results, he reported that "87 percent voted for military use," and when an hour later Washington asked him what he himself thought he replied: "My vote is with the majority." Actually, there was "but one possible honest interpretation of the poll's results": 15 percent of the 150 scientists favored quick military use while 85 percent favored other courses of action, such as a demonstration of the bomb in Japan or elsewhere before "full use" of the weapon.[53]

However, a separate scientific panel had thought of various objections to any demonstration and there was a strong desire in Washington to use the bomb to finally knock Japan out of the war before the Russians entered it on August 8. Accordingly, intense pressure was put upon the scientists at Los Alamos to get the bomb ready for "a date near August tenth,"[54] and at the Potsdam Conference a declaration was published, without informing Molotov, threatening Japan with "immeasurably greater" blows but giving no intimation that a whole new dimension of force was about to be released upon her. Stalin was casually told by Truman of a bomb "far exceeding any known in destructiveness," but he too was not told that the atomic threshold was about to be crossed.

On August 6, 1945, after being balked for five days by bad weather, American airmen arrived over Hiroshima, one of four Japanese cities selected for deathless distinction as the first city to be destroyed by an atomic bomb. As it exploded beneath them—shaking earth, sky, and plane—one of them exclaimed:

---

[53] Davis, pp. 645–46.
[54] Philip Morrison, *The Bulletin of the Atomic Scientists*, February 1949, p. 40.

"My God! What have we done?" What they had done was to kill 80,000 people and burn 37,000 seriously, not counting legions of others who were doomed to die lingering, agonized deaths for decades thereafter. Something else had been done which was of eternal importance: there had been created the presumption that in any future great war atomic bombs would be used—soon to be H-bombs, many thousands of times more powerful. These two A-bombings had given "moral" sanction in the future to any weapon that would "win," or end a war, no matter how destructive it might be, and without being under any overwhelming pressure of self preservation.

But Truman was riding high in the Presidency. When news of the first successful test explosion of a "Fat Man" reached him at the Potsdam Conference, shortly after July 16, 1945, he had mystified the others by his imperious domination of the next session and thereafter he chafed to get home. When the Hiroshima news reached him on shipboard, he exulted: "This is the greatest thing in history." Years later he added that he had "no qualms" about using it and that he had "never lost any sleep over it since."[55]

Countless others have taken his action more seriously. On August 9, 1965, Pope Paul VI described the bombing of Hiroshima as an "infernal massacre" and an "outrage against civilization." Appealing for an end to "dishonorable weapons," he prayed "that the world may never again see such a wretched day as that of Hiroshima" and that all nations "shall ban the awful technique which creates these weapons, multiplies and stores them for the terror of mankind."[56]

During the twenty year anniversary of Hiroshima in 1965 many doubts were expressed about the necessity of the bomb's first use, but nobody questioned the wisdom of destroying Nagasaki on August 9, 1945, with our one remaining "Fat

[55] Fleming, *The Cold War and Its Origins, 1917–1960,* Vol. I, pp. 296–308.
[56] The Portland *Oregonian,* August 9, 1965.

Man," killing 35,000 and dooming 60,000 wounded. Some dire compulsion seemed to determine this act, the day after the Russians entered the war, following years of urgings on our part to do so. There was no waiting for the shock of Hiroshima to bring about Japan's surrender, which came on August 14, greatly embarrassing the Russians, who felt obliged to deny to their people for many days that the war was over, while they completed substantially the occupation of Manchuria—that occupation which Truman himself had strongly urged upon them in the early part of the Potsdam Conference, before the successful test explosion on July 16. Far from waiting for the impact of Russia's entry into the war to bring about Japan's surrender, both atomic bombs were hastily used to accomplish that result. Afterward, the wartime heads of both our Air Force and Navy agreed that the use of the bombs had not been necessary and Admiral William D. Leahy felt that we had "adopted the ethical standard common to the barbarians of the Dark Ages."[57]

The saving of hypothetical *American* lives is a very precious thing. To achieve this objective anything could be justified. Within twenty years some Americans were arguing for a "preëmptive" missile assault upon the Soviet Union to prevent them from surprising us in a missile exchange, thus saving some millions of American lives, perhaps just enough to avert racial extinction. The achieving of a political objective can also come to have inordinate value in a leader's mind, even one chosen democratically. If the death of 200,000 Japanese people by atomic fire, and the lingering death of many more, will prevent an ally from gaining her agreed share of the winnings, who is to stay a president's hand?

ASTRONOMIC WASTES   Who, too, can fully comprehend the incalculable human and material wastes of World War II which came to an end in August 1945? Estimates made by official agencies and the American University in Washington pointed

[57] Fleming, *op. cit.*, p. 297; William D. Leahy, *I Was There*, New York, 1950, pp. 441–42.

toward military expenditures totalling $1,116,991,463,084, and property damage amounting to $230,900,000,000.[58]

What would the world have been like if the more than trillion dollars of military expenditures had been used to build roads, schools, houses and other useful things? Alternatively, this vast expenditure could have gone far to industrialize the backward areas of the world and so reduce greatly the likelihood of future wars, either of revolution or of imperialism.

There were some additions to the world's capital goods, especially in the United States and probably in the U.S.S.R., but against these gains stood the appalling 231 billions in property damage, some 130 cities destroyed which it had taken centuries to build, to mention only the most spectacular losses.

The human losses should also give pause to every person who toys with the idea of just one more war. According to figures released by the Vatican the military and civilian dead of World War II amounted to 22,060,000 and the wounded, 34,400,000.[59] Yet these 56,000,000 lives ended or maimed were only a part of the human cost. Untold millions of people had their lives dislocated and made uncertain, especially with the ominous shadow of the atomic bomb hanging over their heads and promising the swift destruction of hundreds of millions of people if the old deadly cycle of mutual recrimination and fear got started again.

The United Nations
Submerged by the Cold War

What then did the leaders of the victors do after 1945, after this stupendous, unforgivable squandering of life and resources

[58] *World Almanac and Book of Facts for 1950*, New York, 1950, p. 746. The breakdown of military costs showed 330 billion dollars for the United States, 120 billions for Great Britain, 192 billions for the U.S.S.R. and 273 billions for Germany.

[59] *Ibid.*

in a second long and barbarous orgy of destruction within twenty years? Did they then give daily evidence that they had finally been bludgeoned into learning the lessons that were so starkly and pitifully clear at the end of World War I? Did they hasten on their spiritual knees to make *certain* that the old fatal cycle of balance of power rivalries and anarchical national lusts should be ended forever? Did they hurry to demonstrate that neither partisan strife nor blind immaturity would this time destroy man's last chance to live on this planet, in the atomic age which had just dawned so ruthlessly and so gruesomely?

It has to be recorded in any doomsday book that they did not. Even in the best democracies everything depends upon the lottery of elections and of death in high office. Roosevelt's death on April 12, 1945, removed from office a man who had worked with the Russians all during the war, first to win it and then above all to establish a new United Nations in which both would cooperate to keep the peace. They had won. At Yalta he had spent the last reserves of his strength to achieve agreements about the Far East, Eastern Europe and Germany and had succeeded handsomely, as the observers at that Conference have recorded in detail. None of the formulas agreed upon could really restore Eastern Europe to right wing anti-Soviet capitalism, but Roosevelt's wisdom and his very high standing with the Russians would have worked powerfully to smooth the transition to very different social systems in that area. But on April 23, 1945, eleven days after Roosevelt's death, President Truman was tongue-lashing Molotov in the White House about Poland, a country through which the Soviet Union had been invaded disastrously three times since 1914, including the Polish invasion of 1920. Soon there was much talk in the press and elsewhere of inevitable war with Russia, especially from leaders who had never wanted to fight Fascism, but were eager to fight the Russian Communists.

For the third time in our history the swift reversal of a great war President's wise policies for making peace rapidly gathered steam. The same thing had happened to Lincoln and Wilson, establishing a high probability that we are incapable of making peace. By March 5, 1946, Winston Churchill was declaring the Cold War against an alleged all-devouring Russian juggernaut at Fulton, Missouri, in Truman's applauding presence, and after conference with him. A year later Truman enunciated the world-shaking Truman Doctrine, proclaiming the encirclement of the Soviet Union and forbidding, for all practical purposes, revolution anywhere in the world.[60] Within a few years the United States was the head of chains of alliances, including forty-two nations, formed around the Soviet Union and China. Our new leaders rashly over-compensated for our isolationist fiasco by swinging all the way over to assuming responsibility for what went on everywhere in the world.

But the League of Nations—was it never resurrected? All during the war there was deep consciousness in the country that the failure of the League had been everybody's failure. It was keenly realized that no new beginning could be made unless the United States Senate would pledge itself in advance that it would not do again what it had done from 1918 to 1920. This would come hard with the Senate, but on September 21, 1943, the House of Representatives passed, by a vote of 360 to 29, the Fulbright Resolution committing the House to the principle, and on November 5 the Senate itself recognized the necessity of establishing at the earliest practicable date a general international organization "with power to prevent aggression and to preserve the peace of the world." The vote was 85 to 5. Thereafter, Roosevelt and Secretary of State Cordell Hull shepherded, through many negotiations, agreement with the Russians for a new United Nations organization and it was organized at the San Francisco Conference which ended on June 26, 1945, after the Soviets had made the essential concessions.[61]

[60] Fleming, *The Cold War and Its Origins,* Vol. I, pp. 348–57; 433–76.
[61] *Ibid.,* pp. 270–89.

But the UN quickly became a victim of the Cold War. At its very first meeting, there was, against the wishes of the United States, an acrimonious exchange of charges over Russian troops in Iran and Allied troops in Syria-Lebanon which resulted in the first Russian veto in the Security Council. In the spring of 1946 UN sessions in New York forced Russia out of Iran and in 1950 a Russian boycott of the Security Council, in China's behalf, enabled the United States to mobilize the UN to resist the sudden North Korean attack on South Korea. After three years of stalemated, large-scale war a truce was made, but no peace.

Then to prevent the Soviet Union from blocking any future UN action a Uniting for Peace Resolution was passed in the General Assembly, largely transferring the peace keeping function from the Security Council to the Assembly. This resulted in a big UN policing operation in the Congo, during which the leftist leader Lumumba was treacherously murdered by his opponents and UN Secretary General Dag Hammersjkold lost his life, before the UN came to bankruptcy due to the refusal of Russia, France and a dozen other states to pay their share of the costs of the operation assessed against them. Years of deadlock on the question of collecting the disputed arrears resulted in 1965 in a long session of the Assembly during which no vote could be taken on any question lest the issue of the unpaid dues break up the UN. At the end it was apparent that the United States did not have the votes to deprive the Russians and other delinquents of their votes in the Assembly and in August 1965 we abandoned the effort to enforce the collection of Assembly-levied dues against the will of great powers, upon whose unanimity the UN had been founded.

By this time the automatic American majority in the Assembly, based on twenty Latin American votes, no longer existed. The scores of new neutralist Asian and African states had created a situation in which the U.S. was appreciative of its own veto in the Security Council, lest the Assembly might bill it for peace keeping operations of which it disapproved. But without China, one of the permanent members of the Council, still excluded from the UN by the U.S. and increasingly feared by Washington, could the UN be saved? The social and economic services of the League of Nations had been large and highly successful, but they had not saved the League; the corresponding services in the UN were huge, but they too would not prevent some great power from destroying it in a crisis—unless just possibly the great governments could curb their imperial wills until the peaceful functional activities of the UN and its great branches might very gradually create that unity of mankind which can save it.

Pax Americana

But this was a very slender hope in 1965, as U. S. President Lyndon B. Johnson made two decisions which affected all humanity and in effect declared a global *Pax Americana*.

In February 1965 one of the kaleidoscopic client regimes which we had maintained in South Vietnam for ten years, at the cost of billions of dollars, was about to collapse from its own internal corruption and from rebellion aided by the kindred North Vietnamese, who had been assured by the Geneva Treaty of 1954 that the division of their country was only temporary. Accordingly, Johnson suddenly declared, on February 7, that North Vietnam was an aggressor and began to bomb that country, selectively but relentlessly.

Our air strikes mounted into many thousands as this activity continued for many months—thirteen months as this was written —presenting to the most illiterate Asian the clear picture of the huge white man methodically and incessantly beating the small colored boy. This was an image which could not be prevented from entering minds all around the world.[62] Nevertheless, when one of the parts in our China containment ring was about to fall Mr. Johnson completely begged the nature of the conflict in Vietnam and proclaimed, on April 7, that "we will always oppose the effort of one *nation* to conquer another." (Italics added.) Continuing, he warned: "Armed hostility is futile. Our resources are equal to any challenge. . . . Our patience and determination are unending. . . . We have no desire to devastate that which the people of North Vietnam have built with toil and sacrifice. We will use our power with restraint and with all the wisdom we can command. *But we will use it.*" (Italics added.)

The intent to make his will prevail, in Vietnam and wherever else it might be necessary could not have been clearer, as he promptly demonstrated when a revolt broke out in Santo Domingo on April 24, 1965, to restore the only democratic government which had ever existed there, one deposed by rightist elements including some of our corporations. Now Mr. Johnson rapidly threw some 30,000 troops into the island in absolutely clear violation of the Charters of both the Organization of American States and of the United Nations. He would take no chance that a few alleged communists might control the revolution and make another Cuba on our doorstep. To make his Doctrine emphatic and hemispheric he declared that "the American nations cannot, must not and will not permit the establishment of another Communist government in this hemisphere."

These two absolute assertions of our right to crush revolution in small states on any continent made it clear and unmistakable that in Johnson's time the United States would attempt to enforce a *Pax Americana* in the world, at any cost. After watching for two weeks the building of great American military power bases in South Vietnam, Walter Cronkite reported from Saigon

[62] D. F. Fleming, "Can We Play God in Asia?" *The Progressive,* June 1965, pp. 12–15. The article examines the reasons for believing that our efforts to cling to the far shore of the Pacific are self defeating.

on July 21, 1965, that to maintain this Asian power base the U. S. Government was prepared to fight a Korean type war if it must and a world war if necessary.[63]

Having at their fingertips the undoubted power to destroy all nations, the President and his half dozen top advisers feel that they can make effective the prohibition of the Truman Doctrine against any revolution anywhere, lest it turn Red. Yet when several kinds of revolution are running in the world this is a disastrous policy. If it does not end in destroying the world it invites the slow but perhaps inexorable closing in around us of a kind of Fortress America which the earlier isolationist advocates of such a policy never imagined. They thought of a mighty fortress erected inside the country, but the fortress now in preparation is one rising outside our frontiers in the minds of hostile peoples. To the active hostility of some billion and a half Asians which the relentless bombing first of North Vietnam and then of South Vietnam has stirred, was added at once the fear, resentment and opposition of some 300 millions of Latin Americans who had believed that the century-old violent interventions of the Colossus of the North in their affairs had been ended forever.

It goes without saying that the two Johnsonian thunderbolts revived the diminishing hostility of the many Communist peoples, but their effects were also deep in Western Europe, where indignation about our take-overs of their business properties was already strong, along with resentment about our perpetual inability to settle the German problem and evacuate our armies from Europe. Therefore we cannot count upon the continued toleration of our best friends. On the contrary, there is much evidence that West Europe, including Britain, is turning its face toward East Europe and the Soviet Union, thus raising also the Atlantic Wall of a developing Fortress America, one not composed of great rings of armed bases and alliances built closely around us, but of world-wide aversion to our pretensions.

[63] CBS Evening News, July 21, 1965.

As the grisly tragedy in Vietnam continued, the Communist states—the Soviet Union, China and those in Eastern Europe— quietly helped to train and arm the North Vietnamese and the Viet Cong with the weapons essential for a long conflict; one which throttled down President Johnson's Great Society program, deeply divided and embittered our people, created revolutionary conditions at home and deepened our isolation from the great majority of mankind. By February 23, 1968, the *Wall Street Journal* was saying that "the whole Vietnam effort may be doomed" and that "no battle and no war is worth any price, no matter how ruinous."

A month later, on March 31, 1968, Mr. Johnson announced to the nation that he would begin de-escalating the bombing and would not accept renomination for the presidency. Gone was the proud day of April 7, 1965, when he proclaimed that "We will not be defeated. We will use our power with wisdom and restraint. But we will use it!" He *had* used it, and he had been defeated—by the tenacity of the Vietnamese, South and North, and finally by their stunning Tet offensive early in 1968; by steadily rising world opposition; by constantly deepening division at home; by the disintegration of our world position financially, powered by mounting Vietnam deficits piled on top of never ending cold war ones; and finally by the looming evidence that he would be defeated for re-election, either in the Democratic National Convention or in the November election.

The first calamitous failure of the *Pax Americana* generated by the cold war policy of containing the vast bulk of the old world and of forbidding revolution through the "free world" had been registered.

IX. Conclusions

———❧———

What conclusions are justified by fifty years of observation and study of the world's slides and plunges toward oblivion? I believe that the following will stand up.

1. Guilt and Responsibility for World War I

This first armed catastrophe of our time was the natural and almost inevitable product of the international anarchy and the balance of power "system." The *guilt* for it falls clearly upon the Cabinet of the Hapsburg Monarchy, which was determined to crush Serbia in a localized war while Germany held the ring. The *responsibility* for the outbreak of the war rests upon Germany, the controlling power in the Triple Alliance, whose rulers saw a favorable occasion for a general war which would reassert German hegemony and extend it widely.

2. Guilt and Responsibility for World War II

No volumes need be written to determine who was *guilty* of willing and launching this second negation of everything that could be called civilized. The Japanese warlords, the Fascist chiefs of Italy and, above all, the German Nazis successively sought to subdue their neighbors and eventually they made all-out, unlimited efforts to conquer and enslave as much of the world as they could. No one could be unaware of the predatory nature of their plunges for power over other peoples. Among those lusts the German desire for empire in the East stood out starkly, establishing a continuity between World Wars I and II.

Nevertheless, the *responsibility* for permitting this orgiastic return of the deluges of death, destruction and desolation falls back upon those American leaders who gave the first great negation to the deep yearning for a break with the balance of power cycle and for a world organization to keep the peace. This was a rejection of leadership which facilitated, and to an extent justified, the aversion of British and French imperialists to defending the law of the League of Nations against other imperialists. Since power and responsibility are inseparable, there is no escaping the conclusion that the main responsibility for World War II was incurred by the American and British leaders who won World War I and then refused to defend the new International Order which the war and the treaty of peace created.

The Anglo-Saxon powers had it patently in their power to stabilize the world through the League of Nations and lead it in a new direction, and in every major test their leaders rejected responsibility. The responsibility of France is much less, because her power was far less and because the Anglo-Saxons first left her to enforce the Treaty singlehanded and then held her impotent in the decisive pre-war crises.

3. *Munich Irretrievable*

All the earlier rejections of responsibility culminated in the supreme abdication at the Munich Conference in 1938. There Europe was turned over to the most outlandish and rapacious of the Fascist dictators, to do with as he wished. To be sure he was expected to sate his lusts for conquest in the East. As Lord

Rothmere said in the London *Daily Mail* as early as November 18, 1933, "Once Germany has acquired the additional territory she needs in Western Russia, her need for expansion would be satisfied." This would not be too difficult when the furious German warriors met the weak system and troops of the Soviets. It would all be over in about six weeks.

Yet it transpired that the Soviet Union not only survived but mangled the bulk of the German armies for four years. By the time of the Yalta Conference, in February 1945, "the Russians were in military occupation of Bulgaria, Romania, Poland, and East Prussia."[1] They were fighting bloodily in Hungary toward Vienna and on their way to Berlin. Moreover, no one at Yalta wanted them to stop or knew how the war could be ended without them. To the contrary, the aid of the Red Army was urgently wanted in Manchuria, down to the July 16 test A-bomb explosion in the middle of the Potsdam Conference.

There can be no honest understanding either of World War II or of the ensuing Cold War without realizing that the post-war future of East and Central Europe was settled not at Yalta but at Munich. Churchill later yearned and planned mightily to recover by various strategems what Chamberlain had given away at Munich, but it was beyond the power of anyone to reverse its results.

The Munich surrender was so great and so decisive that it is difficult to find a parallel to it. For this reason virtually all alleged analogies to it are false. Its unique character lies in the bludgeoning of a brave and friendly people, by the most brutal diplomatic pressure from its friends, into submission to a ruthless foreign conqueror. This compelled the Czechs to look to the Soviet Union for their protection after the war—not the greatest consequence of Munich, but a major one.

[1] Kenneth Davis, *Experience of War*, New York (Doubleday), 1965, p. 582.

4. *Unconditional Surrender*

This decision of Roosevelt and Churchill at Casablanca, July 24, 1943, was backed by their war chiefs for a compelling reason. The Russians had been pleading for a Second Front in West Europe since our entry into the war in December 1941. One had virtually been promised them for 1942, but due to the great aversion of the British to it, and to other reasons, there was not going to be a second front in 1943 or until mid-1944. Being human, the Soviets wondered if they would ever be relieved or even if a military Munich might be in the making. At the same time, we had to have the continued massive help of the Red Army and to make sure that it did not falter or fail. There was only one way to do that, to give all the Soviet peoples positive public assurance that we were with them to the end.

Less urgent, but of vital importance, was the need to counter any new stab-in-the-back alibis by the Nazis or their successors. One of their chief arguments in rising to power had been the claim that Germany was defeated by the Allies in World War I only by socialist and pacifist treachery at home. It was imperative that any doubts about Germany's defeat be removed, lest a third world war presently be hatched out of some new German myth.

It is now frequently alleged that but for the unconditional surrender policy the German generals and other conservatives would have overthrown Hitler at some point before the Russians got so far into Europe. The great German objective in World War II was still the pre-1914 *Drang Nach Osten*, "the be-all and end-all of Nazism," for which "aristocrats, bureaucrats, generals, industrialists" thought they would use Hitler's demagogic talents. The British historian H. R. Trevor-Roper has shown devastatingly how at various times these elements plotted to overthrow Hitler before his great gambles, but invariably subsided and thought about the jobs, promotions, profits and power that they saw in his winnings. Even if they had been able to over-throw Hitler, the West would have done the world no service to leave them in power.[2] Anyway, Hitler had both prostituted and mastered the German conservatives and, in Churchill's words: "negotiation with Hitler was impossible. He was a maniac with supreme power to play his hand out to the end, which he did."[3]

[2] H. R. Trevor-Roper, "Why Hitler Did not Invade Britain," *The New York Times Magazine,* June 6, 1965, pp. 29, 85–89.

[3] Robert Sherwood, *Roosevelt and Hopkins,* New York, 1948, p. 696.

On August 22, 1965 Louis J. Halle published an article in the *New York Times Magazine* entitled "Our War Aims Were Wrong," in which he argued that it was wrong to think of "permanently" destroying "the power on either side of the Russian Empire, by which it had hitherto been contained," that is, Japan and Germany. He even went so far as to say that we adopted as our World War II "objective the creation of the European power vacuum into which the Russian power would expand." We should have declared, he says, that we were only fighting "the criminal regimes that had usurped power in Germany, Italy and Japan" and played the war to preserve the power of these states against Russia, eschewing all thought of unconditional surrender terms and remembering that the balance of power principle is essential.

This reasoning assumes that a desperate world war for survival could be fought successfully against three "criminal regimes" that were trying to strangle and enslave vast populations on the coldly calculating plane of helping the Russians, but not enough to win. It ignores the fact that Germany was not fighting to retain "essentially its pre-war frontiers and the means to defend them," but to conquer Europe, which she almost did. It ignores also the unavoidable fact that we had to have the full assistance of the Russians down to the end in order to escape great defeat for ourselves.

This is a recurrence of the thinking that Senator Harry S. Truman uttered when he heard that the Germans had attacked the Russians in 1941: "If we see that Germany is winning we ought to help Russia, and if Russia is winning we ought to help Germany, and in that way let them kill as many as possible."—*The New York Times,* July 24, 1941.

It is probable that the 1945 Cold War began with this Truman statement, but no one has ever figured out how to fight a war and be on both sides, above all one against a criminal regime that was waging an all-out struggle to conquer and depopulate its "inferior" neighbors. There was no point at which such an insane onslaught could be halted and defended from punishment, even if all questions of honor were cast aside.

5. *The Hitler-Stalin Analogy*

The consolidation of Soviet power over Eastern Europe and the Balkans was a bitter blow to the West. There had never been, except in Czechoslovakia, anything more than charades of democracy in these areas, but there had been capitalism and these areas had served as sources of raw materials and outlets for the manufactures of West Europe. That they should become communist was almost unbearable and yet unavoidable. It was not possible to undo the main result of the war in Europe.

However, Stalin wanted a little more. Having closed the broad invasion highways from the West into the Soviet Union, he also wanted a base on the Turkish Straits, proverbially Russia's greatest window on the world. It had been closed by the Turks in both world wars, with calamitous effects in the first and tragic ones in the second. Any Russian ruler would have sought to do something about that at the close of a victorious world war. This may safely be taken as a permanent Russian objective.

The Russian desire to detach Iranian Azerbaijan just below their great oil fields was less justifiable and the aid of Communist Bulgaria and Yugoslavia to a massive Communist-led rebellion against the restoration of the Greek Monarchy by Churchill seemed to bring Soviet power into the Mediterranean, around the Straits. Stalin also mentioned a desire to have a base in the Eastern Mediterranean. It may be that the Russian desires to open the Mediterranean window and perhaps to get nearer the Persian Gulf had to be rejected, natural as they would seem to the Russians, but these peripheral questions after World War II hardly justified the charge which mushroomed throughout the West that Stalin was another Hitler, out for world conquest. The terribly ravaged and exhausted Soviet Union was in no condition to conceive and execute great conquests in any direction. Nor is it likely that Roosevelt would have permitted a Soviet world conquest dogma to gain the ascendancy.

6. *The Fascist-Communist Analogy*

That "Communism is just as bad as Fascism" quickly became a dogma in the United States after 1945, one so universal that none dared deny it. From the standpoint of those who established it, Communism was worse. Fascism allied itself with private capitalism, but Communism destroys it. This is one of the main dynamos of the Cold War, another being a belief that the Communists work clandestinely to destroy the areas of capitalism.

Yet there was no denying that Fascism was utterly predatory. It violently attacked both capitalist and communist states until they had to unite to destroy it. On the other hand, Communism has evolved steadily and in many directions since 1945. Beginning in independent Yugoslavia, in defiance of Stalin, it has evolved differently in every East European state and in the Soviet Union itself, until the press files have increasingly showed many innovations that copy some of our practices. Above all, too, the lesser Communist states have asserted their nationalistic independence more and more and multiplied their contacts with the West. Before the American bombing of Vietnam a *détente* was developing between the U.S. and the U.S.S.R. which made the alarms and fears of the earlier cold war years seem very remote. In his epochal encyclical *Pacem in Terris,* Pope John XXIII wrote that "There are no political communities which are superior by nature and none which are inferior by nature," and he insisted that the best juridical structures must evolve, along with the primitive ones. In these immensely significant words, Pope John disavowed the dogma that in our time there is an immutable struggle between the pure white on our side and the red evil of Communism, or that we alone have achieved the perfect society.

Before he spoke in 1963 it had long been clear that there

did not have to be war to the death between us and the many communist states in which the rising desires of the great rank and file so obviously had to be taken into account. At the same time, it was plain that every enlightened democracy was inexorably impelled to adopt more and more socialist welfare measures. Both sides sought better lives for their peoples, and by some of the same measures.

7. *Must We Destroy China?*

Our great ring of containment around the Soviet Communist virus is obviously disintegrating. But there is no denying that the Chinese brand is more disturbing. The Chinese revolution is still comparatively young and they are working actively, though unsuccessfully, both to spread it and to oppose our interests everywhere they can in the vast underdeveloped world.

Yet it is also indisputable that we have prolonged their civil war indefinitely and that we hold a ring of hostile fortresses, manned by hundred of thousands of men and every other kind of military power around them, even to islands in their harbors. They have also achieved the beginnings of industrialism and the explosion of atomic bombs. Therefore it can only be a question of time before they will be able to reach Los Angeles and Chicago with nuclear missiles, and to give us the choice of evacuating their environs or engaging in nuclear war.

In the meantime we have the choice of attacking China, with nuclear weapons "if necessary," or of recognizing the unfairness and untenability of our attempt to police the far shore of the Pacific. The latter choice involves a gradual evacuation of East Asia, the neutralization of areas we now hold, and a moving over into neighborly relations with the Chinese and helping them to achieve their primary objective of a good life for their people —soon to be a billion.

The latter course involves, of course, friendly diplomatic relations and the welcoming of China to her reserved seat in the UN Security Council, but it would also resolve the only looming power fight which is likely to end in a world holocaust. The first course—attempting to maintain a military, diplomatic, economic stranglehold and boycott of the world's biggest people, and probably the ablest—involves either enormous "conventional" bombing of China and a giant ground war in Asia or the use of H-bombs to save us this distasteful prospect.

Which road shall we take? On our past record we will choose to commit genocide in China, even if a couple of hundred million people are killed. We used our very first A-bombs to wipe out 200,000 Japanese civilians, after having done the same thing with fire bombs, and there will be no lack of powerful "realists" and hardliners among us who will demand both the destruction of China and the "saving of American lives." The road to moral oblivion, and probably to national death, is wide open to us and we already have both military and civilian strategists who think calmly in terms of the death of many millions. We await only a presidential decision to start the final escalation.[4]

8. *Can We Enforce Pax Americana?*

Our destructive military power is unlimited, but our economic, political and moral powers are not. We can abort a number of revolutions in the Caribbean and in upper South America, occupying the troubled lands indefinitely, but Latin America contains some vast countries that are far away, in which the explosive forces may be too much for either their tiny privileged classes or our troops to control. This is also the second half of the Twentieth Century and it is far too late to restore a supergunboat control over our Latin neighbors. They are more numerous than we are and not with capacity for ever increasing hatred.

[4] See Herman Kahn, *On Thermonuclear War*, Princeton, 1961.

Nor will the suppression of some revolutions avert others when the grievances are deep enough. In a time when the disease of nationalism has become universal and the smaller peoples demand the right to manage or mismanage their own affairs, it is too late for Uncle Sam to forbid all violent social change, lest it turn Red.

Colonialism and neo-colonialism have also seen their day, killed by the two terrible wars which the white men (and their Japanese imitators) visited upon humanity. It was natural for Great Britain to seek to cling to a few valuable properties in Asia, but teetering constantly on the brink of bankruptcy forced her to withdraw. With our greater resources we can doubtless hold for a while, fringe spots in Asia, but that is a rearguard action, untenable for long against the gathering might of China and the will of the smaller Asian peoples. We may maintain control of South Vietnam and South Korea for a time by subsidizing vast native armies in each (600,000 in South Korea), and by keeping divisions of American troops in both, but in the end Korean and Vietnamese nationalism will achieve the reunification of these tragically divided, frightfully scourged and impoverished peoples.

At the end of August 1965 James Reston wrote from Saigon in an article portraying our wholesale bombing of *South* Vietnam that "we could win the war and lose the people, and that would be the final irony of the story." But his article fully justified the conclusion that we had already lost the people of all Vietnam, and with them the opinion of the world. On the same day Nasser called our air raids on *North* Vietnam "aggression which arouses the indignation of the world." Bombing Vietnam, from one end to the other, may seem to pacify the country, but as Governor Mark O. Hatfield of Oregon observed in a statement on July 23, 1965: "A war of liberation cannot liberate if its result is to annihilate."

We can bring ourselves to bankruptcy, visit misery upon various small peoples and perhaps initiate the final destruction of humanity, but we cannot police the world. To be sure there is in Washington a mighty determination that we *will* learn how to defeat guerrilla wars, that we will learn how to suppress what the Communists call wars of national liberation and that we will preserve what is left of our capitalist living rooms. Nevertheless, the law of social change is inexorable, and if it does not come by orderly processes it will come by violent ones. This is a law which will defeat any government which tries to suppress it, no matter how much raw power it may have. Certainly that is a strange attempt for a nation to make which was born by revolution and whose revolution lighted the world for more than a century.

It will be infinitely more conservative to remember: (a) that it is very difficult to name a successful revolution that turned Communist because of outside infiltration; (b) that all Communist societies do evolve rapidly in directions more palatable to us; and (c) that all the other non-Communist states, and especially West Germany, are finding increasingly that they can trade profitably with Communist states, and even form 50-50 partnerships with them. There is no grinding, ineluctable necessity which compels us to demolish every revolutionary barricade that may be raised in the non-Communist part of the earth, to make certain that the revolution does not turn Red.

9. *The Costs of the Cold War and of the Military-Industrial Complex*

There has been too little awareness that the United States had been moving steadily toward international bankruptcy, before the Vietnamese hemorrhage brought us to the verge in 1968. For many years previously we had approached a $3 billion deficit each year, roughly the equivalent of the cost of maintaining some 400,000 troops abroad, many scores of foreign bases, two huge navies and all the other foreign costs of the Cold War. This, too, is an unproductive drain which is seldom mentioned in deploring the deficits. The only returns that it is possible to calculate from it are the intangibles of power politics. These do not balance our international books or slow the gold drain. It is only prudent to foresee that the $3,000,000,000 annual cold war drain will bankrupt the mightiest of the nations in the not very long run.

We have led the world in spending well over a trillion, three hundred billion dollars of military cold war expenditures, mainly since the Korean War began, but our own share of the total exceeds $800,000,000,000 while the Soviets have squandered half as much. This means that they have, by necessity or good judgment, not indulged in enormous over-kill spending. It means, too, that, Britain excepted, our European and Japanese allies have not followed our example of overspending for "defense." On the contrary, they have poured their research money into creating new products, for living instead of dying, and are steadily gaining the world's markets.[5]

In plain terms we are sterilizing such a huge segment of our energies in carrying on the Cold War that we are falling behind the rest of the world in the real sinews of power.

During the fifties and sixties, also, the Soviet Union not only created the best system of health care in the world for its entire people, but probably the best educational system. They spent about twice as large a proportion of the national income on education, and this immensely significant difference presaged that during the 1970s "the technical preparation of the Soviet population will be far more advanced than any other Western country, while the numbers of Soviet scientists and engineers will be several times larger than the American."[6]

On our present course we will still be squandering the great bulk of our scientific brains on inventing new means for destroy-

[5] In 1962 Fred J. Cook published his pioneering book *The Warfare State* (Macmillan, New York) in which he described the growth of our militarism, our demand for 99.9 percent security, how the warfare state runs, the vitiation of all disarmament efforts, the program to bury us in underground shelters and the role of the radical right in the military-industrial complex.

[6] Robert G. Wesson, *The American Problem: The Cold War in Perspective*, New York, 1963, pp. 20, 36, 107, 110, 154.

ing man and for spectacular space exploits, and we shall still be pouring out great sums in trying to control "the areas of weakness" on earth, where "the modern ferment is uncontainable."[7]

While other nations have concentrated lately on making the earth a good place for living, we have spent for the Cold War and let our schools run down, our cities fester with ghettos, foul air and putrid waters. We have let vast rural slums develop, left our elderly largely at the mercy of ill health, let our hospitals grow inadequate and hopeless poverty rise in the midst of affluence. In other words, the Cold War ran on year after year as the national welfare declined.

The processes by which first $50,000,000,000 a year of war spending after the Korean War, then $100,000,000,000 planned for the post-Vietnam period, debilitate our nation and doom its future have been set forth in the most hard-headed terms by Professor Seymour Melman in *Our Depleted Society*, a book which ought to reverse our downward plunge. As an industrial engineer he finds that "Entire industries are falling into technical disrepair, and there is massive loss of productive employment because of inability to hold even domestic markets." As the "parasitic and malignant processes" of military growth and technology flourish we import physicians, leave our railroads in the nineteenth century, build forty merchant ships to the Soviets 673, bury thousands of nuclear missiles deep in the earth, give the Defense Department title to installations and equipment worth $171,000,000,000, give it a total capacity to deliver 19,584 megatons of nuclear death and spend many billions to *overkill* the Soviet Union—"that is, to do an impossible thing." Yet the direct spending on overkill prompted by fictitious "gaps" in our defense, especially "the missile gap," "amounted to between $110 to $146,000,000,000."[8]

[7] *Ibid.*, pp. 278, 280.
[8] Seymour Melman, *Our Depleted Society*, New York, 1965, especially pp. 3, 4, 8, 18, 42. He discovered that the U.S. pays for our 400,000 troops in Germany three times: (1) through the defense budget; (2) in

Other deeply disturbing chapters show: (1) how we have induced poor underdeveloped countries around the world to accept "military aid," meaning plentiful military equipment the maintenance of which depletes their own nascent economies; (2) how dying civilian industries still produce profits by buying up a variety of factories abroad—"profits without productivity"; (3) how our universities are gorged with federal research funds for war purposes, involving enticing 43,000 foreign scientists and engineers to come to the U.S. since 1949, "thereby imposing our priorities on other nations"; and (4) how great numbers of military-industrial firms, small and huge, have become "Firms Without Enterprise." Engulfed by a giant military socialism, they do not have to compete, killing what is supposed to be the central virtue and mainspring of our entire economic system.

We then face the strange paradox that our competitors in the world, including the Communist states, hold down the wastes of their military spending and insist on giving primacy to expenditures that are economically productive, while we indulge in wholesale fashion in the worst form of socialism, the military brand, which acts as a national drug. Since it finances payrolls and makes tills jingle, whole communities want some of it—forever.

Accordingly we are driven to the somber conclusion that we are firmly in the grip of that military-industrial complex against which General Eisenhower so strongly warned us in his farewell address as President. Nor is there any hope that we can escape from this inexorably debilitating stranglehold if we continue to assume it to be our bounden duty to enforce a *Pax Americana* in the world, crushing revolution in Vietnam because it is Communist-led and attempting to stamp out all other revolutions lest they too might be. This role must promote our debilitization by

---

the loss of goods and services the men could have produced; and (3) the sale of weapons abroad in order to get some of the dollars spent abroad back. These three costs total about $9.1 billion a year.—p. 140.

the military socialism route and end in imposing an authoritarian regime on us, to stifle the dissent from this form of national suicide and enforce the increasingly onerous sacrifices which are inherent and inescapable in the follies of *Pax Americana.*

Our military machine is inherently incapable of suppressing social discontent abroad for various reasons, but especially because it does not understand it. One of our ace reporters in Vietnam has demonstrated not only that our military command fights the Vietnamese with World War II methods but that it insulates itself from all news that would cast doubt upon its success.[9]

Much less is the military mind capable of understanding the complex revolutionary thinking that is sweeping through the entire developed world. Finding that "the revolutionary condition seems to be present almost everywhere," Walter Lippmann warned on June 9, 1968, from France, the center of revolutionary turmoil at the moment, that "the revolutionary forces that are loose in the modern age are greater than our conventional wisdom."

In such a time there can only be disaster in trusting to military solutions of world problems and in spending ever increasing billions on scientific "weapon systems" for "defense" against scientific doom—up to the point of national collapse or the final use of the "weapons."

10. *Can We Produce for Human Welfare?*

On the record of these fifty years the answer is negative. We had booming prosperity during World War I and while the ravages of war were being repaired—as the gambling in land, stocks and with foreign loans continued. Then after the great collapse in 1929 all the measures of the New Deal never really got the

[9] David Halberstam, "Bargaining With Hanoi," *The New Republic,* May 11, 1968, pp. 14–15.

economy under way until the 1940 war boom came. Once more much of the world was in ruins, only more so, and there was prosperity for us in rebuilding it. In 1950 the Korean War came and after it we entered permanently on a war-oriented economy, powered by huge annual military budgets.

This is apparently to go on until the gadgets of destruction are used, for the last time. Of course that is not necessary. All we have to do is to make a comparable amount of planning for useful goods that will meet human needs. But it is much easier to produce military "goods" that do not need to be sold, or to spend $20 billion in shooting for the moon—literally. It is this propensity to spend violently for uneconomic ends that promises to end our capitalism, if the same urge does not end humanity first.

11. Is the Population Explosion Inexorable?

Many demographers believe that it is. Certainly too many countries are doomed to suffocate themselves unless they can manage, or be helped, to achieve an educated, industrial life on an adequate agricultural base in time.

This points up the monumental error of spending nearly a trillion dollars on the Cold War in the years when a part of this sum might have made viable many parts of the Latin American world that we ignored until Cuba went Communist. Now desperate revolutions may well be unavoidable and unquenchable, and it will not avail us to continue perpetually our post-war practice of buttressing on three continents the rule of tiny oligarchies over depressed and suppressed populations, while talking always of freedom and democracy.

As Professor Neal D. Houghton, one of the far seeing men of our time, has often pointed out, meeting in some acceptable manner the needs of the enormous populations now being created will require the best efforts of all governments and of all progressive social systems. It may be added that planning for life on a world scale will also be required, if death on the same scale from over-population or over-militarization is to be avoided.

12. *Is Our National Life to Be Short?*

Most of this chapter was written in 1965, when our national outlook was grave enough, but in the following three years we looked for the first time over the brink, beyond which lies national decline, if not oblivion.

At the end of World War I, Paul Valery wrote that "We later civilizations now know too that we are mortal. We had long heard tell of whole worlds that had vanished, of empires sunk without a trace . . . and now we see that the abyss of history is deep enough to hold us all. We are aware that a civilization has the same fragility as a life."[10]

This was painfully evident in 1918, yet one was unable to think that it would apply to us Americans. Since then we have seen our leaders set us up as a world policeman and push this role until even in mid-1966 a perceptive observer could write that against us "animosity—when it isn't hatred—burns around the world."[11]

Nevertheless, in mid-1968, after the fiasco in Vietnam had become evident to all except our military command in Vietnam, there were extremely powerful forces in this country that did not intend to give up the *Pax Americana* role. In 1967 the Pentagon proposed the building of 30 huge FDLS—fast deployment logistic ships—each designed to hold the big weapons for two divisions, such as artillery, trucks, tanks, helicopters, etc. These ships, loaded for instant action would be stationed around the underdeveloped world, perhaps patrolling it, ready to meet thousands of U.S. troops coming in C-5 transport planes, each carrying 500

[10] James Reston, *The San Francisco Chronicle*, April 14, 1968.
[11] Royce Brier, *The San Francisco Chronicle*, July 6, 1966.

men. This plan for crushing insurrection anywhere was defeated for the 1967 and 1968 budgets by Senator Richard B. Russell, Senate Chairman of the Armed Forces Committee, but in June, 1968, while he was ill, it passed the Senate for the 1969 budget.

Nothing could demonstrate more clearly the determination of the military-industrial complex to continue its world police role. It is backed, too, by the tremendous expansive power of the American economic system, which generates large corporate profits each year, to be invested and the profits on profits reinvested indefinitely into the future. This is one of the greatest forces in the world, one which turned outward can bring us rapidly to national downfall.

After the two world wars have ended imperialism the world over, except in Portuguese Africa, it is too late for any white people, even the most powerful, to assert its control over the colored peoples. A new imperium by the United States, resting at home on a foundation of great social ills, can only be short and calamitous for us.

We may be sure also that the continuance of a powerful American outthrust in the world must involve the loss of our individual liberties at home. Our government cannot continue to suppress social dissent abroad and permit us indefinitely to protest at home. Some kind of fascist rule would be required.

It is not reassuring either to learn, after the assassinations of Dr. Martin Luther King, Jr. and Senator Robert F. Kennedy, in rapid succession, that in our private lives we are the most violent and gun-prone people in the world. Between 1900 and 1966, guns caused 795,000 American deaths—while 550,000 war deaths occurred—and each year 100,000 people are wounded, maimed, or assaulted by firearms who are not killed. By contrast, Britain and Japan have about 30 gun murders a year, Germany only a trifle more and the Netherlands had none at all during a recent three-year period.[12]

After the 1968 assassinations, the playwright Arthur Miller

[12] *The Christian Science Monitor,* June 8, 1968.

described our plight succinctly in this sentence: "We are 200 millions now. Either we begin to construct a civilization, which means a common consciousness of social responsibility, or the predator within us will devour us all." And: "A country where people cannot walk safely in their own streets has not earned the right to tell any other people how to govern itself, let alone to bomb and burn that people."[13]

No one has put more strikingly the shame of our conduct in Vietnam, while our cities festered and burned at home. Both developments spell out for us a highly uncertain future.

13. *Can We Find a Viable, Long Term Role in the World?*

These tragic fifty years have demonstrated in blood, tears and sinful wastes of wealth:

(1) that balance of power struggles laid the world low in World War I;

(2) that the refusal of the three great democracies to back collective security led to the ravaging of the world even more sadly in World War II;

(3) that these convulsions brought Communism to Russia and China, the big bulk of Eurasia;

(4) that in war even the most "enlightened" governments will use any weapon on which they can lay hands;

(5) that several governments will soon have the power to touch off a nuclear holocaust, to wage chemical and bacteriological war and to discover ever newer and cheaper means of ending humanity; and

(6) that in this convulsive advance toward doomsday the

[13] *San Francisco Sunday Examiner and Chronicle,* June 16, 1968. Professor Richard Hofstadter suggested in *The New York Times Magazine,* on May 19, that it would be "a tax on our maturity to absorb the sense of guilt and failure that we will take away from Vietnam."

world's largest democracy, and its most powerful state, has been unable to find a viable role in the world.

In these fifty years we have oscillated violently through almost every possible extreme: from relatively innocent isolation in 1914 into World War I; back into isolation by will power and rampant money making until 1929, only to be catapulted into World War II; out of it all the way over to building giant rings of containment, of every kind, close around the Soviet Union and China, on the other side of the world; and finally on to the attempt to suppress all rebellion in the non-Communist world and to enforce a *Pax Americana* in it.

It is evident from these gyrations that the United States has become a great danger both to the world and to itself. Wesson suggests that there are three long-term alternatives before us and the world: one is "the imposition of a world state," a role toward which we have moved since he wrote. The second is "the degradation of civilization," that is, the final culmination of the giant lurches in this direction described in these pages. But there does remain a third alternative which is still open to us, "the establishment of a multilateral equilibrium."[14]

Are we big enough to welcome this third alternative? Having seen with our own eyes that the Soviet Union and the Communist states of East Europe have become more palatable and less fearsome to us as they have become stronger and richer, can we now apply the same saving lesson in China? Can we cease to antagonize her, make peace with her by stages and finally welcome her as a great trading partner? Can we recognize that the giant underdeveloped world is too big for us to handle and that "to propel the famished and unhappy nations (of this vast area) toward a liberal, American-style society is a task beyond the highest projection of American abilities?"

If we can make these shifts and abandon the post-Roosevelt

[14] Wesson, *supra*, p. 278. I have changed the order of his three alternatives.

urge to "contain" our great rivals and to restrain revolution everywhere else, a great future awaits us as still the strongest power, but one of several leaders toward a better and safer life for humanity. If we can do these things and stop stultifying our national life through military spending, we could even find the funds to bring the Negro nation that lives in ghettos among us into our American civilization, and to make ourselves an example of decent living that all the world would appreciate. After all, it is only the example and knowledge of what we are, here at home, that can give us real world leadership. Everything else will fail, and perhaps with disastrous results to ourselves.

Historically speaking, our rise in the world has been meteoric and, judging from our conduct during these fifty years, there is nothing to prevent our flashing out of the pages of history even faster than we came in—nothing except the eternal vigilance and growing maturity of the American people. We have demonstrated that we can produce great leaders occasionally, but we do not get them often enough to keep us on an even course for the long pull and it is that which matters if the American dream is not to fizzle in the skies of Earth, or perhaps in those of the Moon and Mars. An alternative powerfully urged among us is that we should bury ourselves in huge underground cities in the name of "civil defense." Or, if both of these ways of self-immolation can be avoided, the pursuance of a *Pax Americana* policy can lead the peoples of the three continents which surround us to form federations around their leading states for defense against us, all armed with nuclear deterrents.

14. *Is a World Community Attainable?*

There can be no doubt that the cooperation of the leading states—the United States and the Soviet Union, West Europe, and China—is essential if civilization is to be saved. This is the foundation. This is the principle on which the United Nations was founded. But something more is imperative. The big powers must lead in the formation of a true world community.

Most students of world politics also see a way to do it, the method of functional international organization. This is an old approach. We have used it ever since the Universal Postal Union was formed nearly a century ago. The problem of narcotic drugs is world-wide, so a branch of the League of Nations or the United Nations wrestles with it. Contagious diseases are international, so organization to deal with them is readily conceded, and so on through a wide variety of economic functions. We have the International Labor Organization, the Food and Agriculture Organization, and many others.

All of these bodies do work which the world needs. They are "non-political" and so are not thought to interfere with the mighty sovereignty of the national state, as exercised by a few men at the top. Let us go on assigning functions to international bodies and gradually the world will be so knit together that the power of the top rulers to send the marines or all the armed forces overseas, or to hurl nuclear thunderbolts, will gradually become irrelevant and wither away.

I would not for a moment depreciate the functional approach. It is beneficent, and if we had plenty of time it would finally knit the world community together. Let it go on as rapidly as possible. But the fatal fact is that we do not have time. We have never had time since August 1914 and we have less of it each year. What is required is some real breakthroughs toward world unity, such as a treaty renouncing the use of atomic and nuclear weapons, providing for their destruction, and a decision by all the big powers to channel a major part of their foreign aid funds through the United Nations, where the spending of the money would not promote the interests of any given nation or bring deep resentment upon it.

It could be, also, that our financial troubles, flowing mainly from our perpetual cold war expenditures, will force a first step in world government. In June 1968 three different world organizations dealing with world monetary affairs were meeting in Europe, all fearing a big monetary crisis, the third in a year. The day of reckoning seemed to be "approaching with totally unexpected rapidity." The situation was so grave that Lord Robbins, head of *The Financial Times* of London, suggested that a central bank might have to be created to control the volume of cash and credit throughout the Western world. But, he pointed out, this means world government. "It involves a surrender of sovereignty on a scale not contemplated hitherto in the whole history of the world."

He thought this could not happen quickly, but a leading New York banker doubted that any currency in the world was freely usable and a high Belgian authority warned that in the absence of drastic action "an increasingly chaotic situation" would develop, "the greatest set back the free world could suffer."[15]

Such pressures might force a step toward world government that would otherwise be unthinkable.

If the world community is to gain the ability to keep the peace before it is too late, there must be a rapid return to using the United Nations to hold the world level, and to submerging the clashing wills of big governments into common endeavors for the good of all. If we used half the time that we spend in planning to destroy humanity, ever more efficiently, in socially useful planning, we would soon have a long list of essentially thrilling undertakings for the benefit of humanity. We might even meet the critical needs of large populations for water.

On the record of this disastrous half century we will not turn aside from the escalations of war and from gigantic preparations for universal death. Nevertheless, each of us must do what he can. In the last paragraph of his book, Robert Wesson wrote:

[15] John Allan May writing from London to *The Christian Science Monitor*, June 10, 1968.

"The fixation of the Cold War obscures vision, but reason can still play a part in making the best of our unpromising and worsening situation. With cool thought, much can still be done to bring it to pass that civilization shall mean good, not evil."[16]

Since 1914 civilization has made great advances in many good directions, but our appalling immaturities have led to even greater advances of unlimited evil. On July 26, 1963, President Kennedy made one of the greatest addresses of this tragic period in behalf of the partial test ban treaty, a small step toward salvation but an essential one. In it he pictured vividly what the final nuclear world war would be like. Then he pleaded: "So let us turn the world from war. Let us make the most of this opportunity and every opportunity to reduce tension, to slow down the perilous nuclear arms race, and to check the world's slide to final annihilation."

This is man's first priority and the end is highly uncertain. At the close of their fine survey of the problems left unsolved by twenty years of Cold War, Barnet and Raskin wrote: "Whether we shall learn fast enough to find new ways to control our passion for destruction and chaos is by no means clear. Perhaps a growing awareness that his problems are too vast for either a parochial community or a parochial ideology may help man to come to terms with his trembling existence."[17]

This is the only way of escape. We must rapidly stretch our minds beyond changing ideologies and evanescent power urges and advance into the world community, where the really exciting tasks of saving and advancing our civilization lie.

[16] Wesson, *The American Problem: The Cold War in Perspective*, p. 280.

[17] Richard J. Barnet and Marcus G. Raskin, *After 20 Years: Alternatives to the Cold War in Europe*, New York, 1965, p. 204.